Zhao Hongqin

赵宏琴　著

Developing Professional Knowledge about Teachers

发展关于教师的
专业知识

ZHEJIANG UNIVERSITY PRESS
浙江大学出版社

图书在版编目(CIP)数据

发展关于教师的专业知识 = Developing Professional Knowledge about Teachers：英文 / 赵宏琴著. —杭州：浙江大学出版社，2009.6

ISBN 978-7-308-06854-3

I. 发… II. 赵… III. 师资培训—中国—英文 IV. G451.2

中国版本图书馆 CIP 数据核字(2009)第 096014 号

发展关于教师的专业知识

Developing Professional Knowledge about Teachers

赵宏琴　著

责任编辑	张颖琪	
封面设计	俞亚彤	
出版发行	浙江大学出版社	
	（杭州天目山路 148 号　邮政编码 310028）	
	（网址: http://www.zjupress.com）	
排　版	杭州中大图文设计有限公司	
印　刷	浙江中恒世纪印务有限公司	
开　本	640mm×960mm　1/16	
印　张	12.5	
字　数	281 千	
版 印 次	2009 年 6 月第 1 版　2009 年 6 月第 1 次印刷	
书　号	ISBN 978-7-308-06854-3	
定　价	30.00 元	

Preface

INTRODUCTION TO
DEVELOPING PROFESSIONAL KNOWLEDGE
ABOUT TEACHERS

BY **IVOR GOODSON**

PROFESSOR OF LEARNING THEORY

UNIVERSITY OF BRIGHTON

The book *Developing Professional Knowledge about Teachers* represents a significant step forward in our work with teachers. This book provides a vital link between work on teachers' voices, life-history and new patterns of analysis and pedagogy. The book fits into our growing understanding of the crisis of teacher education and of the representational crisis at the root of some of the problems.

The Representational Crisis

Educational study is again undergoing one of those recurrent swings of the pendulum for which the field is noted. But, as the contemporary world and global economies are transformed by rapid and accelerating change, such pendulum swings in scholarly paradigms seem to be alarmingly exacerbated.

Hence, we see a set of responses to a specific structural dilemma in which educational study has become enmeshed. But alongside this, the field is becoming engulfed (though more slowly than in many fields) by a crisis of scholarly representation. A specific structural dilemma now becomes allied with a wider representational crisis. Jameson (1984: viii) has summarized the latter crisis succinctly, as arising from the growing challenge to "an essentially realistic epistemology, which conceives of representation as the production, for subjectivity, of an objectivity that lies outside it". Jameson wrote this in the foreword to Lyotard's *The Postmodern Condition*. For Lyotard, the old modes of representation no longer work. He calls for an incredulity towards these old canonical meta-narratives and says, "the grand narrative has lost its credibility, regardless of what mode of unification is used, regardless of whether it is a speculative narrative or a narrative of emancipation." (Lyotard, 1984, p. 37)

> Returning to the field of educational study, we see that in response to the distant, divorced and disengaged nature of aspects of educational study in universities, some scholars have responded by embracing the "practical", by celebrating the teacher as practitioner.

My intention here is to explore in details one of these movements aiming to focus on teachers' knowledge – particularly the genre which focuses on teachers' stories and narratives. This movement has arisen from the crises of structural displacement and of representation briefly outlined. Hence the reasons for this new genre are understandable, the motivations creditable. As we see, the representational crisis arises from the central dilemma of trying to capture the lived experience of scholars and of teachers within a text. The experience of other lives is, therefore, rendered textual by an author. At root, this is a perilously difficult act and Denzin has cogently inveighed against the very aspiration:

> If the text becomes the agency that records and represents the voices of the other, then the other becomes a person who is spoken for. They do not talk, the text talks for them. It is the agency that interprets their words, thoughts, intentions, and meanings. So a doubling of agency occurs, for behind the text as agent-for-the-other, is the author of the text doing the interpreting. (Denzin, 1993, p. 17)

Denzin, then, is arguing that we have a classic case of academic colonization, or even cannibalization, "The other becomes an extension of the author's voice. The authority of their 'original' voice is now subsumed within the larger text and its double-agency." (1993, p. 17)

Given the scale of this representational crisis, one can quickly see how the sympathetic academic might wish to reduce interpretation, even collaboration, and return to the role of "scribe". At least in such passivity sits the aspiration to reduce colonization. In this moment of representational crisis, the doors open to the educational scholar as facilitator, as conduit for the teacher, to tell her/his story or narrative. The genuine voice of the oppressed subject, uncontaminated by active human collaboration; teachers talking about their practice, providing us with personal and practical insights into their expertise.

Here, maybe, is a sanctuary, an inner sanctum, beyond the representational crisis, beyond academic colonization. The nirvana of the narrative, the Valhalla of voice; it is an understandable and appealing project.

The Narrative Turn / The Turn to Narrative

So the turn to teachers' narratives and stories is, at one level, a thoroughly understandable response to the way in which teachers have tended to be represented in so much educational study. The teacher has been represented to serve our scholarly purposes.

Given this history and the goal displacement of educational study noted, it is therefore laudable that new narrative movements are concentrating on the teachers' presentation of themselves. This is a welcome antidote to so much misrepresentation and representation in past scholarship, and it opens up avenues of fruitful investigation and debate. The narrative movement provides then a catalyst for pursuing understandings of the teacher's life and work. In many ways, the movement reminds me of the point raised by Molly Andrews in her elegant study of elderly political activists. She summarizes the posture of those psychologists who have studied such activists:

> When political psychology has been taken to analysing the behaviour of political activists it has tended to do so from a thoroughly external perspective That is to say, that rarely have their thought processes been described, much less analysed, from their own point of view. Yet it is at least possible that a very good way to learn about the psychology of political activists is to listen to what they have to say about their own lives. (Andrews, 1991, p. 20)

What Andrews said can be seen as analogous to a good deal of our scholarly representation of teachers where they are seen as interchangeable and essentially depersonalized. In 1981, I argued that many accounts presented teachers as timeless and interchangeable role incumbents. But that:

The pursuit of personal and biographical data might rapidly challenge the assumption of interchangeability. Likewise, by tracing the teachers' life as it evolved over time – throughout the teachers' career and through several generations – the assumption of timelessness might also be remedied. *In understanding something so intensely personal teaching it is critical we know about the person the teacher is.* Our paucity of knowledge in this area is a manifest indictment of the range of our sociological imagination. (Goodson, 1981, p. 69)

The argument for listening to teachers is, therefore, a substantial and long overdue one. Narratives, stories, journals, action research and phenomenology have all contributed to a growing movement to provide opportunities for teacher representations. In the case of stories and narratives, Kathy Carter has provided a valuable summary of this growing movement *in the early years of its educational incarnation:*

With increasing frequency over the past several years we, as members of a community of investigator–practitioners, have been telling stories about teaching and teacher education rather than simply reporting correlation coefficients or generating lists of findings. This trend has been upsetting to some who mourn the loss of quantitative precision and, they would argue, scientific rigour. For many of us, however, these stories capture, more than scores or mathematical formulae ever can, the richness and indeterminacy of our experiences as teachers and the complexity of our understandings of what teaching is and how others can be prepared to engage in this profession.

It is not altogether surprising, then, that this attraction to stories has evolved into an explicit attempt to use the literatures on "story" or "narrative" to define both the method and the object of inquiry in teaching and teacher education. Story has become, in other words, more than simply a rhetorical device for expressing sentiments about teachers or candidates for the teaching profession. It is now, rather, a central focus for conducting research in the field. (Carter, 1993, p. 5)

Story and History

The emphasis upon teachers' stories and narratives encouragingly signifies a new turn in presenting teachers. It is a turn that deserves to be taken very seriously, for we have to be sure that we are turning in the right direction. Like all new genres, stories and narratives are Janus-faced; they may move us forward into new insights or backwards into constrained consciousness – and sometimes simultaneously.

This uncertainty is well stated in Carter's summary of "The place of story in the study of teaching and teacher education":

> Anyone with even a passing familiarity with the literatures on story soon realizes, however, that these are quite turbulent intellectual waters and quickly abandons the expectation of safe passage toward the resolution, once and for all, of the many puzzles and dilemmas we face in advancing our knowledge of teaching. Much needs to be learned about the nature of story and its value to our common enterprise, and about the wide range of purposes, approaches, and claims made by those who have adopted story as a central analytical framework. What does story capture and what does it leave out? How does this notion fit within the emerging sense of the nature of teaching and what it means to educate teachers? These and many other critical questions need to be faced if story is to become more than a loose metaphor for everything from a paradigm or world view to a technique for bringing home a point in a lecture on a Thursday afternoon. (Carter, 1993, p. 5)

But what is the nature of the turbulence in the intellectual waters surrounding stories, and will they serve to drown the new genre? The turbulence is multifaceted, but here I want to focus on the relationship between stories and the social context in which they are embedded. For stories exist in history – they are, in fact, deeply located in time and space. Stories work differently in different social contexts and historical times – they can be put to work in different ways. Stories then should not only be *narrated* but also *located*. This argues that we should move beyond the self-referential individual narration to a wider contextualized, collaborative mode. Again, Carter hints at both the enormous appeal and the underlying worry about narrative and story. At the moment, the appeal is substantial after long years of silencing, but the dangers are more shadowy. I believe that unless those dangers are confronted now, narrative and story may end up silencing, or at least marginalizing in new ways, the very people to whom it appears to give voice.

For many of us, these arguments about the personal, storied nature of teaching and about voice, gender, and power in our professional lives ring very true. We can readily point to instances in which we have felt excluded by researchers' language or powerless in the face of administrative decrees and evaluation instruments presumably bolstered by scientific evidence. And we have experienced the indignities of gender bias and presumptions. We feel these issues deeply, and opening them to public scrutiny, especially through the literature in our field, is a cause for celebration.

At the same time, we must recognize that this line of argument creates a very serious crisis for our community. One can easily imagine that the analysis summarized here, if pushed ever so slightly forward, leads directly to a rejection of all generalizations about teaching as distortions of teachers' real stories and as complicity with the power elite, who would make teachers subservient. From this perspective, only the teacher owns her or his story and its meaning. As researchers and teacher educators, we can only serve by getting this message across to the larger society and, perhaps, by helping teachers to come to know their own stories. Seen in this light, much of the activity in which we engage as scholars in teaching becomes illegitimate if not actually harmful. (Carter, 1993, p. 8)

Carolyn Steedman, in her marvelous work, Landscape for a Good Woman, speaks of this danger. She says, "Once a story is told, it ceases to story: it becomes a piece of history, an interpretative device" (Steedman, 1986, p. 143). In this sense, a story "works" when its rationale is comprehended and its historical significance grasped. As Bristow (1991, p. 117) has argued, "The more skilled we become at understanding the history involved in these very broadly defined stories, the more able will we be to identify the ideological function of narratives – how they designate a place for us within their structure of telling." In reviewing Steedman's work and its power to understand patriarchy and the dignity of women's lives, Bristow talks about her unswerving attention to the ways in which life writing can bring its writers to the point of understanding how their lives have already been narrated – according to a pre-figurative script, Steedman never loses sight of how writers may develop skills to rewrite the life script in which they find themselves. (Bristow, 1991, p. 114)

This, I think, focuses acutely on the dangers of a belief that merely by allowing people to "narrate", we in any serious way give them voice and agency. The narration of a pre-figurative script is a celebration of an existing power relation. More often, and this is profoundly true for teachers, the question is how to "rewrite the life script". Narration, then, can work in many ways, but clearly it can work to give voice to a celebration of scripts of domination. Narration can both reinforce domination and rewrite domination. Stories and narratives are not an unquestioned good: it all depends. And above all, it depends on how they relate to history and to social context.

Again, Andrews' work on the lives of political activists captures the limitation of so much of the developmental psychologists' study of lives, and it is analogous to so much work on teacher narratives:

> In Western capitalist democracies, where most of the work on development originates, many researchers tend to ignore the importance of the society– individual dialectic, choosing to focus instead on more particularized elements, be they personality idiosyncrasies, parental relationships, or cognitive structures, as if such aspects of the individual's make-up could be neatly compartmentalized, existing in a contextual vacuum. (Andrews, 1991, p. 13)

The version of "personal" that has been constructed and worked for in some Western countries is a particular version, an individualistic version, of being a person. It is unrecognizable to much of the rest of the world. But so many of the stories and narratives we have of teachers work unproblematically and without comment with this version of personal being and personal knowledge. Masking the limits of individualism, such accounts often present "isolation, estrangement, and loneliness... as autonomy, independence and self-reliance" (Andrews, 1991, p. 13). Andrews concludes that if we ignore social context, we deprive ourselves and our collaborators of meaning and understanding. She says:

> It would seem apparent that the context in which human lives are lived is central to the core of meaning in those lives. Researchers should not, therefore, feel at liberty to discuss or analyse how individuals perceive meaning in their lives and in the world around them, while ignoring the content and context of that meaning. (Andrews, 1991, p. 13)

This, I believe, has been all too common a response among these educational researchers working with teachers' stories and narratives. Content has been embraced and celebrated; context has not been sufficiently developed. Cynthia Chambers has summarized this posture and its dangers in reviewing *Work on Teachers' Narratives*:

> These authors offer us the naive hope that if teachers learn "to tell and understand their *own* story" they will be returned to their rightful place at the centre of curriculum planning and reform. And yet, their method leaves each teacher a "blackbird singing in the dead of night"; isolated, and sadly ignorant of how his/her song is part of a much larger singing of the world. If everyone is singing their own song, who is listening? How can we hear the larger conversation of humankind in which our own history teacher is embedded and perhaps concealed? (Chambers 1991, p. 354)

Likewise, Salina Shrofel, in reviewing the same book, highlights the dangers:

> Focus on the personal and on practice does not appear to lead practitioners or researchers/writers to analyse practice as theory, as social structure, or as a manifestation of political and economic systems. This limitation of vision implicit in the narrative approach serves as a constraint on curriculum reform. Teachers will, as did the teachers cited by Connelly and Clandinin, make changes in their own classroom curricula but will not perform the questioning and challenging of theory, structure, and ideology that will lead to radical and extensive curriculum reform.
>
> It can be argued that the challenge of running a classroom fully occupies the teachers and that questions of theory, structure, and ideology don't affect the everyday lives (practical knowledge) of teachers and are relegated to "experts". However, there are many dangers in separating practice from these other questions. First, as Connelly and Clandinin point out, it ignores the dynamic relationship of theory and practice. Second, it ignores the fact that schools are intricately and inextricably part of the social fabric and of the political and economic system which dominates. Third, because curriculum reform is implemented in the classroom by teachers, separating teachers from these other aspects might negatively affect radical and widespread curriculum reform. To avoid these dangers, either the narrative method will have to be extended, or it will need to be supplemented with a process that encourages teachers to look beyond the personal. (Shrofel, 1991, pp. 64–65)

In summary, should stories and narratives be a way of giving voice to a particular way of being, or should the genre serve as an introduction to alternative ways of being? Consciousness is constructed rather than autonomously produced; hence, giving voice to consciousness may give voice to the constructor at least as much as the speaker. If social context is left out, this will likely happen.

The truth is that many times a life storyteller will neglect the structural context of their lives, or interpret such contextual forces from a biased point of view. As Denzin (1989, p. 74) says, "Many times a person will act as if he or she made his or her own history when, in fact, he or she was forced to make the history he or she lived." He gives an example from his 1986 study of alcoholics: "You know I made the last four months by myself. I haven't used or drank. I'm really proud of myself. I did it." (Denzin, 1989, pp. 74–75) A friend, listening to this account commented:

> You know you were under a court order all last year. You didn't do this on your own. You were forced to, whether you want to accept this fact or not. You also went to AA and NA. Listen Buster, you did what you did because you had help and because you were afraid and thought you had no other choice. Don't give me this, "I did it on my own" crap. (1989, pp. 74–75).

The speaker replies, "I know. I just don't like to admit it." Denzin concludes:

> This listener invokes two structural forces, the state and AA, which accounted in part for this speaker's experience. To have secured only the speaker's account, without a knowledge of his biography and personal history, would have produced a biased interpretation of his situation. (1989, pp. 74–75)

The great virtue of stories is that they particularize and make concrete our experiences. This, however, should be the *starting point* in our social and educational study. Stories can so richly move us into the terrain of the social, into insights into the socially constructed nature of our experiences. Feminist sociology has often treated stories in this way. As Hilary Graham says, "Stories are pre-eminently ways of relating individuals and events to social contexts, ways of weaving personal experiences into their social fabric" (see Armstrong, 1987, p. 14). Again, Carolyn Steedman speaks of this two-step process. First the story particularizes details and historicizes – then at second stage, the "urgent need" to develop theories of context:

The fixed townscapes of Northampton and Leeds that Hoggart and Seabrook have described show endless streets of houses, where mothers who don't go out to work order the domestic day, where men are masters, and children, when they grow older, express gratitude for the harsh discipline meted out to them. The first task is to particularize this profoundly a-historical landscape (and so this book details a mother who was a working woman and a single parent, and a father who wasn't a patriarch). And once the landscape is detailed and historicized in this way, the urgent need becomes to find a way of theorizing the result of such difference and particularity, not in order to find a description that can be universally applied (the point is *not* to say that all working-class childhoods are the same, nor that experience of them produces unique psychic structures) but so that the people in exile, the inhabitants of the long streets, may start to use the auto-biographical "I", and tell the stories of their life. (Steedman, 1986, p. 16)

The story, then, provides a starting point for developing further understandings of the social construction of subjectivity. If the teachers' stories stay at the level of the personal and practical, we forego that opportunity. Speaking of the narrative method focusing on personal and practical teachers' knowledge, Willinsky writes: "I am concerned that a research process intended to recover the personal and experiential (aspects or not?) would pave over this construction site in its search for an overarching unity in the individual's narrative." (Willinsky, 1989, p. 259)

Personal and practical teachers' stories may, therefore, act not to further our understandings, but merely to celebrate the particular constructions of the "teacher" which have been wrought by political and social contestation. Teachers' stories can be stories of particular political victories and political settlements. Because of their limitation of focus, teachers' stories – as stories of the personal and practical – are likely to be limited in this manner.

A Story of Action within a Story of Context

This section comes from a phrase often used by Lawrence Stenhouse (1975), who was concerned in much of his work to introduce a historical dimension to our studies of schooling and curriculum. While himself a leading advocate of the teacher as researcher and pioneer of that method, he was worried about the proliferation of practical stories of action, individualized and isolated, unique and idiosyncratic, as our stories of action and our lives are. But as we have seen, lives and stories link with broader social scripts – they are not just individual productions, they are also social constructions. We must make sure that individual and practical stories do not reduce, seduce and reproduce particular teacher mentalities, and lead us away from broader patterns of understanding.

Let us try to situate the narrative moment in the historical moment – for the narrative movement itself could be located in a theory of context. In some ways the movement has analogies with the existential movement of the 1940s. Existentialists believed that only through our actions could we define ourselves. Our role, existentialists judged, was to invent ourselves as individuals, then, as in Sartre's (1961) trilogy *Les Chemins de la Liberté*, we would be "free", especially from the claims of society and the "others".

Existentialism existed at a particular historical moment following the massive trauma of the Second World War, and in France, where it developed most strongly, of the protracted German occupation. George Melly judges that existentialism grew out of this historical context.

> My retrospective explanation is that it provided a way of exorcising the collective guilt of the occupation, to reduce the betrayals, the collaboration, the blind eye, the unjustified compromise, to an acceptable level. We know now that the official post-war picture of France under the Nazis was a deliberate whitewash and that almost everyone knew it, and suppressed the knowledge. Existentialism, by insisting on the complete isolation of the individual as free to act, but free to do nothing else, as culpable or heroic but *only* within those limits, helped absolve the notion of corporate and national ignominy. (Melly, 1993, p. 9)

Above all, then, an individualizing existentialism freed people from the battle of ideologies, freed them from the awfulness of political and military conflict. Individualized existentialism provided a breathing space away from power and politics.

But the end of the Second World War did not provide an end to politics, only a move from hot war to cold war. As we know, ideologies continued their contest in the most potentially deadly manner. During this period, narratives of personal life began to blossom. Brightman (see Sage, 1994) has developed a fascinating picture of how Mary McCarthy's personal narratives grew out of the witch-hunting period of Joe

McCarthy. Her narratives moved us from the "contagion of ideas" to the personal "material world". Mary McCarthy could "strip ideas of their abstract character and return them to the social world from whence they came" (quoted in Sage, 1994, p. 5). In Irving Howes's memorable phrase, as "ideology crumbled, personality bloomed" (Sage, 1994, p. 5).

And so with the end of ideology, the end of the cold war, we see the proliferate blooming of personality, not least in the movement towards personal narratives and stories. Once again, the personal narrative, the practical story, celebrates the end of the trauma of the cold war and the need for a human space away from politics, away from power. It is a thoroughly understandable nirvana, but it assumes that power and politics have somehow ended. It assumes, in that wishful phrase, "the end of history".

In educational bureaucracies, power continues to be hierarchically administered. I have often asked administrators and educational bureaucrats why they support personal and practical forms of knowledge for teachers in the form of narratives and stories. Their comments often echo those of the "true believers" in narrative method. But I always go on, after suitable pause and diversion to ask, "What do you do on your leadership courses?" There, it is always "politics as usual" management skills, quality assurance, micro-political strategies, personnel training. Personal and practical stories for some, cognitive maps of power for others. So while the use of stories and narratives can provide a useful breathing space away from power, it does not suspend the continuing administration of power; indeed, it could well make this so much easier. Especially as, over time, teachers' knowledge would become more and more personal and practical – different "mentalities". Wholly different understandings of power would emerge, as between, say, teachers and school managers, teachers and administrators, teachers and some educational scholars.

Teachers' individual and practical stories certainly provide a breathing space. However, at one and the same time, they reduce the oxygen of broader understandings. The breathing space comes to look awfully like a vacuum, where history and social construction are somehow suspended.

In this way, teachers become divorced from what might be called the "vernacular of power", the ways of talking and knowing which then become the prerogative of managers, administrators and academics. In this discourse, politics and micro-politics are the essence and currency of the interchange. Alongside this and in a sense facilitating this, a new "vernacular of the particular, the personal and the practical" arises, which is specific to teachers.

This form of apartheid could easily emerge if teachers' stories and narratives remain singular and specific, personal and practical, particular and apolitical. Hence, it is a matter of some urgency that we develop stories of action within theories of context – contextualizing stories, if you like – which act against the kinds of divorce of the discourses that are all too readily imaginable.

Carter had begun to worry about just such a problem in her work on *The Place of Story in the Study of Teaching and Teacher Education*:

> And for those of us telling stories in our work, we will not serve the community well if we sanctify story-telling work and build an epistemology on it to the point that we simply substitute one paradigmatic domination for another *without challenging domination itself.* We must, then, become much more self-conscious than we have been in the past about the issues involved in narrative and story, such as interpretation, authenticity, normative value, and what our purposes are for telling stories in the first place. (Carter, 1993, p. 11)

Some of these worries about stories can be explored in scrutinizing the way in which powerful interest groups in society actually promote and employ storied material.

Looking at the ocean, at the bottom, representing long-term time, are deep currents which, although apparently quite stable, are moving all the time. Such long-term time covers major structural factors: worldviews, forms of the state, etc. The movement from pre-modern to modern, or modern to post-modern forms can be understood in terms of these broad epochal shifts (Bell, 1973; Denzin, 1991; Lyotard, 1984; Wright Mills, 1959). The effects of the emerging social, economic and political conditions of the post-modern era upon the organization and practices of schooling might be understood in these terms (e.g. Aronowitz & Giroux, 1991; Hargreaves, 1994).

Above this level are the swells and tides of particular cycles representing medium time. Such medium-term time has been conceived in boom-bust like spans of 50 years or so – although, with the compression of time and space in the post-modern age, these cycles may themselves undergo compression (Giddens, 1991). It is within these medium-term cycles that one might explain the establishment of the current "grammar of schooling", for example, as classroom-based, graded and subject-specialized schooling in the latter years of the 19th and early years of the 20th centuries. As Tyack and Tobin (1994) admonish, unless reformers begin to talk the historical "grammar of schooling", their attempts to initiate educational change will be forever thwarted.

At the top of the ocean, representing the waves and froth, is short-term, every day time: the everyday events and human actions of ordinary daily life. Proponents of this view of history often celebrate its empirical specifics against the grander theoretical claims of epochal shifts between different historical periods (e.g. McCulloch, 1995). These theorizations of history should not be treated as competitive, though. Fine-grained empirical detail and broad-based theoretical sensibility are complementary forces in history and complementary resources for interpreting such history. Much of contemporary change positions itself here "at the top of the ocean" in the waves and froth: the legacy is therefore unlikely to be enduring.

REFERENCES

[1]   ANDREWS, Molly. (1991) *Lifetimes of Commitment: Aging, Politics, Psychology.* Cambridge: Cambridge University Press.

[2]   ARMSTRONG, P. F. (1987) *Qualitative Strategies in Social and Educational Research: The Life-history Method in Theory and Practice.* In Newland Papers No. 14, The University of Hill, School of Adult and Continuing Education.

[3]   ARONOWITZ, S. & GIROUX, H. (1991) *Post-modern Education: Politics, Culture and Social Criticism.* Minneapolis: University of Minnesota Press.

[4]   BELL, D. (1973) *The Coming of Post-industrial Society.* New York: Basic Books.

[5]   BRISTOW, J. (1991) Life Stories: Carolyn Steedman's History Writing. *New Formations,* No. 13, Spring, pp. 113-130.

[6]   CARTER, Kathy. (1993) The Place of Story in the Study of Teaching and Teacher Education. *Educational Researcher,* 22(1), pp. 5-12, 18.

[7]   CHAMBERS, Cynthia. (1991) Review of Teachers as Curriculum Planners: Narratives of Experience. *Journal of Education Policy,* 6(3), pp. 353-354.

[8]   DENZIN, Norman K. (1989) Interpretive Biography. *Qualitative Research Methods*

Series 17. Newbury Park, London and New Delhi: Sage Publications.

[9]   DENZIN, Norman K. (1993) *Review Essay – On Hearing the Voices of Educational Research.* Mimeo: University of Illinois at Urbana – Champaign.

[10] DENZIN, N. (1991) *Images of Post-modern Society: Social Theory & Contemporary Cinema.* London: Sage.

[11] GOODSON, I. F. & SIKES. (2001) *Life-history Research in Educational Settings: Learning from Lives.* Buckingham: Open University Press.

[12] GOODSON, I. F. (1981) Life History and the Study of Schooling. *Interchange,* II(4).

[13] HARGREAVES, A. (1994) *Changing Teachers, Changing Times: Teachers' Work and Culture in the Post-modern Age.* New York: Teachers' College Press.

[14] JAMESON, F. (1984) Forward. In Lyotard, J. F. *The Post-modern Condition: A Report on Knowledge* (pp. vii-xxi). Minneapolis: University of Minnesota Press.

[15] LYOTARD, J. F. (1984) *The Post-modern Condition: A Report on Knowledge.* Minneapolis: University of Minnesota Press.

[16] MELLY, George. (1993) Look back in Angst. *The Sunday Times,* June 13.

[17] SAGE, L. (1994) How to Do the Life: Review of C. Brightman's *Writing Dangerously: Mary McCarthy and Her World. London Review of Books,* Feb. 10.

[18] SHROFEL, Salina. (1991) Review Essay: School Reform, Professionalism, and Control. *Journal of Educational Thought,* 25(1), pp. 58-70.

[19] STEEDMAN, Carolyn. (1986) *Landscape for a Good Woman.* London: Virago Press.

[20] STENHOUSE, L. (1975) *An Introduction to Curriculum Research and Development.* London: Heinemann.

[21] WILLINSKY, J. (1989) Getting Personal and Practical with Personal Practical Knowledge. *Curriculum Inquiry,* 19(3), pp. 247-264.

[22] WRIGHT MILLS, C. (1959) *The Sociological Imagination.* London: Oxford University Press.

Contents

Chapter One

Introduction: Understanding Teachers in Changing Contexts

That Chinese people, in general, value education seems to be a widely observed cultural significant in China and beyond (Ross et al, 2000; Hu, 2002b; Yang, 2002; Gao, 2008), which perhaps is influenced by the Confucian philosophy on education. This has resulted in the perceived role of education as being to cultivate people and strengthen the nation. Education as a goal in itself has been shared by the whole of Chinese society (Cheng, 2000; Hu, 2002), as a Confucian saying goes: "Everything else is low, only education is high." Education is regarded as a means to an individual's success, and a foundation for national revitalization and modernization (Hu, 2002b: 97; Zhao, 2008a, b).

This valuing of, and belief in, education and learning has a strong influence on educational practices, parenting, and teachers and students' lives, across all sectors in China. In the case of teachers, these valuable cultural traditions used to serve as teachers' key power sources and foundations of teachers' professional authority and, as a consequence, their ability to influence students' beliefs, attitudes, and behaviour (Gao, 2008; Kelchtermans, 2005). In the traditional Chinese cultural discourses, teachers used to enjoy high social status and are regarded as being in the same league as other key cultural figures, including heaven, earth, the emperor and parents, and highly valued as intellectuals as seen in Gao's (2008) work:

"In the government's ideological propaganda as well as in public discourses, teachers are consistently portrayed as 'soul engineers'."

While bearing in mind these cultural traditions of reverence for education and teachers, the economic and industrial development in China in recent decades, alone with globalization around the world, have been profoundly impacting on education, peculiarly on teachers' work and life. Specifically, at a macro-economic level the national economy of China has reoriented towards an industrial and a market-driven model, which has achieved astounding economic success very rapidly. Part of the effect of the radical industrialization and commercialization on the education system is seen in the increased marketization of education, arrived at over a relatively short span of time in the last fifteen years or so, which is historically very brief given the long history of Chinese civilization.

It seems that the same social-economic and industrial approach has been applied to the school system, driven by the ontological belief and assumptions of developing a market-driven educational model. This "marketization" model of education encourages the delivery of educational services to parental consumers and other public sector stakeholders, who, in turn, have some degree of freedom in choosing and bargaining over the educational provision (see also Goodson, 2001: 51). The problem is not so much with the concept of choice, but with the desires that underpin parental choice, i.e. the end result of examination scores and grades and the fact that this becomes the pure goal and perceived status of an educational "service sector".

The radical changes in the wider social contexts have therefore caused a sort of paradoxes in education, which in one way challenges education and teachers to adapt to the changes undergoing in the wider society, in another, has inevitably resulted in some kind of unintended outcomes in teaching and learning, in the process of social transition in this country, which is manifested in terms of deskilling of teaching, marginalized learning and teacher vulnerability, etc. (Gao, 2008; Goodson, 2003; Ball, 2003).

Schools, in this system, are not only places to cultivate people and mark out potential university students, but also act as:

"locomotives of education development and are showcases for local educational achievement" (Wong and Ysui, 2007: 467; Ball, 2003).

which rests a lot upon the instrument of teachers' performances, and engenders a type of culture of "performativity" present in both public and private schools, and in how teachers then work within them. The performances of individual teachers serve as measures of productivity and displays of "quality" (Ball, 2008). Thus accountability and judgments are used as means of control of the value and worth of teacher's work, which consequently affects the teacher's feelings when the value of judgement and the teacher's personal view of worth and mission are in conflict. It is often identified by teachers themselves as coming from specific areas (Zhao, 2009): the relatively low standing of teachers in society, the concomitant relatively modest rate of pay, the emotional and physical exhaustion resulting from a teacher's workload, and the feeling that they are not truly capable of functioning properly as a teacher, when they are driven away from their professional mission as developing people toward a professional culture of performance and accountability. As a result, teachers become deskilled and somewhat vulnerable.

When the resources, thoughts and time are channelled into examinations and competitions, and when teachers are occupied by the thought of examination results, it inevitably marginalizes genuine learning. For instance, Gardner (1989: 250) insightfully points out that the educational system is competitive, after having been to China several times to visit schools and universities; he says, "in China, education is considered a race", where students start education as early as possible and try to reach to the end as soon as possible. Ironically, what is missing is perhaps the process and love of learning. And maybe this is the "cost" of such competitions. This kind of cognition of Chinese education may appear to be generalized. But, in reality, to some degree, it is still evident in forms of teaching competitions, various mandated student examinations and all kinds of student contests.

These outcomes of the recent socio-economic development and its impact on education in turn pose challenges for the whole society and education to attend to.

> "This draws attention to the impact of changing educational conditions, in particular, educational reforms related to devolution and commercialization, on the teaching profession in many countries, which makes teachers feel ever more deskilled and threatened." (Gao, 2008: 155)

The teacher population is large, and the starting points vary between regions, specific schools and individual teachers, for historical reasons. There is still much to do to draw attention to the quality of teachers' work and life, so that they can enjoy and gain more satisfaction from teaching, and reduce professional frustration or stagnation. What teachers know, and how they express their knowledge, determines, to a large degree, what, and how students learn in the classroom. Only when teachers are empowered with knowledge and flexibility, can they increase students' learning opportunities, by creating alternative conditions for students' learning. The understanding and advancement of knowledge about teachers and education may play a role in the improvement and transformation of educational practices in China.

Providing adequate education and teacher development for such a huge population is an extremely hard task for the system, while the government has realized that they cannot afford to ignore teachers and teacher education (Yang, 2002), as they did during the "Cultural Revolution" (1966-1976). The government and the public have realized that, to improve the education of its people, China has to create a large number of teachers who are well-motivated individuals with skills and adaptability to match developments in China and the world (Yang and Wu, 1999). Teachers are perceived to be the foundation of education itself. In the similar line, Xu and Connelly (2009: 221) emphasize that:

> "Teachers are at the human-to-human curriculum and teaching intersection, at the point where formal curriculum, students, teachers and culture intersect into. They are, as the idea of teacher proof curriculum ironically implies, vital to educational success and reform. But instead of teacher proofing the process, it is important to understand how teachers relate to external forces like policy and curriculum materials as they teach. Educational reform comes down always to teachers and students acting together in curricular settings."

Consequently, teachers and teacher education have received a great deal of attention, which has mainly taken the form of legislation, increasing financial subsidies, and attempts to elevate teachers' social and professional status (Hu, 2005; Goodson, 2003). This indicates a noticeable tendency to recognize the centrality of teachers in theory and understanding, which is a sign of a humanistic growth in education around the world (Goodson, 1992; 2003).

In reality, teachers as persons who teach and learn and the major workforce in education have received, however, less professional understanding (e.g. Goodson, 1992; 2007). In order for the reform of curriculum and educational system to produce sustainable and positive effect on its future – children and young people, those who directly work with our future generations and carry out the national curriculum play a crucial role in influencing our education and the future of this nation. Developing professional knowledge about teachers will forge a new direction for education and policymaking in order to move education at both basic level and tertiary level forward through the agency of teaching and teachers (Goodson and Ball, 1985; Goodson, 1992, 2003).

At the micro level, my experience of teaching and then doing academic work in China, has allowed me to witness the system and many teachers striving for, and seeking, knowledge to improve their understanding and expertise in teaching. As a result, it leads me to think – what actually makes a teacher? What inspires us to teach? How are we experiencing this changing world as teachers? Studies on teachers' thinking and knowledge through narrative inquiries (e.g. Elbaz, 1983; Connelly, Clandinin & He, 1997), and teachers' professional lives through life-history (e.g. Sikes and Goodson, 2001; Goodson, 2003) in the recent two decades, have established approaches to these fundamental questions and set up the groundwork for professional knowledge about teachers. Along these streams of research, this book attempts to advance the area by linking up knowledge about teachers and teachers' knowledge by joining the context and teachers themselves, from outside in and inside out, in order to transform teaching practice in the changing context. Goodson (2003: 7) puts it this way:

> "The joining of 'stories of action' to 'theories of context' is especially imperative… Without this kind of knowledge, teaching becomes the technical delivery of other people's purposes. Such a mission is unlikely to appeal to the creative and caring people we need to educate our children."

This form of professional knowledge is created through the new traditions of research that seek to broaden the focus of the work with teachers established as life-history and biographical studies to include the social and political, the contextual and the collective of teachers' work and life (e.g. Goodson and Sikes, 2001; Roberts, 2002). The understanding and advancement of knowledge about teachers will play a role in the improvement and transformation of educational practices at all levels in China, as Goodson (2003: xiii) elaborates:

> "While a broader conception of professional knowledge and professional development is a worthwhile end in itself, there are further benefits from a wider focus on professional life and work in terms of elaboration and delivery of educational reforms and change initiatives."

Therefore, this work is dedicated to the Chinese educational system and people work in it for better understanding of teachers, taking advantage of my inter-cultural experience and dual position as both insider and outsider (Ellis and Bochner, 2000). Having studied and worked in China for most of my life so far and worked and studied outside of China for nearly six years, I use the reflexivity and the benefit of my expertise in this field to provide insight into what is said in this book, in the way that the interpretation is grounded in the author's authentic experience, and the teachers' lived experiences through research. This may also facilitate understanding why it is that some teachers remain trapped in underlying beliefs and notions of teaching, often continuing in the same way in which they were taught; how we can go about breaking that cycle; how teachers interact with the contexts in which they work; how teachers exactly carry out their work, and how they feel about the way they are doing their job. Through life-history narrative, I can listen to teachers and hear what they expressed about these issues, in terms of what they did, and do, and why, and how, they think, feel, and aspire, in their continuous experience with the society. The wholeness of the individual's educational life as the most significant part of their life-history serves as a crucial way to develop professional knowledge about teachers (Goodson, 2003).

It has been recognized that teachers stand at the interface of the transmission of knowledge, skills and traditional values of our cultures. Support for their well-being and knowledge development is, therefore, a fundamental and integral part of efforts to raise standards of teaching and to improve learning, and, in a broader sense, to progress education (Day 1999; Fullan, 2001; Goodson, 2003; Zhao,

2008a). Yet, teaching occurs in different cultures, the variety of which is stunning (Bruner, 1996). We need to provide teachers with some insight about their own folk theories that guide their teaching, to facilitate reflection on their own practice, in order for them to understand their own pedagogy and take a step forward (Bruner, 1996; Zhao, 2008a). In China, perhaps effort should be made to provide a more relaxed, creative, and flexible exploratory curriculum and environment, which may lead to a new horizon of education. Education, rather than revolution, is the catalyst for social change.

To the extent that change occurs in each society, the mode may differ (Gardner, 1989). This work will contribute to the knowledge and understanding of the reality of Chinese teachers' learning and work, particularly from English as a foreign language area, based on their own accounts. It will make the effort to identify the characteristics (nature) of their knowledge of teaching in their own words. It serves that audience looking for the present experience of, and humanistic understanding of, teachers' learning and working life.

Hence, the importance and purpose of this book must be seen as giving voice to the teachers' experience and knowledge, as a first step towards making further change possible, and fostering development toward a desired form of practice, in relation to English as a foreign language (EFL) education in particular, and in relation to education in general. This is achieved through teachers' description in research of their learning and teaching experiences in the form of pedagogical stories, incidents, and metaphorical thinking. I hope this kind of work can interest teachers, and make a difference in their practice. This is also a part of the value I can see in academic practice and that research can make a difference to society and to the individual's quality of life.

This book synthesizes what has been done for knowledge about teachers with an empirical study conducted by myself and philosophical discussions about it, by connecting the Western literature to the teaching practice in China (see also Zhao, 2007). This will bridge the gap between the life-history methodology and teaching practice under Confucian tradition by setting out to investigate Chinese teachers' understanding about teaching and developing knowledge about their work. As a result, given the context of the book written in English, there is the hope that this work will contribute to cross-cultural communication, human knowledge and understanding of teaching and learning.

The book is organized into seven chapters. Chapter Two looks at the relevant literature and maps the field of knowledge about teachers, aiming to establish the conceptual framework for this work by introducing the key concepts in this area, such as teachers' knowledge, teachers' voices, stories, and critical incidents in their life-history. The purpose is to provide the language and knowledge, established from the literature, to cater to the developing knowledge about teachers by linking up teachers' knowledge.

Chapter Three concentrates on the basic methodological considerations in order to best explore professional knowledge about teachers. It revolves around understanding the life-history narrative perspective in relation to understanding teacher's knowledge as a starting point to develop professional knowledge about teachers. This chapter clarifies a few concepts, such as narrative and life-history, to establish and justify the narrative of life-history perspective that underpins knowledge about teachers.

Chapters Four and Five demonstrate how the life-history narrative methodology is applied in studying about Chinese teachers, focusing on the diachronic and synchronic framework for narrative analysis. It is illustrated with an intergenerational case along the diachronic dimension, and the key metaphors and critical incidents derived from life-history narrative of individual teachers along the synchronic dimension. Chapter Six discusses the theme from both synchronic and diachronic analysis which characterizes Chinese teachers' pedagogy intertwined with caring and grammar teaching. Chapter Seven shares some of my philosophical reflection on research for knowledge about teachers. I put a sample biographical interview and a follow-up conversation transcript translated from Mandarin to English in the appendix.

Chapter Two

Navigating the Conceptual Landscape

This chapter surveys the relevant works on teachers' knowledge research and sets up the theoretical framework and the conceptual landscape for developing knowledge about teachers, by introducing the key concepts, such as the teachers' voices, stories and folkways; image and/or metaphor. These notions are further linked up with life-history synthesized to generate professional knowledge in the field.

Educational research has long been studying teachers and the nature of teaching, and it has been increasingly recognized that teachers themselves, as well as the methods and materials they use, are central to improving teaching and students' learning (Calderhead, 1987; 1988; 1996; Elbaz, 1983; Shulman, 1987; Freeman and Johnson, 1998, 2006). Studies of teachers' knowledge and professional lives (e.g. Ball and Goodson, 1985; Goodson, 1992; Goodson and Sikes, 2001; Huberman, 1989; Clandinin and Connelly, 1996, 2000; Wu, 2005; Zhao, 2008a) have further developed the knowledge base for recognizing the dialectic relationship between teachers' understanding of teaching and the wider social contexts in which they teach and live. That, to some extent, has established a baseline foundation for developing professional knowledge about teachers and their work.

The question as to what makes someone a good and able teacher provoked the study into the nature of the knowledge for, and of, teachers, and the sources of that knowledge. Their understanding of teaching and learning results from various learning experiences constitutes the major sources for teachers' underlying knowledge that guide their day-to-day practice (Calderhead, 1988; Elbaz, 1983; Grossman, 1990; Shulman, 1999, 2006). Until the 1980s, research on teaching and teachers appeared largely focused on teachers' performance and cognition, rather than on teachers' knowledge and understanding of teaching (Grossman, 1990: 4; Calderhead, 1996). Teacher knowledge, in the arena of research, was identified as a "neglected area" (Calderhead, 1996: 710) or "missing paradigm" (Shulman, 1986: 87; Poulson, 2001, 2003: 2). Likewise, Freeman (1996b: 351) identified this as an "unstudied problem" in research on teacher learning in language teaching. Since then, research on teacher knowledge in general, or on EFL education in particular, has proliferated (see Connelly et al, 1997; Calderhead, 1996; Freeman, 1996a, b). Calderhead (1996: 709) identifies research in this area as now:

> "…constituting a substantial area of inquiry in explorations of the nature of teaching."

Specifically, his (ibid) overview indicates that research in the recent two decades has been particularly characterized by an emphasis on the content and nature of teachers' knowledge and beliefs, and on the processes involved in the growth of professional knowledge in teaching:

> "…because teachers' knowledge has necessitated research to investigate teaching and teachers by embracing both cognitive and affective aspects of teachers' working life."

Within the area of educational research on teachers' knowledge, there is considerable diversity in both the contents and methods (Rosiek and Atkinson, 2005). In actuality, there exist variant views on, and differentiated approaches involving, both philosophical discussions and empirical research, from specialized researchers on teaching to more teacher-centred case studies and stories, aiming at theorizing and articulating teaching, understanding, and sharing teachers' knowledge and experience (Elbaz, 1983; Calderhead and Shorrock, 1997; Woods, 1987; Freeman 1991, 1993, 1994; Carter, 1990a).

Research on teachers' knowledge has a tradition of evolution. The increasing interest and recognition of the importance of teachers and their knowledge in relation to students' learning in education has generated debate about the repertoire of the research knowledge of teaching, understanding of teachers and their pedagogy. However, so far, there is no single consensus as to what teachers' knowledge should be, and how it should be studied. Also, to chart a human knowledge base in the area of teachers' knowledge and therefore forms of knowledge about teachers have been recognized as an ambitious and actually very challenging work (Calderhead, 1996).

Mapping the Field

Many researchers and scholars (e.g. Rosiek and Atkinson, 2005; Fenstermacher, 1994; Carter, 1990a) have attempted to survey the field and give an overview picture of the perspectives and approaches. However, they have made it apparent there has been a tendency towards division or polarization of this research area into two major streams. One is largely concerned with knowledge for teachers – termed as a knowledge base and/or formal knowledge (Shulman, 1987; Fenstermacher, 1994; Poulson, 2001) regarding what knowledge teachers should or need to have, as well as the nature of the knowledge necessary for teaching and the sources of that knowledge. The other is concerned more with teachers' experience-based knowledge, what teachers actually hold and how they display their knowledge in practice – this can be termed as teacher knowledge-in-use, or teachers' knowledge, and is also described as practical knowledge (Elbaz, 1983) and personal practical knowledge (Connelly et al, 1997; Connelly and Clandinin, 1999; Meijer et al, 1999; Golombek, 1998). Still, Fenstermacher (1994: 3) acknowledges in his review on the known and the knower, and notions of knowledge on teachers and teaching:

> "Of particular interest is the growing research literature on the knowledge that teachers generate as a result of their experience as teachers, in contrast to the knowledge of teaching that is generated by those who specialize in research on teaching. This distinction, as will become apparent, is one that divides more conventional scientific approaches to the study of teaching."

The above charting of the literature is not ideal, according to Fenstermacher (1994), because distinguishing teacher knowledge into formal and practical knowledge is hard to define. For example, knowledge on teaching and teachers can be gained in formal and informal ways, such as through degree courses and training programmes, and in actual teaching practice and experience. On the other hand, knowledge of teaching as understanding and contemplation can be tacit, but not necessarily less formal, or more practical (Buchmann, 1987, 1989), and debate on what counts as knowledge is still open and on-going (Irme, 1982; Sikes, 2004). In addition, what can be defined as formal knowledge does not have final legitimacy. For example, it would be inappropriate for a scholar to regard knowledge embedded in experience as not being formal.

Being aware of these dilemmas and dynamics in relation to teacher knowledge studies, scholars such as Carter (1990a), and Doyle (Doyle and Carter, 1996), have tried to avoid the term "knowledge" which has been recognized as problematic when defining or setting boundaries (Carter, 1990a, see also Wu, 2005). For example, when reviewing the literature on teacher knowledge, Carter and Doyle (Doyle and Carter, 1996; Carter 1990a) use "learning to teach", using the teacher's personal narrative and life-history, to indicate a connotation of the scale of teacher knowledge, laying much emphasis on teachers' knowledge which is derived from biographical and personal narrative studies of teachers. They discovered the amalgamated nature of the topic of teachers' knowledge using methodological considerations of life-history and personal experience, merging them into one domain. They tend to gloss over and blur the boundary of theory and practice (Clandinin and Connelly 2000; Goodson and Sikes, 2001).

However, this reconciled view of conducting research has disturbed and challenged the view that sees research as divided distinctly into theory and practice. This strand of research, yet, is not without criticisms about its shortcomings. The major debate is that research can achieve the fullest success in connecting individual narrative and biography to wider social and cultural change and development (see also Hargreaves, 1996; Goodson, 1995). Therefore, scholars such as Fenstermacher (1994) call attention to the usefulness of talking about and promoting understanding of the field in alternative ways that break down the distinction between formal knowledge and practical knowledge. Likewise, after having navigated the multiple perspectives of teacher knowledge with four approaches such as:

"...the scholarship of teaching, action research and teacher research, narrative inquiry, and critical-cultural teacher research."

Rosiek and Atkinson (2005: 422) realize that this divides the field of teacher knowledge in even more unproductive and over-simplified ways. Therefore, they (ibid: 442) suggest bridging the divide with a

> "...semiotic theory that acknowledges the way in which teacher knowledge is irreducibly mediated by multiple discourses while preserving a commitment to the idea that individual teachers' experiences can be a source of novel and useful knowledge."

In navigation the literature on teachers' knowledge and learning to teach, a few commentators, such as Goodson (1992) and Cortazzi (1993), have created new ways to bridge the divides and formed a new approach to recognizing the significant work in the literature by identifying and highlighting the most prominent concepts, in order to connect them together and inform new research.

Further into this navigation of the literature, the organization and focus is on identifying a few significant concepts in relation to teacher knowledge studies, aiming at establishing the language and knowledge derived from the existing literature (e.g. Goodson and Sikes, 2001; Calderhead, 1996; Fenstermacher, 1994; Wu, 2005; Carter, 1990a; Carter and Doyle, 1996; Feldman, 1997). The purpose is to establish a conceptual framework and background for developing professional knowledge about teachers, within which disciplines in educational research will inevitably overlap. Research has yielded a number of key concepts in this area, such as the knowledge-base, teachers' voices, images and/or metaphors, stories and folkways, critical incidents and life-history (e.g. Goodson and Sikes, 2001; Calderhead, 1996; Doyle and Carter, 1996; Cortazzi, 1993; Buchmann, 1987; Bruner, 1996).

The Knowledge-base for Teachers

The question as to what knowledge teachers should and/or need to have has provoked the study on the nature – the content and character – of the knowledge necessary for teaching, and the sources of that knowledge. Part of the effort is to conceptualize, codify and articulate teaching knowledge in order to enhance the quality and status of teaching and care for student learning (e.g. Grossman,

1990; Shulman, 1987; Freeman and Johnson, 1998). Shulman (1986, 1987) and his colleagues, such as Grossman (1990), have tried to conceptualize the knowledge for teaching within a frame of a knowledge-base and asserted that it should, at minimum, include the following knowledge domains: content/subject-matter, general pedagogy, pedagogical content, curricula and students, purposes, and context. Among which it is regarded that pedagogical content knowledge and subject knowledge are specific and essential for teaching well (Shulman, 1987; Grossman, 1990). The conceptualization of a knowledge-base for teaching and teachers has been highly influential in generating educational studies to explore how it can better influence policy and practice, for instance, by drawing attention to the importance of teachers' subject knowledge in classroom teaching (Calderhead, 1996; Poulson, 2003), or how pre-service teachers develop, and how experienced teachers express these aspects of teaching knowledge in practice (see e.g. Bishop, 2000; Poulson, 2003; Gudmundsdottir, 1995). Specific to EFL teachers, Freeman and Johnson (1998) have argued that the core of language teacher knowledge must include the activity of the teaching itself, the teacher who does it, the context in which it is done, and the pedagogy by which it is done. On the other hand, the knowledge-base is regarded by other scholars as "normatively oriented" (e.g. Fenstermacher, 1994: 17) or "low-context" knowledge, which is more explicitly prescriptive and less tied to any particular context (Cortazzi, 1993). This is in contrast to the knowledge used by the teacher in practice, which is thought of as "high-context knowledge", in the sense that most of the relevant information necessary to interpret what teachers say and do is either related to the physical environment or internalized in the person (ibid: 9).

The conceptualization of the knowledge-base for teaching and teachers is a useful tool for thinking about and informing teacher education and teaching practice, when applied for understanding the teaching process, and improving teaching, rather than just using it to assess teaching for accountability. Other scholars, such as Lather (1986), Goodson and Hargreaves (1996: 9), also have pointed out that this notion of knowledge-base has limitations in that it does not include other significant aspects of teaching knowledge, such as the moral, aesthetic, political, cultural, and personal dimensions. When teachers themselves, and the context in which they teach, are detached from each other, the capacity of such principles to inform and transform classroom practice, or teacher education, would be limited.

In addition, Goodson and Hargreaves (1996: 9) point out that the discussion of knowledge-base tends to privilege knowledge and cognition above care as the foundation of school-teaching. They (ibid) continue to stress that

"...care, as well as cognition, should be at the heart of the teaching profession, and, for many teachers, is so."

Further on, Cochran-Smith and Lytle, (1996, cited in Day, 1999: 44; see also Cochran-Smith and Lytle, 1990) also recognize that:

"What is missing from the knowledge-base for teaching are the voices of teachers themselves."

Scholars, such as Shulman (1987) and Grossman (1990), aim to codify and conceptualize a knowledge-base for teaching for the purpose of raising the standard of teaching and teacher education, the endeavour of the advocates of the knowledge-base for teaching seems also to generate professional reforms and to elevate the professional status of teaching and teachers, by articulating and communicating what teachers should know and be able to do. However, if the authentic voice of the teacher is not obvious, an important aspect remains missing in the knowledge-base. Freeman and Johnson (1998) argue for reconceptualising the knowledge-base for teachers in language teaching. They believe that a knowledge-base for language teaching needs to account for the teacher as a learner of teaching; it should centre on the teacher who does it, and the social context of schools, and schooling, within which teacher-learning and teaching occur. In a similar line, Golombek (1998) suggests opening windows on possibilities in studying second and foreign language teachers' ways of knowing and how they use their knowledge in their language classroom.

The Teachers' Voices

The notion of knowledge-base no doubt has contributed to the debate about knowledge for teaching and teachers, which contrasts with what knowledge teachers actually use in their practice. Research on the nature and the scope of teaching knowledge in use is focused on what teachers actually know, and how they come to know it (see Calderhead, 1996; Elbaz, 1983, 1991; Carter, 1990a;

Doyle and Carter, 1996; Poulson, 2001). In other words, it examines the substance and characters of the knowledge held and applied by teachers, as well as its influential factors. Therefore, the centrality of teachers and their voices are recognized as important in order to understand their practice, to present their knowledge and its growth (Elbaz, 1983, 1991). Not until recently, is the term "voice" increasingly used by those concerned with developing education through listening to voices from various participants in education (see e.g. Calderhead, 1996; Martin et al, 2002; Goodson, 1994, 1995; Goodson and Sikes, 2001; Carter and Doyle, 1996; Elbaz, 1983, 1991, 1997; Cortazzi, 1993; Richardson, 1994; Hargreaves, 1996; Jensen et al, 1997). When discussing teachers' voices in relation to teachers' knowledge, Cortazzi (1993: 10), for instance, refers teachers' voices to teachers' own accounts and narrative stories that teachers themselves describe, and through them understand their working lives. He continues

"...the term emphasizes the need for teachers to talk about their experiences and perspectives on teaching in their own words, as part of the current debate and process of change in education which affects, among others, the teachers themselves."

In a consistent line, Butt et al, 1992, in Goodson (1994: 31), argued:

"The teacher's voice is important in that it carries the tone, the language, the quality, the feelings that are conveyed by the way a teacher speaks or writes. In a political sense the notion of the teacher's voice addresses the right to speak and be presented. It can present both the unique individual and the collective voice."

What is needed is just to use the sense of ears to listen to the voices of teachers and voices of research about teachers when making policies. However, about teachers' voices, there is no agreement in the field yet (Elbaz, 1991). For many researchers, teachers' voicing their thinking, and their action, are seen as two separate domains; we study teachers' thinking and listen to teachers' voices in order to learn more about teachers' action, since the teachers' thinking is assumed to direct her teaching. Teachers' speaking, thought and action are regarded as one interrelated domain in many studies about teachers' knowledge (Clark and Peterson, 1986, in Elbaz, 1991). A critical stance of studies in teachers' knowledge incorporating teachers' own voices is that of an epistemological demand and methodological consideration (Freeman, 1994, 1996a; Goodson and Sikes, 2001; Sparkes 1994a, 1999, 2002), because teachers know a great deal as a result of their own learning experiences, teacher education courses, teaching practices, instincts and personal interests; teachers are particularly knowledgeable about their own teaching, themselves, their ideals of education, the students they teach, and the context in which they teach. What teachers know, and how their knowing is expressed in teaching, is very important as a source for teaching knowledge and knowledge about teachers (see Elbaz, 1983). On this assumption, "teacher knowledge and knowing affects every aspect of the teaching act" which impacts on student learning (Connelly et al, 1997: 666; Cortazzi, 1993). And this is an essential part of knowledge about teachers.

The importance of listening to teachers' accounts is simple, for it is an ongoing attempt to understand teachers and their teaching, in order, ultimately, to improve their engagement with educational development through the improvement of their practice; they are key components that influence the quality of student learning (Cortazzi, 1993; Goodson and Numan, 2002; Poulson, 2001; Hargreaves, 1993, 2003; J. Olson, 2002a, b). Therefore, research on developing professional knowledge about teachers perhaps should, to some extent, include more of "teachers' perspective" and "teachers' point of view" about their own practice of teaching and learning, in other words, "from the inside" of teachers and their culture (Elbaz, 1991: 10; Cortazzi, 1993: 5; Freeman, 1994).

The value, therefore, of recognizing teachers' centrality and voices is multifold (Calderhead, 1996). First of all, it contributes to the epistemic scope, in a way the knower and the known extend from university, with its specialist scholars, to school teachers and their knowledge. Secondly, by using teachers' accounts, taking information from teachers' experience into consideration, it contributes to understanding something so intensely personal as teaching, and the person who teaches (Goodson, 1992, 1994; Goodson and Sikes, 2001; Fenstermacher, 1994). Thirdly, attending to teachers, and including teachers' perspective on, and participation in, educational improvement and teacher development is essential for these attempts to be successful and really effective (Hargreaves, 1996, 2003; Goodson, 2001). Hence, listening to teachers articulating their educational experiences and understandings and their needs, making them available and accessible to policy makers and teacher educators, as well as teachers in practice, or for sharing ideas and bridging cultures, is an empathic means of enabling, and then empowering, teachers in their process of improvement and development of education.

In this sense, teachers as intelligent agents, with personal agency, and their voices, can be a source of knowledge for practices and policies, and therefore can illuminate teaching and learning (Carter and Doyle, 1996; Goodson, 1992; Sparkes, 1999; Bateson, 1990; J. Olson 2002b; Hargreaves and Woods, 1984). Jackson (1968, in Carter, 1990a), from another angle, has reminded us that the characteristics of the teachers' language and thought may be conceptually simple and lacking in technical vocabulary, caught up with the here-and-now and in emotional ties with their students, they adopt an intuitive rather than a technical approach to classroom events, and are quite opinionated and perceptive about their classroom practices. Their account is one of "technical naïveté". He also acknowledges that what teachers' know is perhaps appropriate to the complexity and unpredictability of the settings in which they work. This seems to be what Cortazzi (1993) called the unpredictability-routine polarity in teachers' narratives of their practice. Also, researchers such as Doyle (1990, in Cortazzi, 1993: 9) and Carter (1993) suggest that teachers' knowledge is context-embedded and "event-structured" case knowledge:

> "What teachers know about chunks of context, instructional actions, or management strategies are tied to specific events they have experienced ... teacher knowledge is fundamentally particularistic and situational. Their knowledge is, in other words, case knowledge."

Despite this, educational thinkers and researchers may take this feature as an advantage in educational research, drawing closer to participants' real and working life situation and circumstances (see Pring 2000; Sparkes 1994a, b, 2002; Sikes, 2004; Tripp, 1993, 1994; Cortazzi, 1993). For instance, Pring (2000: 120), argues that it is an epistemic as much as a practical point to study teachers, for only he or she, on a day-to-day basis, has access to the data crucial for an understanding of the classroom; in addition, an understanding of the situation calls for reference to the accepted social rules and values within which the teachers are operating. It requires, too, reference to the teachers' interpretation of these rules and to the constant, often minute, judgements by which teachers adapt to evolving situations. This demands of us an understanding of the new ways that are already in plain view, and to look at the commonsense or commonplace practices critically, to unpack the underpinning values that characterize teachers' teaching (Wittgenstein, 1953, in Latham, 2004; Trip, 1993). One of the concerns in research on teachers' knowledge, in including teachers' accounts, is that researchers have to find ways of learning what teachers know without employing methods that distort or destroy this knowledge, while aiming at presenting teachers' knowledge and then knowledge about teachers (see Black and Halliwell, 2000). Knowledge also differs in how widely it is distributed, how it is gained and held, and how it is seen as warranted (Buchmann, 1987, 1988; Sikes, 2004). This is indicated in Goodson's (1997) work:

> "There is a belief that we can facilitate the genuine voice of the oppressed subject, uncontaminated by active human collaboration. Teachers talking about their practice – providing us with personal and practical insights into their expertise, avoid academic colonization."

While teachers' narratives and stories are employed as alternative ways to present their knowledge and understanding, also the genre of representing this form of research needs to adapt to the characteristics of the participants and their worlds. At times, academic investigators have to create a way by telling tales, or relating folklore, to safeguard the participant's and the author's genuine and authentic voices and knowledge (e.g. Sikes, 2005; Sparkes, 2002, 2003; Geertz, 1988; Denison, 1998; Denison and Rinehart, 2000). Therefore, what the teachers know, and how they know it, very much needs preserving, in order to get closer to the reality of their world and worldview, as a departure point to understand and improve their situated, intimate and tacit knowledge (Goodson, 2003; J. Olson, 2002a).

A question remains: can researchers take them at their word? (Freeman, 1994, 1996a; Connery, 1999). This concern is not unique to this form of research though – almost any research has to rely on what and how the researcher and/or participants say, do, or write, in forms of language – even in research that uses quantitative data, the numbers, symbols, and statistics are interpreted using linguistic expressions too. Therefore, the participants' voices and knowledge are fore grounded as much as possible. When necessary, the role of the researcher is to offer interpretations with the assistance of knowledge from the wider literature, to bridge understanding by making their telling more overt and accessible to the audience, from different backgrounds and different cultural origins.

Development in teachers' knowledge studies incorporating teachers' voices has been firmly linked to narratives such as of life experiences (Cortazzi, 1993; Calderhead, 1996: 712; Goodson and Sikes; Freeman, 1994). Teachers' knowledge, along with narrative research, has fruitfully pushed the boundaries of educational research, contributing to broadening the ways and the scope of understanding teaching and teachers, as well as human knowledge about teachers (see Fenstermacher, 1994; Calderhead, 1996; Goodson, 1994; Freeman, 1996a; Carter and Doyle, 1996; Huberman, 1995).

Images and Metaphors

Knowledge originated from teachers' voices and practices is termed as practical knowledge (e.g. Elbaz, 1983, 1991) and personal practical knowledge by Clandinin and Connelly (1996; see also Connelly et al, 1997). They contend that narrative seems to be particularly fitting to make public teachers' voices. They need to use narrative to adequately constitute and present teachers' knowledge, which contains the teachers' rules, principles, personal philosophies and everyday work, in order to depict teachers' images of teaching, and of themselves (Calderhead, 1996; Cortazzi, 1993). Elbaz (1983) adopted the term practical knowledge in her case study, over a two-year period, of a high school teacher she called Sarah, perhaps one of the earliest empirical studies to explicitly embark on the tacit dimension of human knowledge from the teacher's perspective (Elbaz, 1991; Calderhead, 1996; Clandinin and Connelly, 1988, 1994, 1996, 2000; Goodson, 1994; Conle, 2000a, b; Golombek and Johnson, 2004).

Elbaz (1983) attempts to define the character of knowledge used by the teacher in practice. She refers broadly to practical knowledge as the knowledge teachers have of classroom situations and the practical dilemmas they face in carrying out purposeful action in these settings. Elbaz (1983: 5) maintains that:

"This knowledge encompasses first-hand experience of students' learning styles, interests, needs, strengths and difficulties, and a repertoire of instructional techniques and classroom management skills."

She identifies five broad domains of the content of the practical knowledge of the teacher: (a) knowledge of self; (b) the milieu of teaching; (c) subject matter; (d) curriculum development; and, (e) instruction. Moreover, Elbaz tries to organize such a reservoir of practical knowledge using a structure of three levels. First, as rules of practice, which are decisions on what actions to take in particular situations? For example, when a novice teacher faces a distraction in class caused by a few students – her rule in dealing with this classroom incident is not to make the whole class unhappy because of a minority, instead, her decision is to talk to the specific students after class and lightly criticize them. Second, as practical principles, which are broader statements for reflecting upon situations or selecting from among practices which apply to specific circumstances; Zhao and Poulson (2006) illustrate this point with the veteran teacher in their study, Ms. Tang, who holds a dual role in her work, as an English teacher as well as deputy-head. Her principle priority is given to teaching rather than administration, whenever she is in circumstances where she has to make a decision between the two. Third, as images, which is a general orienting framework, in the case of Sarah (Elbaz, 1983), they are defined as:

"…brief, descriptive, and sometimes, metaphoric statements which seem to capture some essential aspect of Sarah's perceptions of herself, her teaching, her situation in the classroom or her subject matter."

For another example of images of teaching and teachers, in Calderhead and Shorrock's (1997: 39) case studies of learning to teach, one of the novice teachers in their study, Adam, has an image of teaching which is of two aspects – personal and professional. The personal dimension of his image of teaching is concerned with his own personal quality as a teacher, being moral and caring; while the professional dimension is related to his "professional qualities", being able to ensure a suitable environment for students to learn effectively. The teachers' feelings, values, needs, experience and school folklore gives substance to these images (Elbaz, 1983; Calderhead and Shorrock, 1997).

Carter (1990: 300) comments on Elbaz's study of practical knowledge that it

"...provides insights into the overall scope and organization of teachers' knowledge. And the focus tends to be on the characteristics, rather than the substance, of what teachers know."

However, Webb and Blond (1995: 611) indicate that Elbaz's (1983) structures of teachers' practical knowledge are found to "be too neat and the boundaries too well defined." Despite this, it is recognizable that Elbaz's (e.g. 1983, 1991, Elbaz-Luwisch, 1997) work has contributed substantively to the establishment of this tradition of research. This tacit dimension of human knowledge is also referred to in various ways, for example "craft knowledge" (see Calderhead, 1996: 717), "situated knowledge" (Leinhardt, 1988: 146, 1990) or "wisdom in the practice" (Feldman, 1997: 757) that guides teachers' day-to-day practices.

From another angle, Webb and Blond (1995: 613) look at Elbaz's (1983) study of the case of Sarah, and see how her attitude of caring influences Sarah's knowing, in the image of Sarah as "ally" (helping the students beat the system) and "good energetic teacher" (who takes responsibility for student learning), as well as looking at her struggles, when she is sometimes "giving too much and challenging too little". They also (ibid: 613) recognize that, in their own study of teachers' narratives, teacher's knowledge is actually relational and dynamic, as "nested knowing" between students and teachers in their educational settings, and their interactions. They continue, to argue for recognition of an epistemological position for caring in teaching, because the teacher knows from caring about, and being in a relationship with, her/his students.

However, Webb and Blond (1995: 612) also recognize that it is a real challenge to connect caring and knowing in teacher' knowledge which has to do with the question: what is counted to be knowledge by its nature. Is it knowledge of objects? Is knowing people regarded as knowledge? How is knowledge expressed or represented (see also Sikes, 2004)? They take Code's (1991, in ibid: 612) stance and claim that knowing other people is a worthy contender for knowledge, and, in their study, lay stress on caring for the person (see also Noddings, 1984), and this is revealed as being central to what the teacher knows. This is consistent with Tirri et al's (1999) research finding, in which they assert that a teacher's professional and moral character and knowledge were interrelated and could not be separated from each other. Furthermore, Calderhead (1996: 718) also emphasizes that images and/or metaphors are important elements in the understanding of teachers' knowledge, which are non-propositional, holistic, and embrace emotionality and ethics.

Images touch on various aspects of practices as mentioned above. Teachers may portray their roles, ways of teaching, or their understanding of learning, by using expressions of imagery, which are conceptions that teachers have of their work that account for what they do, both in their roles in the classroom and in relation to students. Images as metaphors have emerged in the literature as a theme and a way of generating meaning in the study of teacher knowledge and its development (Calderhead, 1996; Carter, 1990b; Munby and Russell, 1990; Connelly et al, 1997). Teaching metaphors can be seen as "archetypes" of teachers' thinking and teaching knowledge. They have exploratory power and ability to structure information, articulate and conceptualize teachers' experiences, and illuminate understanding (Martinez et al, 2001). Carter (1990b: 110) argues that metaphors can be used as a vehicle for "modelling teachers' comprehension of their work" and for communicating messages and meanings, which are difficult to access in literal language (see Chomsky, 1972; Lakoff and Johnson, 1980). Therefore, metaphor is the 'what' and 'how' of teachers' knowledge, and is a valid source for gaining insights into teachers' thoughts and feelings regarding their teaching. This can be further linked to teacher education by reflecting upon their beliefs and negotiating their new roles in the classroom (also Tobin, 1990; Berliner, 1990; Yero, 2002). In my own study, metaphors embedded in the participants' life-history accounts stand out as a useful medium to discern their knowledge, which will be further discussed later as one of the techniques of analysis. I will return to metaphor as an element of analysis later in the methodology section.

Stories and Folkways

A group of researchers including Connelly and Clandinin and their colleagues (see, e.g. Connelly et al, 1997; Clandinin and Connelly, 1994, 1996, 2000; Xu and Connelly, 2009), have extended the notion of teachers' knowledge and represent it through teachers' experiential stories. They aim at exploring teachers' knowledge, termed as personal practical knowledge; using narrative inquiry:

"...the study of the ways humans experience the world." (Clandinin and Connelly, 1990: 2, 1994)

They have worked collaboratively with teachers over long periods of time to achieve an understanding of how they interpret and give meaning to practice and come to terms with the communication of self and the situation. They have studied teachers through observation, journal-writing, conversation, documents, and mutual construction of experiential narratives. Central to the process is the teacher's story containing personal practical knowledge (see Clandinin and Connelly, 2000; Carter, 1993; Carter and Doyle, 1996). They draw on theoretical and philosophical resources such as Dewey's work (e.g. 1929, 1938) on education in relation to time, experience and society, based on which they developed experiential stories that combine the social and the personal, and the temporal and the spatial. Through experiential stories they attempt to give voice to tacitly-held personal knowledge (Polanyi, 1958, 1962) and its practical complexity (Schwab, 1969). This personal knowledge has a practical function for deliberation; instinctive decisions, daily actions and moral wisdom (see also Eraut, 1994, 2000).

Connelly and Clandinin's conception of personal practical knowledge combined Polanyi's (e.g. 1962) sense of the personal with Schwab's (e.g. 1969) notion of the practical, and MacIntyre (1984) and Johnson's (1993) ethical intent (Conle, 2000a).The constructs Connelly, Clandinin and their colleagues (see e.g. Connelly et al, 1997: 666) developed to conceptualize personal practical knowledge through telling stories using narrative inquiry, are:

"...image, rules, practical principles, personal philosophy, metaphor, cycles, rhythms and narrative unities."

through which teachers know and structure their knowledge. Among these terms, the rules, practical principles and personal philosophies are very much consistent with Elbaz's (1983) three levels, which organized Sarah's practical knowledge, elaborated above. The content of personal theories or philosophies is very much specific to the individual knower, conceived in experiences and developed throughout their career (e.g. Ritchie, 1998; Mangubhai et al, 2004).

The notion of narrative story, according to Connelly et al (1997), is the key thread that teachers construct their knowledge along, which underscores the coherence and continuity of an individual's accounts of lived experience. The notion of story and unity, employed by the researchers, is a way of avoiding the excessive imposition of external theories or constructs. However, this may confine professional knowledge entirely within the practical terrain which would not seem a well-thought strategy for raising general professional standards.

"A much wider conception of professional knowledge would need to be defined and advocated (Goodson, 2003: xii)."

Attempting to present teachers' knowledge blended in their teaching practice and experience, remains a "puzzling" concept for many people who are not familiar with this line of research, while narrative unity, or story tries to avoid too much analytic focus on what might be seen as discrete images, which would lose the holistic sense of an individual person and his or her experiential knowledge (Clandinin and Connelly, 2000). Part of another reason might be that some stories make the presupposition that they communicate meaning in a transparent way (Conle, 2000b).

However, this may not be the case, in particular, when researchers' intentions and readers' interpretations are not universally in agreement, for things may seem obvious within one socio-cultural environment, but not in another (See Sikes, 2005). The open-endedness of the pursuit by some theorizing stories concerning working reality/ies may result in lack of certainty and precision. Sometimes, it can be risky while being very useful (Sikes, 2006).

In fact, Fenstermacher (1997: 124) asserts that story is one of the most truly useful ways of helping the understanding of teachers and their knowledge. He also points out that narrative stories are "difficult" to unpack with precision, (Fenstermacher, 1994: 12), therefore, he (1997) demands to know more about what counts as a story or narrative. My own understanding of this concern is that the sophistication of the educational practices at the level of school and classroom is intrinsically involved with people and their traditions. Dealing with ambiguity and contradictions and learning along the way is a working theory in this stream of research (e.g. Sikes, 2006; Clandinin and Connelly, 2000). One thing known with certainty and precision about teachers' perceived understanding is that the teachers change and grow over the life of their career (Goodson and Sikes, 2001). As for the issue of precision, some educational thinkers and researchers, such as Clandinin and Connelly (2000: 9), have tried to avoid theoretical precision, and confess that "certainty is not a goal", because they think theoretical precision is troublesome when the centrality of the inquiry is people and the sophistication of their practice (see also Bruner, 1996; Sikes, 2006). This concern has also long been debated in philosophy, for instance by Aristotle (in Irme, 1982: 139):

> "It is the mark of the educated man and proof of his culture that in every subject he looks for only so much precision as its nature permits."

A possible solution is to pursue precision methodologically, when presenting narrative knowledge in research on human experience in education and the social sciences, by avoiding excessive jargon, or too much human imposition, and by being faithful to the narrative data. I endorse Silverman's idea (1998: 111, in Sikes, 2005: 90):

> "All we sociologists have are stories. Some come from other people, some from us. What matters is to understand how and where the stories are produced, what sort of stories they are, and how we can put them to intelligent use in theorizing about social life."

Some researchers may turn to alternative terms to avoid the ambiguity caused by terms such as "narrative unity" or "story". For example, Gudmundsdottir (1990) uses curriculum stories to tell about teachers' knowledge of pedagogy; in Cortazzi's (see 1993: 123) study of British primary teachers' narratives, he identified 10 dualities from teachers' descriptions of their teaching experience, such as in the polarity of "enjoyment-grind", where teaching was reported as being "hard work", while also permeated with enjoyment. This notion is important for understanding the teachers' narratives, where teachers experience teaching as being "tiring", giving them "bitter joy", or making them "painfully happy" (e.g. Zhao and Poulson, 2006; Zhao, 2008a). While many researchers in teachers' knowledge studies have striven to theorize human experience, representing teachers' knowledge with narratives, and sponsoring teachers' voice, the notion of personal practical knowledge tends to concentrate on the personal dimension, and to focus on teachers' narratives, and has not moved too much beyond that. Poulson (2001: 52) highlights that there is still much to be learned, for example, she (see 2001: 49-50) points to the scarcity of:

"...reference to the socio-cultural and historical contexts of teachers' knowledge, or to teaching as social practice."

And of cultural practice (see also Goodson, 1992, 2001; and Hargreaves, 1999), which deserves more attention and connections. E. Thomas (1997) also asserts that certain key contextual values and culture-specific features are part of the cultural context of both learners and teachers. People such as teachers, and their knowledge, are relational to others and their environment, because they do not exist in isolation. Teachers exist in relation to students, and the institution in which they teach. They create and conduct their practice underlined by their knowledge, such as the values and beliefs derived from their experience and cultural traditions.

For instance, Bruner (1996, see also S. Strauss, 2001) uses the concept of folk psychology and identifies a further concept in education, which he terms as folk pedagogy, or folkways of teaching to illustrate some human tendencies and deeply ingrained socio-cultural beliefs about teaching as cultural practice, such as how learning takes place in the mind, and assumptions teachers have about children (Bruner, 1996; S. Strauss, 2001).

"Folkways" of teachers' teaching refer to those skills which teachers picked up from the acquaintance and observation of others and absorbed into their own practice (Buchmann, 1987; Lortie, 1975). Generally speaking, folkways are not even noticed until they have existed a long time, and then mostly by outsiders; insiders feel that folkways are "true" and "right" (Sumner, 1906/1979, 1960; Buchmann, 1987). From Sumner's work (1906/1979, in Buchmann, 1987): "The tradition is its own warrant... The notion of right is in the folkways". In relation to teacher's knowledge, Buchmann (1987: 3-7) refers to "folkways" of teaching as the base from which teachers' knowledge is derived. They are an "integral part of personal biography and collective tradition", such as cultural norms and manifestations of education. According to Bruner (1996: 60), the importance of knowledge accumulated in the past is underestimated, and cultures preserve past reliable knowledge much as the common law preserves a record of how past communal conflicts were adjudicated. Therefore, Bruner (1996) asserts that in theorizing about the practice of education in the classroom and other settings, it is better to take into account the folk theories of those engaged in teaching and learning, because these culturally-coloured ways of teaching, theories and beliefs, may determine the educational practices that take place in classrooms. Reforms and innovations in teaching will achieve more if they involve changing the folk psychology and folk pedagogy of educational practitioners (Bruner, 1996).

In a consistent line, Buchmann (1987, 1989) contends that local mores, folkways, private views, and expertise of teaching are teaching knowledge, the lights teachers live by. Buchmann (1987, 1989) describes the folkways of teaching as "teaching as usual", part of the learned and practiced half-conscious way in which people go about their everyday lives. This can often be envisaged through teachers' talk about a typical day, or how they teach a typical lesson, which constitutes the tradition of teaching. Local mores overlap with folkways of teaching to some extent, as she claims it reflects the customs, moral attitudes, and manners in teaching. Teachers' private views arise from particular experiences, feelings, and characteristics of individuals, who, nevertheless, are members of groups sharing a culture. Teachers' knowledge and teaching, therefore, carries their culture and traditions. Folkways and local mores are embedded in the common practice of individual teachers' everyday teaching, educational events and customs, and signify the integration of formal knowledge, personal aspirations and goals, and cumulative experience and understanding of local situations.

The folkways and expertise of teachers' knowledge are embedded in the teacher's past experience, in the teacher's present mind and body, and in their plans and actions. It can be found in teachers' practices which rejects the segregation of thinking from action, and emphasizes that theory can be found in practice, with respect to the complications of working reality (Buchmann, 1987). Therefore, education is also a cultural practice, a process of communication of cultural values (see, Bruner, 1996; Yuan, 2003). Hence, it is imperative to acknowledge both the cultural bearings in teachers' knowledge, particularly in the cross-cultural context, such as in this study. People are part of their culture, and it will not be fruitful to divorce teachers and their understanding from their cultural background

(Perkinson, 1984).

Still, most cultural manifestations are not directly quantifiable. As a result, it is necessary to draw attention to the risk and rationale of a mere focus on personal experience and knowledge, because it can rupture the links to theoretical and contextual knowledge when not appropriately conducted. Only if these new modes link to wider narratives about social change with a global view, will teachers' knowledge become fully generative and socially and politically efficacious (Goodson and Numan, 2002: 272). Goodson (1995) (see also, Goodson and Sikes, 2001; Hargreaves, 1999) further points out that studies which locate these lives in their full context have been much less common, and sadly neglected, until recently:

> "Researchers had not confronted the complexity of the schoolteachers
> as an active agent making his or her own history."

His admonition is to "tell the story of action within a theory of context" with life-history methods (Goodson, 1992: 4, 1995: 98; 2003). Therefore, a study that links teachers' knowledge to the wider society will no doubt contribute to the literature, and to a better understanding of teachers and their knowledge development.

Life-history and Critical Incidents

These issues that emerged in the mapping of literature point to the need to connect teacher knowledge studies to the wider cultural and historical environment, and to the interaction between the conditions and factors that either enable or constrain teachers' knowledge, to provide a wider view of teachers and teaching (e.g. Bruner, 1996). Amongst the varied aspects of teachers' knowledge, it seems that one unifying avenue is the perspective of listening to the subject teachers speaking for themselves, as Goodson (1992, 1995, 1997, 2008) has advocated, and to place the narrative action in the context of life-history, because life-history shares the grounding in teachers' stories. Also, emphasis is placed on the socio-historical contexts as to what values teachers have, and how they conduct and interpret educational situations (Goodson, 1992; Tripp, 1994; Woods, 1987; Calderhead and Shorrock, 1997; Carter and Doyle, 1996). Life-history narrative has been recognized as both the content and method of research into teachers' knowledge and experience (Clandinin and Connelly, 2000; Woods, 1987). According to Bertaux (1981), life-history is a person's socially read biography (see also Measor and Sikes, 1992). Life-history and biography in research on teachers and teaching knowledge usually refer to the formative experiences, which are the basis for, and have influenced, the ways in which teachers think about teaching, and subsequently their actions in their practice (Knowles, 1992; Tripp, 1994; Woods, 1987). Calderhead (1988) and Knowles (1992) assert that life-history is increasingly believed to have a significant bearing on the practice of teachers. It is a significant source of, and has a powerful effect on, the development and formation of a teacher's knowledge, such as beliefs, images and role understanding that manifest in her/his practice. Knowles (1992: 105) further finds, through his case studies of how biography affects beginning teachers' teaching, that there are a number of ways in which teachers' life-history and biography influence their classroom practice:

"...confidence displayed in the classroom; relationship with students; and personal work habits, planning and organizational skills."

The capacity of life-history and biographical materials, according to Sparkes (1995, in Hatch and Wisniewski, 1995: 116), lies in the strength that both can focus on the individual in relation to the context and relationships into which the individual is nested:

"The ability of life-history to focus upon central moments, critical incidents, or fateful moments that revolve around indecision, confusions, contradictions, and ironies, gives a greater sense of process to a life and gives more ambiguous, complex, and chaotic view of reality."

The specialty of life-history in research lies in the fact that it is both the content and method in study. A life-history narrative of educational experiences will potentially tell where teachers come from, who they are, and what their future might be as educators. It will help to reach teachers fully, to engage them and make learning possible and effective, by teacher reflection, teacher education and professional development or reforms. Information from a group of teachers' life-histories will open a window onto their educational culture (Cortazzi, 1993).

Life-history begins with, and builds on, life stories, or looking at critical incidents and events as the educational life experience that the teacher tells. With this wide range of data, a contextual background is brought in for developing joint understanding of the teacher's knowledge. This life experience includes what they strive for, love, and endure, and how people act and are acted upon, the ways in which they act, desire and enjoy, see, believe, inspire – in short, processes of experiencing the educational world (see Dewey, 1929).

Life histories can also inform our thinking about the personal engagement with social context, with implications for some of the most prominent public issues of the day (Woods, 1987; Goodson, 1995, 2007). Furthermore, Tripp (1994: 67) and Goodson (1994, 1995; see also Woods, 1987; Pomson, 2004) assert that the use of biographical information to understand the broader aspects of teaching practices is in order to understand a teacher's teaching through knowledge about the person that the teacher is, within other constraints. Therefore, life-history is the junction and anchor of the teacher's life and work, including private views and personal philosophies (Elbaz-Luwisch, 1997; Goodson and Sikes, 2001; Goodson, 2007). However, a narrative incorporating biographical information and life-history data, as a body of evidence, has been sadly neglected until recently and insufficiently explored in educational studies so far (Goodson and Numan, 2002; Stables, 2002). It is also worth noticing that the use of life-history data is not to produce continuous chronological accounts of whole lives, but to contextualize teachers' present practice in their whole life, and to produce an ongoing piecemeal examination of teachers' fragmental accounts of their past, up to their present, to uncover professionally formative and educational experiences as critical incidents (Tripp 1993, 1994: 65; Measor, 1985; Woods 1987; Pomson, 2004).

According to Tripp (1993: 25), the term "critical incident" comes from life-history:

"…where it refers to some event or situation which marked a significant turning-point or change in the life of a person or an institution (such as a political party) or in some social phenomenon"

(e.g. industrialization, war, etc). This is analogous to what Denzin (1989: 70) called the "epiphany" – the interaction moment and experience that leaves an impact on people's lives. Epiphany can take the form of a major historical event or incident. However, this kind of critical incident as a major event occurs so rarely in a teacher's lifetime that it alone could not constitute an adequate basis for a professional research file.

For example, in Measor's (1985: 62) study of critical incidents in the classroom in relation to the teachers' identities, choices, and careers, she identified some "extrinsic" incidents as historical events, such as the Second World War, in the participants' biographies that forced decisions and actions upon people. She also identified some "intrinsic" and "personal" incidents within the participants' career and personal life that confronted the individual with choices and decisions. The "Cultural Revolution" and other political campaigns in the 1960s and 1970s in China were critical incidents in that period of history in China; three senior participants in the study experienced it, which dramatically redirected their personal and professional lives and led them to become teachers. China is undergoing a process of industrialization, its impact on teachers' work and life is ongoing. When applied to other teachers' working lives and lived experience, of those who entered teaching more recently, critical incidents take the form of more localized changes, such as policy turnabouts; significant life experiences, or classroom anecdotes or vignettes (Tripp, 1993: 25; see also Measor, 1985), and textbook stories that they remember. These are critical in a rather different sense, in that they had very important consequences, and they are indicative of underlying trends, motives in teachers' life-histories or social process. The incident itself probably presents the:

> "...culmination of a decision-making, it crystallizes the individual thinking, rather than of itself being responsible for that decision."

which indicates the individual's values and beliefs (Measor, 1985: 62). They seem to be "typical" rather than "critical" at first sight, but are rendered critical through analysis. Tripp (1993: xv, 1994) uses the notion of critical incident to work with teachers to examine and reflect on "exceptional incidents" or "routine phenomena", critically, to foster a self-monitoring practice, so that teachers can improve their professional judgment in a circumstance in which there is no single right answer to tackling contingencies and uncertainties in teaching. A critical incident cannot be assumed to communicate meaning on its own; it involves diagnosis, analysis, and drawing up of positions, in short, explicit interpretation. Teachers learn a great deal by teaching, critical incidents, as a practical instrument, has great potential for them and for researchers to gain knowledge by examining their daily work as a reflective teacher. They are congruent with the forms of knowledge-in-action that under-gird the varieties of, and multifaceted practices in, teaching and other fields. Critical incidents are the substance of case knowledge, which builds up teachers' comprehension of teaching in context. In this sense, teachers' wisdom of practice is demonstrated in relation to a specific incident or particular experiences that constitute teachers' professional life. On the other hand, critical incidents can serve as a fruitful technique to analyze teachers' narrative in a life-history context (Tripp, 1994; Woods 1987; Miles and Huberman, 1994). I will return to this point in the methodology a little later.

Therefore, life-history is used to contextualize the present within the framework of individuals' lives through teachers' voices and narratives (Goodson and Sikes, 2001; Tripp, 1994; Cortazzi, 1993). With critical incidents or life stories, the piecemeal examination of teachers' experience and current practice is to uncover professionally formative and educational experiences, and tease out their understanding of teaching through teachers' own words (Tripp, 1994; Woods, 1986).

The navigating of the key concepts and the major concerns has provided the conceptual background – there is strong evidence that what teachers know about teaching derives from the links between their life-history and their cultural context, throughout their professional career (Goodson, 2003; Calderhead, 1988; Calderhead and Shorrock, 1997; Carter and Doyle, 1996; Huberman, 1995). The key argument is that the knowledge that teachers have, and how they acquire it, is the most important element in the evolution of modern teaching practice and this in turn forms the knowledge base about teachers' professional lives.

Chapter Three

Life-history Narrative Perspective

This chapter introduces the life-history narrative perspective as the methodology in studying teachers' knowledge and developing professional knowledge about teachers. It clarifies what life-history narrative is, and justifies its use in the context of social sciences. This section also draws attention to the words of caution and the ethical issues in applying this perspective in research.

Approaches to Studying Teachers

In the searching for the best approach to studying about teachers, my starting point is to follow in the footprints of how other scholars have studied teachers and their knowledge, and then to find the common ground where knowledge about teachers and teaching is rooted and grows up.

I have started from the topic of teachers' knowledge which has become, in the recent two and half decades, an area of growing interest for research for various reasons, in particular, for its importance in relation to the quality of students' learning, and its potential contribution to educational development. It has been approached by diverse methods with differing emphases (e.g. Calderhead, 1996; Fenstermacher, 1994; Carter, 1990a; Carter and Doyle, 1996; Gudmundsdottir, 1995). The major methods employed to approach this topic have also been synthesized from a number of comprehensive reviews of research in relation to teachers' professional knowledge (i.e. Calderhead, 1996; Fenstermacher, 1994; Carter, 1990a; Carter and Doyle, 1996; Poulson, 2001; Goodson, 2003). Meanwhile, Denzin and Lincoln, (2000: 19) have realized and reminded social science researchers of that:

"...no single method can grasp all of the subtle variations in ongoing human experience."

This rings true with studying of teachers and teaching. Researchers are always seeking better ways to make more understandable the aspects of the world they have studied. There are diverse approaches and methods available. This area of research has involved both quantitative and qualitative methods and data. For example, Gatbonton (1999) in Canada, has investigated the hypothesis that it is possible to access the pattern of knowledge about teaching and learning (pedagogical knowledge) that a few experienced ESL (English as Second Language) teachers utilize in classrooms while they teach, through both qualitative and quantitative analyses of verbal protocols obtained from teachers who watched videotaped segments of themselves in teaching and simultaneously reported on the thoughts they had as they taught these segments. This method is termed "stimulated recall commentaries", as a thinking-aloud technique to capture teachers' thinking-in-action (e.g. Calderhead, 1996: 711). Other methods, which might be less common, such as concept mapping (Calderhead, 1996: 711), drama plays and drawings, as more visual data, accompanied with verbal interpretations, have also been used to explore participants' images of teachers and concepts of teaching, and its biographical and cultural connotations (e.g. Weber and Mitchell, 1996). Poulson and Avramidis (2003) have also used both qualitative and quantitative data in their case studies about effective teachers of literacy in Britain, to find out how they gained knowledge and experience through their professional development, that is interwoven with both contextual and personal factors. The strength of such approaches is that they may engage directly with teachers – and to some extent represent their voices. They have realized in their study that the biographical dimension is important in teachers' knowledge development, in order to understand how they have come to do what they do and know what they know. To explore a more ontological issue – teaching as a way of being (Feldman, 1997; Cortazzi, 1993) can unpack some fundamental, underpinning values, assumptions, beliefs and principles that constitute a teacher's persona and ways of teaching using teachers' voices (Cortazzi, 1993).

The common methods are largely qualitative. They are closely associated with stimulated recall, ethnographical case studies, and narratives of biographies and life histories (e.g. Elbaz, 1983; Calderhead, 1996; Calderhead and Shorrock, 1997;

Cortazzi, 1993; Carter and Doyle, 1996; Bishop, 2000). It has been argued by Cortazzi (1993) that teachers' voices and understanding may emerge at its strongest in teachers' narrative accounts, as tested in his narrative study of more than one hundred British school teachers (Cortazzi, 1993: 10, 12). This is consistent with Calderhead's (1996) cognition. He (ibid: 712) says:

> "...narrative of accounts of teaching aim to describe teaching in teachers'
> own words and to represent the real-life complexity of teaching."

Likewise, Elbaz (1992, in Calderhead, 1996: 713) also gives insight on this point:

> "...narrative research allows teachers a voice in how they themselves
> are portrayed, a voice that, she argues, is denied in much social scientific
> research." (see also Goodson, 1994, 1995, 1997)

It has been asserted by Calderhead (1996: 713) about those narratives:

> "...will no doubt contribute further to the development of teachers'
> knowledge research...narrative studies are sources of teachers' perspectives
> on their teaching and often take a broader focus, examining teachers'
> practice in the context of other life experiences."

This may be the reason why narrative has been increasingly taking prominence and significance in studying teachers. Likewise, Carter and Doyle (1996: 124) contend that a vigorous tradition of studying teachers' knowledge has developed since the mid-1980s, and stress that two complementary methods have been widely used – narratives and life-history. This mode of research is concerned with describing an individual's experience of reality, and aims for highly detailed studies of individuals, for the purpose of understanding human action in context, which is characterized as part of the interpretive tradition of research (Denison and Rinehart, 2000; Calderhead, 1996: 713; Neuman, 2000; Bryman, 2001; Denzin, 1989; Roberts, 2002).

Therefore, knowledge about teachers is now understood as best carried and studied through teachers' voices – their own accounts of their experiences, including their own interpretation. This is also linked to teachers' narratives, and it connotes that what is said is characteristic of teachers (Calderhead, 1996; Cortazzi, 1993: 11). The teacher's life-history of learning and teaching, and the context – for instance in terms of the culture, politics, history and economy, as well as geography, or the type of school – may constrain and entail certain ways of understanding teaching and learning, in terms of presence, provision, access and interactions. Teachers' narratives of their life-history can link their understanding to the contextual, social and private congruencies of the teacher's knowledge, and its growth, as pinpointed in the previous chapter. Hence, the new perspective to underpin studies of knowledge about teachers is that of life-history narrative. Roberts (2002: 1) has recognized that research with life-history narrative is a broad and developing area of study:

> "…the collection and interpretation of 'personal' or 'human' documents… stimulating and fast-moving field which seeks to understand the changing experiences and outlooks of individuals in their daily lives, what they see as important, and how to provide interpretations of the accounts they give of their past, present and future."

Similarly, according to Sikes and Goodson (2001, see also Carter and Doyle, 1996: 121), a teacher's biography and life-history serve as a way of making sense of the personal meanings teachers associate with the incidents and circumstances of teaching practice, and they assert that a life-history narrative perspective shares the grounding of biography, but emphasis is also placed on the social and historical context that influenced what values teachers hold and how they interpret educational issues and situations (see also Goodson, 1992; Goodson and Sikes, 2001; Woods, 1987).

What Is Life-history Narrative Perspective?

Life-history narrative is also known as the biographical narrative research approach in the literature (Wengraf, 2001; Denzin, 1989; Roberts, 2002; Bertaux, 1981). The relationship of life-history and biography, according to Measor and Sikes (1992: 209), is best defined as life-history being "sociologically read biography" (see also Bertaux, 1981), as mentioned earlier, which can be interpreted as biographical information used as data to study people and their experience, in a dialogical relation to the movement and development of the wider society (Tripp, 1994; Ferrarotti, 1981; Wengraf, 2001; Denzin, 1989; Denison, 2003; Roberts, 2002). Quite often, life-history perspective and methods do not hold a clear-cut boundary with biographical research; on the contrary, they share similarities. As Roberts (2002: 1) acknowledges in his book *Biographical Research*, he says:

> "...the book title *Biographical Research* is not intended to be associated with a precise definition but to indicate various, often interrelated, approaches to the study of individuals." (see also Bertaux, 1981; Denzin, 1989)

According to Kohli, (1981: 61; see also Denzin, 1989, Denzin and Lincoln, 2005), the analogy rests on the fundamental premise of "interpretive" or "communicative" social research:

> "...that research acts are social acts, that researchers therefore cannot create their own set of rules but are bound by the rules of everyday social action."

Mead (2002: iii) agrees with Lyotard (1984) that post-modern writers:

> "...work without rules in order to formulate the rules of what will have been done."

The different use of the terms is, however, realized as an initial challenge in the field of life-history narrative and biographical research (Roberts, 2002: 4). It has to be pointed out that researchers may use slightly different terms when referring to the same method.

For instance, when Kelchtermans (1994: 93) claims to use "narrative-biographical research" in the study of teachers' professional development, he specifies it as biographical-methods" to collect and analyze teachers' career stories in understanding how teachers give meaning to their experiences and how their experiences influence their practice. Consequently, while this book takes a life-history narrative perspective, the primary method for data collection remains, as what Wengraf (2001: 110) called, a "Biographic-Narrative Interview" accompanied by observation. According to Wengraf (2001: 111), this is utilized as a "lightly-structured in-depth interview" design. Given their nature, the boundaries of qualitative perspectives and approaches, such as ethnography, case study, life-history and action research, blur together and overlap, and the life-history narrative perspective using biographic-narrative interview, accompanied by observation, as a form of qualitative approach, is but one of many possibilities that this perspective can be used in research. Still, Polkinghorne (1995) has also recognized that narrative in research has a variety of meanings, which have caused some ambiguity to be associated with the term, and have sometimes led to a lack of clarity in its use. It is often simply equated to a story, which does not satisfy those of the audience who expect a more analytical discussion. Therefore, the concept of life-history narrative can be further clarified and explored.

On Narrative

Quite often narrative is connected with story and storytelling (e.g. Sparkes, 1999: 19; Elbaz, 1991). It is also associated with literary fictions such as the novel and the poem, or drama. Derived from the Latin word "gnarus" stemming from the Indo-European root "gnu" – "to know", it came into English via the French language and it is used in a number of specialized applications (Wikipedia, n.d.). In human activity and conduct, narrative is ubiquitous in human life in the way people think, ask, tell and write (Bruner 1996; Riessman, 2002b). In the context of this book, narrative refers to narrative non-fiction, for it is about real people and true happenings, and told as factual stories or accounts in the form of concrete events, critical incidents, vignettes and anecdotes, or dialogues. They are accompanied with what these mean to the teller, the participant, with metaphors, perceptions, opinions and views. In this sense, it can be understood as fictionalized facts, in the way that it employs words and numbers with contextual properties, such as time, place, and characters as persons, to describe a sequence of events or incidents with reflections and reasons. In Josselson's (1996a: xii) words, narrative work is born on "hermeneutic" soil. Narrative is related to, and is the product of, a narrator – in research it is narrative data from sample participants. It implies an interpretation of some aspect of the world that is historically and culturally grounded and shaped by human personality (Polkinghorne, 1988, 1995; Wikipedia, n.d.).

Essential to understanding narrative studies as a form of qualitative research is the understanding of narrative as a way of knowing (Polkinghorne, 1988); and a mode of thinking (Bruner, 1996: 119). Polkinghorne (1988) and Bruner (1996) both argue that narrative is a vital human activity, and is the primary means through which human beings convey valuable cultural information, and by which they create meaning in their lives. The narrative enables us to understand the actions of others in relation to our own, helping us to make sense of our lives in relation to, and in conjunction with, the experience of others (Sparkes, 1994a, 1999; Measor and Sikes; 1992). People translate and demonstrate knowing by telling, writing or doing. Narrative has been used as both strategy and technique to get good qualitative data (Riessman, 1993; Sikes, 2005; Sparkes, 1999; Cortazzi, 1993; Denison and Markula, 2003). Narrative as a structure for organizing our knowledge, and to construe reality, is a repertoire of cognition and meta-cognition (Polkinghorne, 1988, 1995; Bruner, 1996: 130-149; Markula and Denison, 2005). Bruner (1996: 121) asserts that:

"...narrative is justified or warranted by virtue of the sequence of events it recounts being a violation of canonicity."

Which means it is open-ended. One of the nine universals of narrative construal of reality sampled by Bruner (1996: 143) is its "inherent negotiability". According to Bruner (ibid), a narrative has dual sides: a sequence of events and an implied evaluation of the events or incidents recounted, which carries a meaning, and is always open to alternative interpretation. As a research approach, it offers an effective way to undertake the: "...systematic study of personal experiences and meaning." (Riessman, 1993: 78; Polkinghorne, 1988; Clandinin and Connelly, 2000; Sparkes, 1999)

The narrative of people's life experience and teachers' knowledge has gained wide legitimacy and space in the research world. Sparkes (2002) and Roberts (2002) have indicated and suggested an informative way of understanding narrative in research in humanities and social sciences from a historical perspective. They highlight that narrative research which involves the technique of storytelling has also been situated in a qualitative approach by Denzin and Lincoln (2005).

Through the tradition of research into social sciences and humanities, Denzin and Lincoln (2005: 3) map the recent history of qualitative research in the North American sphere over the past century into eight moments (from 1900-now, and into the future) that overlap, and simultaneously operate at the present. The fifth (1990-1994) and the sixth (1995-1999) moments, characterized as post-modern and post-experimental, were defined, in part, by a concern with literary and rhetorical tropes and narrative turn – a concern of storytelling. The seventh moment (2000-2004) and eighth moment (2005-), referring to now and the future, confronting a methodological backlash, reflect an evidence-based social and humane research movement, and a moral discourse, aimed at serving a more democratic society, and the individual's good quality of life. In relation to narratives, Denzin and Lincoln (2005), in their third edition of *The SAGE Handbook of Qualitative Research*, placed two chapters related to narratives, under the themes of strategies of inquiry, and clinical inquiry, as methods of collecting and analyzing empirical materials. The social scientists Riessman (2005: 473; 2002b) and Sikes (2005) – speaking as scholars who have been working for many years in the field of narrative analysis – claim that the study using narrative is inherently interdisciplinary, and penetrates into almost every discipline. There is an increasing interest in the narrative genre of research among researchers. This interest is merited because:

"...narrative is the linguistic form uniquely suited for displaying human existence as situated action." (Polkinghorne, 1988, 1995: 5; Goodson, 1992)

Specific to research on teachers and teaching, *The International Journal of Teaching and Teacher Education* had a theme issue (Gudmundsdottir, 1997) on "narrative perspectives on research on teaching and teacher education", it invites and opens up debate about this perspective on, and approach to, research into teaching and teacher education, including teachers' working lives. Doyle and Carter (2003) affirm that the use of narrative as a perspective within which to understand teacher development has gained considerable momentum in the last decade, and this perspective has led to several important innovations in the pedagogy of teacher development: the study of cases, the writing of personal narratives, and the like. There is however, a variety in studies that use narratives as a research strategy and method in educational research. One of the distinctions is known as narrative inquiry, which is widely associated with a particular group of educational researchers, such as Clandinin and Connelly (e.g. 1994, 1996, 2000). It is defined as: "...the study of the ways humans experience the world" (Connelly and Clandinin, 1990: 2; Kramp, 2004). This is identified in the literature review. It has been used in studying teachers, teacher education and teaching (e.g. Clandinin and Connelly, 2000; Beattie, 1995; Conle, 2000a, b; Golombek and Johnson, 2004), which uses personal experiences and stories to present teachers' knowledge, conceptualized as personal practical knowledge, as has been elaborated in the previous chapter (Clandinin and Connelly, 1994, 1996, 2000; Connelly et al, 1997). What distinguishes this column of narrative inquiry as a form of qualitative research is that it is both the process – a participant telling or narrating – and the content or the product – the accounts or narrative told, used as data for a research purpose. That is to say, narrative inquiry is understood with:

"...a rough sense that narrative is both phenomena under study and method of study." (Clandinin and Connelly, 2000: 4, 18; see also Bruner, 1996)

Stories are especially used to integrate the complexity of teachers' practice. Another characteristic in narrative studies is that they can be understood as auto/ biography and/or autoethnography, when a researcher looks at, and reflects on, their own practices and the story of their own personal experiences, to demonstrate their professional and personal growth and development, through sharing their self-knowledge, or self-narrative (Sparkes, 2003; Cortazzi, 1993; Denison, 2002; Roberts, 2002; Kohli, 1981; Sikes, 2004, 2005). Auto-ethnographical narrative researchers and scholars have also broken down the boundaries of narrative and other methods in order to understand other individuals in a broader social and historical context, embracing the biographical information and life-history materials to contextualize the individual's present in terms of their whole life, and in the larger society, and studying their interactions and relationships (Huberman, 1995; Sparkes 1994a, 2002; Hatch and Wisniewski, 1995; Denison and Markula, 2003; Markula and Denison, 2005; Roberts, 2002; Denzin, 1989).

Life-history

In relation to narrative, some researchers such as Ayers (1995, in Hatch and

Wisniewski, 1995) see no distinction from life-history; it is just a matter of whose life-history the narrative is about. Others take life-history as a form of narrative (Hatch and Wisniewski, 1995). It may be neither possible nor necessary to define and clearly cut the boundary between narrative and life-history, however, it is important to give accounts to render understanding of these concepts in use. In the previous chapter, I have put forward life-history as one of the concepts in terms of evidence base for teachers' knowledge in relation to critical incidents, in this section; deeper layers of meaning are further revealed as a general term and a methodological perspective, as life-history narrative is both the content and primary method of this line of research, as referred to earlier.

A deeper layer of meaning of life-history can be traced back to Dewey (1929). Life and history, according to Dewey (1929: 10-11), are congeners of "experience" which is "double-barrelled". Life and history have the same fullness and undivided meaning. "Life" denotes a function, a comprehensive activity, in which an organism and its environment are included, while "history" indicates a scope of deeds enacted – it is the human comment, record, and interpretation that inevitably follow (Dewey, 1929: 11). Every person, including every teacher, has his or her unique experience of life, including their education. The base of life-history is a pedagogical encyclopaedia, composed of a teacher's learning and teaching. The meaning of experience as a general concept is closely associated with knowledge (Wikipedia, n.d.). Experience comprises knowledge of skill, or skill in observation of something, or some event, gained through involvement in, or exposure to, that thing or event. For instance, a person with considerable experience in a certain field can gain a reputation as an expert.

In relation to education, in a broad sense, all genuine education involves experience, which is part of human life (Dewey, 1929, 1938). And "every experience is a moving force" in learning for many people (Dewey, 1938: 38). Therefore, the knowledge, experience and education of a teacher are interrelated. However, Dewey (1938) also points out that not all experiences are equally educative. The conditions for experience to be educative have to meet the criteria of continuity of growth relevant to learning, and interaction, and that all human life experience is ultimately social: that it involves contact and communication (Dewey, ibid; Measor and Sikes, 1992). In fact, Carter and Doyle (2003: 134) find in their case studies that "experience is a knowledge base" in teachers' learning to teach. When life-history is utilized as a research perspective and method, then life-history means any:

> "...retrospective accounts by the individual of his [/her] life in whole or in part, in written or oral form, that has been elicited or prompted by another person." (Watson and Watson-Franke, 1985, in Hatch and Wisniewski, 1995: 125)

According to Roberts (2002: 3), life-history perspective is:

> "...usually taken to refer to the collection, interpretation and report writing of the 'life'."

Life-history as a research perspective emerged in research in the 1920s and 1930s, associated with a group of such as some of the Chicago sociologists (Bertaux, 1981: 5; Goodson and Sikes, 2001; Roberts, 2002: 37). However, life-history appeared then to be "relatively expensive, long-winded and cumbersome" while surveys were prominent and regarded as providing more accurate representative information in a much shorter time (Roberts, 2002: 37). As a result, this approach was almost abandoned in the 1940s (Bertaux and Bertaux-Wiame, 1981). Recently it has become much more accepted and commonplace in research into people and their well-being, experience and the meaning of their life, in relation to social and historical contexts at a micro level (Bertaux, 1981; Denzin, 1989; Sparkes, 1994a; Goodson and Sikes, 2001; Atkinson, 1998; Roberts, 2002; Wengraf, 2001).

Life-history is distinct from life stories. Our life-story is the story we tell about our life, while the crucial focus of life-history is to "locate the teacher's own life story alongside a broader contextual analysis", which is a collaborative venture of participants and others, reviewing a wider range of evidence (Goodson, 1992: 4; Sikes and Everington, 2004; Sparkes, 1994a; Roberts, 2002). Goodson and Sikes (2001: 88) further recognize that:

> "Life-history pushes the question whether private issues are also public matters; the life story individualizes and personalizes; the life-history contextualizes and politicizes."

A life-history is thus a very personal document, yet, at the same time, its attention to the historical, social, political, cultural and economic contexts of that life offers a means for a fully contextualized view, one that is sensitive to the social structure and culture that have a general influence (Woods, 1987; Goodson and Sikes, 2001) as reviewed in Chapter Two. However, in this work, it must be pointed out that the narrative of life-history is not so ambitious as to take everything in, but only to contextualize the analysis in the participants' whole life, limited to that part that is educational experience, more specifically, to their experience of learning and teaching. By life-history, I mean the learning and working experiences, such as turning-points and critical incidents, lived by the participants. In particular, those that influenced their ways of thinking about teaching, which constitute their images as teachers or of teaching, and became the basis of their pedagogy, as teaching knowledge that guides their common practices.

Life-history narrative perspective combines narrative and life-history (Hatch and Wisniewski, 1995). The endeavour to explore life-history narrative is to explore their collective virtues and narrow down the scope of narrative to a form of life-history. The life-history narrative research has enriched research perspectives in studies of understanding human beings and their healthy relationships in humanities and social sciences, as a qualitative mode of research (Goodson and Sikes, 2001; Polkinghorne, 1988, 1995; Sparkes, 1994b, 2002, 2005; M. Olson, 1995). A life-history narrative perspective has its part to play in the study of meaningful, relevant, and living teacher knowledge. It has strengths, to be further fore grounded later, and it has weaknesses, which are many. Our research must be for a way to contain this awareness, rather than to silence it (Goodson and Sikes, 2001), which is touched upon below.

The Main Issues with Narrative Perspectives

Within the research practice characterized as narrative inquiry or study, some pitfalls need to be looked at. It is worthwhile being circumspect before putting life-history narrative into use. This is, however, opposite to devaluing this perspective. Educational thinker Bruner (1996) reminds narrative researchers that when many in education suddenly become so interested in the narrative construction of reality, including his own latest turn to narrative and culture, it must be regarded with caution (see also Goodson and Sikes, 2001; Goodson, 1995, 1997; Conle, 2001; Convery, 1999). For instance, the voice issues, identified in Chapter Two (see also Sparkes, 1994a, b, 1999, 2002; Freeman, 1996a; Elbaz, 1991; Hargreaves, 1996), concerning why the voice matters, and whose voice it is, in studies on teachers and their knowledge in the context of their life-histories, are worth clarifying. Goodson (1997: 111) has warned about the turn to narrative or stories to elucidate teachers' knowledge; he points to what life-history narrative inquiry can do better, with caution:

"Given this history, and the goal displacement of education study noted, it is therefore laudable that new narrative movements are concentrating on the teachers' presentation of themselves. This is a welcome antidote to so much misrepresentation and re-presentation in past scholarship and it opens up avenues of fruitful investigation and debate." (Goodson, 1997: 112)

However, it is increasingly less promising as a focus and reflection. Goodson (1995: 90) sounds a note of caution about the upsurge of narrative in the study of teachers' knowledge, and points out that it may not always be as progressive or humanistic as it appears. Noting the politics and shifts in the output of a global media, he says:

"...the life story presents a form of cultural apparatus that accompanies an aggrandising state and market system."

Sparkes (1999: 19-20), speaking from the area of sports education and sociology, also calls attention to confusions surrounding the issue of using narrative forms in research. He (ibid) points to a tendency that has often led to exaggerated claims about this approach – the understanding of others in ways that endorse a romanticized approach to research. Bearing these caveats in mind, there follow other words of caution.

First of all, much needs to be learned about the nature of the story as a form or representation of narrative, and its value to our common ground and interest (Sparkes, 1994a, 2002; Goodson, 1997: 113). When researchers are assertive about the value brought by the narrative approach, some become so favourable to it that they make statements such as "teaching can only be known through story" Fenstermacher (1997: 121). This unquestioning attitude of undoubted certainty might make the researcher lose sight of being "self-critical" (see Wallace and Poulson, 2004: 6) and reflective on what he/she is doing and risk turning a blind eye to the tenets of other approaches and possibilities. This may inhibit diversifying the research. Probably this is what Conle (2000b; see also Goodson, 1995; Sikes, 2005) realizes, that narrative inquiry is endangered by the way that narratives or stories become context-free, portable, and ready to be used anywhere and anytime for any purposes. Such statements as "all human discourse takes the story form" are uncomfortable, given the fact that the virtue of narrative has not been everybody's recognition or experience. While there is a place for story in the study of others, the self, teaching, and teacher education (Carter, 1993), inquiries should be alert to the fact that:

> "...experiential stories can become 'frozen' and entrap the teller into an
> unchanging image, reinforcing stereotypes of others and of self." (Conle,
> 2000b: 57; see also Goodson, 1995, 1997)

In a sense, all narratives ought to be subject to deconstruction, responding to questions such as where do the stories come from, and to what end they work toward, which demands validation from a methodological, as well as an ethical, angle, with responsibility, giving ways and leaving space for the audience to make their own judgment and draw their own interpretation of the meaning (Sparkes, 1994a, 1999, 2002; Sikes, 2004, 2005). Therefore, Denison (2003: 201, 2006) advocates that research with narrative can evolve and develop as "movement practices" overcoming the rigidity, in a way that narrative in academic research should recognize, and capture the ever-changing interactions and dialogical relationships between society and individuals, and among people. The context of the story and narrative is essential in bestowing its meaningfulness. The nature and the spirit of the open-endedness of many narrative inquiries, in forms of research stories, have attraction, and at the same time a respect for uncertainty, when investigating the immense complexity of practices. In reality, it is hard to know whether it is better to live in the illusion of certainty or the reality of great uncertainty, and it is not easy to keep a balance when doing research unless the researcher has flexible designs, attitudes, and a critical mind. Thus far, this kind of tension and dilemma in qualitative inquiry do not have fundamental solutions yet (Denzin and Lincoln, 2005; Sparkes, 2002). Perhaps ascribing to open-and- critical-mindedness and responsibility to an ethically sound inquiry is of importance (Sikes, 2004). For example, as a researcher using qualitative data, in particular, the life-history narrative, I would not include a nation-wide survey as a narrative inquiry if it needs statistics; even though it involves interpretation and the report has a narrative element.

At other times, when narrative approach is suitable, some researchers assume, at least when they write, that their participants, or narrators, are perfect storytellers, and the stories they present come neatly from the participants, in a secret way, which may inhibit communication. Little account of how their narrative story is constructed from the raw data is given, or little is made available, giving no research testimony of the process. As Denzin and Lincoln (2000) point out, no wonder it results in puzzles or ambiguity among the audience. Fenstermacher (1997) agrees that story is one of the most truly useful ways of learning about teachers; but he still wants to know more about what counts as a story or narrative, and what happened as they are told by the tellers of the stories (see also Convery, 1999).

The role of the researcher in analysis and interpretation should foreground what point of view the data conveys, and how it is influenced by the cultural conventions of telling, the motivations of the tellers, and other social contexts (Sikes, 2004). Secondly, the issue of whose voice it is within a specific research needs boundaries to reduce ambiguity and build up trustworthiness; it is also of ethical importance. For example, Clandinin and Connelly (2000: 146) recognize that:

> "In its broadest sense, voice may be thought of as belonging to the participant, researcher, and other participants, and other researchers, for whom the text speaks."

Issues such as "too-personalized" (Carter and Doyle, 1996: 138; Riessman, 2002a, b, c) or "de-personalized" (Goodson, 1997: 111) can easily erode the credibility and quality of a study with a narrative perspective. Too-personalized a situation in narrative research appears to be lacking in the researcher's orientation on social structural and cultural context, within which the teacher's work is embedded and conducted, just throwing a story around and assuming it would communicate meaning on its own; while the opposite can be de-personalized, where the participants' voice is silenced, the research failing to see their point of view or recognizing them as persons. In research into teachers' knowledge, Bishop (2000) and Gudmundsdottir (1991) are aware of the danger of lacking boundaries between the voices of the researcher and the researched, where there is no explicit interpretation; and the other danger that they might not merge where the message is not clear who speaks for whom (Sparkes, 2002; Sikes, 2005).

Narrative research – such as that of Riessman (2002b, c) and Sikes (2000, 2004, 2005) – can be seen as trustworthy and just, because throughout their research, they give voice to their participants and raise attention to their ways of existence and forms of living, to enhance human understanding and acceptance; therefore they render worthwhile studies; they spend pages in their articles, and even a whole book, elaborating on how they (e.g. Sparkes, 1994a, 2002; Riessman, 1993; Sikes, 2004, 2005) positioned himself or herself in relation to others as the researched and the audience.

Why Life-history Narrative Perspective?

Informed and illuminated by the information and knowledge from the literature and practice, in particular, the issues and words of caution discussed above, I assume that Chinese teachers' knowledge and understanding of teaching is not only affected by contextual factors, but also by their related experiences of teaching and learning in their life-history, hence, life-history narrative perspective and methods are appropriate to approach it.

The reason and rationale for implementing a life-history narrative perspective for developing professional knowledge about teachers also lies in the increasing dissatisfaction with studies where teachers' knowledge is limited to, and obsessed with, personal practical knowledge (Goodson, 2003), which has not fully incorporated the context of narratives with teachers' life-history. It has demanded research with narrative methods to find ways to make the connections and broaden the focus. Kirk and Miller (1986) recognize the truth that the more diffuse and less focused the approach, the wider the net it can cast. Embracing biographical information, to avoid isolating individuals from the world in which they live, has recently thrived in the literature, and has been increasingly used in studies about teachers and their knowledge in education, and other disciplines, moving from a sole focus on classroom or curriculum stories towards a range of more exploratory and contextual procedures and processes (Woods, 1987; Goodson 1992: 7, 1995; Sparkes, 1994a, 2005, 1995, in Hatch and Wisniewski, 1995; Tripp, 1994). This, too, is a basic argument for the value of life-history narrative perspective. Goodson (1992: 4) takes this further and asserts that life-history perspective is needed:

> "The pursuit of personal and biographical data might rapidly challenge the assumption of interchangeability. Likewise, by tracing the teacher's life as it evolved over time – throughout the teachers' career and through several generations – the assumption of timelessness might also be remedied. In understanding something so intensely personal as teaching it is critical we know about the person the teacher is. Our paucity of knowledge in this area is a manifest indictment of the range of our sociological imaginations. The life historian pursues the job from his [sic] own perspective, a perspective which emphasizes the value of the person's own story."

The importance of biographical and life-history narrative in qualitative research, according to Wengraf (2001: 115), derives from the tenet that it conveys tacit and unconscious assumptions, feelings and knowledge, about, and norms of, the individual, or of a cultural group, which constitute the "actual world", but they are difficult to access directly by other methods. In a similar vein, Kohli (1981) represents individual life histories – the biographical data is meant to give access to the reality of life of social aggregates, such as cultures. In some respects, they are less subject to the individual's conscious control, but comprise traditions, commonsense, and personal experience. For example, the study reported in this book sets out to look into everyday practices, and examine what seems to be "normal" or "taken-for-granted", as elicited by the conversational probes used, such as "How did you learn English at secondary school?", "Please tell me about a typical day" or "Please describe how you go about a usual lesson". Narratives can encapsulate mundane facts, actions, and routines which may appear to be everyday and commonplace, such as you can see and hear in any corner of a school or in any staffroom. This natural and intimate manner of narrative research can also generate life experiences, such as intuitions, folklore, sacred and secret stories, which otherwise could not be obtained (Cortazzi, 1993; Goodson and Walker, 1995; Sparkes, 2002). The culture speaks itself through an individual's life (Riessman, 1993; Cortazzi, 1993).

However, the level of disclosure of these materials should follow ethical conventions, even though it constitutes part of the reality. Wengraf (2001: 116) goes on to contend that life-history narratives are "powerfully expressive" of the natures of particular persons, cultures and milieus, and they are "valuable instruments" for a wide range of social research. It is not restricted to the sociological understanding of persons, but is also aimed at the understanding of society in its historical and social structures (constraining and enabling interaction). This perspective has been increasingly used in studies of teachers' knowledge and life (Goodson, 1992, 1994, 1995, 1997; Goodson and Sikes, 2001; Calderhead, 1996; Carter and Doyle, 1996; Huberman, 1995; Hargreaves, 1996).

The value and merit of life-history narrative perspective and biographical materials have long, and widely, been verified in research into people and their practices in general, and about teachers and their knowledge in particular. Foremost, as the essence of research using life-history narrative, is respect for persons, as has been attested by Measor and Sikes (1992: 211; see also Sikes and Everington, 2004):

"...the objects studied are in fact subjects, and such subjects produce accounts of the world."

When this is applied in this study, it means that an object, such as knowledge, experience of teaching, or learning, is attached to the participant teachers who possess it. Denzin (1989: 17) asserts that the life-history narrative is a distinct approach to the study of human experience. He further maintains that it is the approach by which the "real" appearance of "real" people is presented. Following a similar line, Atkinson (1998, in Neuman, 2000: 373) affirms that life-history narrative perspective serve several purposes:

● First, they can assist the participants being interviewed in reconstructing his or her own memories.
● Second, these interviews can create new qualitative data on the life-cycle,

the development of self, and how people experience events.

● Third, the life-history can provide the interviewer with an in-depth look at another's life. This is often an enriching experience that creates a close personal relationship and encourages self-reflection in ways that enhance personal integrity.

What distinguishes life-history narrative research from other qualitative research in studying teachers' knowledge is that it has proved to have two main benefits (Connery, 1999: 131): first, it provides access to privileged information that will improve our knowledge of education, and second, the very process of engaging in discussion about teaching experience provides reflective opportunities for the teacher that lead to personal and professional development (see also Goodson and Sikes, 2001). Therefore, teachers' life histories can contribute a deeper and fuller understanding of the educational process and produce a more democratic and useful teacher knowledge (Woods, 1987). The metaphor of "three-dimensional narrative inquiry space", coined by Clandinin and Connelly (2000: 49), can further crystallize the nature of the narrative of life-history, as personal and social (interaction) along one dimension; past, present and future (continuity) as a second dimension; and place (situation) as a third, as illustrated in Diagram 1.

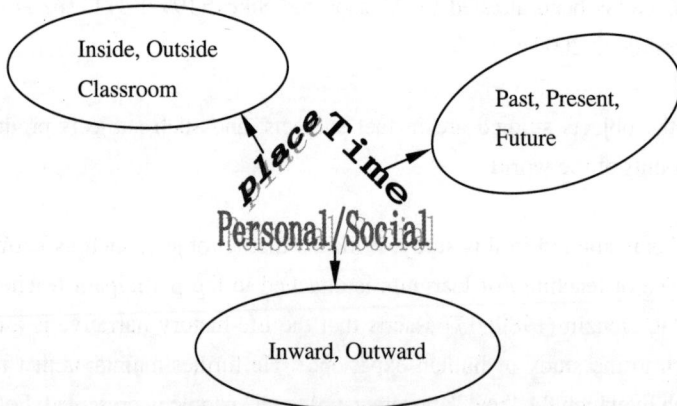

Diagram 1: Narrative research: three-dimensional nature

In other words, in studying teachers and their knowledge, narrative data can capture the multi-faceted nature of teaching practice, that is to say, any attempt to pin them down in one direction or side is at the risk of overlooking other sides. As Josselson (1996b: 35) recognizes:

"Narratives include a multitude of discourses, and it is this multiplicity of discourses that resists being reduced to a single voice."

Polkinghorne (1988) contends that it is the narrative scheme that displays purpose and direction, and makes individual human lives comprehensible as a whole. However, it does not work this way on its own, as language is uncommunicative of anything other than itself. In my research, the participant teacher's life-history is obtained through the participant's telling or narrating about their learning and teaching experience, accompanied by observation, which is recorded and transcribed, and also used as life-history narrative data to be analysed and interpreted. It lays a factual ground for interpretive activities to study about people, and explore questions, such as: how do people live and give meaning to their lives and capture these meanings in written or oral narrative forms; who are these people who are making their own history? (Denzin, 1989: 10; Measor and Sikes, 1992)

As a whole, life-history narrative perspective shares the tradition of interpretative research with qualitative data of life-history accounts (Calderhead, 1996; Bryman, 2001; Neuman, 2000, 2006; Denzin, 1989; Sparkes, 2002; Roberts, 2002; Wengraf, 2001; Measor and Sikes, 1992), which is further pinned down, below, with the following characteristics: first, it is to include individual teachers' perspectives through their voices, to see the world through the participants' eyes. It is to understand why they teach the way they do, with an emphasis on the context of their life-history in relation to the wider changes of society; second, this perspective intends to describe the phenomenon of interest in great detail, in the original language of the participant, for understanding, instead of aiming at generalization, proceeding from the particular to the general characteristics inductively. Furthermore, it is reflexive rather than standardized, because understanding the nature of teacher and teaching as socially constructed over time, and the acknowledgement of the centrality of the teacher, and teachers' knowledge as interpretation and understanding, determines that the approach to exploring and studying is qualitative.

Life-history narrative research is situated in a matrix of wider qualitative research practice, and the tradition of the interpretative for understanding (Denzin, 1989;

Goodson and Sikes, 2001; Wengraf, 2001; Sparkes, 2002). Finally, this work moves on to life-history narrative, by connecting the individual participants with the cultural and historical context in which they live and work, towards a modality that embraces stories of action within theories of context, by "locating the teachers' lives within a wider contextual understanding." (Goodson, 1992: 234, 1995: 98; Measor and Sikes, 1992; Goodson and Numan, 2002; Tripp, 1994; Kelchtermans, 1994; Knowles, 1992; Carter and Doyle, 1996)

Ethics and Trustworthiness

Research is eventually understood through communication. Perhaps, this can be viewed, in part, as the purpose of doing research. Denzin and Lincoln, (2000: 11) stress that qualitative research can (like all research) always be looked at on the:

> "...standard of whether the work communicates or says something to us."

The quality of communication is assisted and achieved through an ethically sound study, with considerations and actions of validation and reliability. Quality life-history narrative research should make no compromise on this standard.

Ethics

An ethical inquiry should not only be valid and reliable to the participants but also to whoever reads it and uses it. These issues are not dealt with once-and-for-all in life-history narrative research, but in the whole process of doing research and its aftermath. Grbich (1999: 71) states that the current dimensions of research ethics range from:

> "...basic protection of participants' rights to active endeavours to improve their lives. Accountability and relationship between research and the researched is the key issue."

For example, the informed consent form should be conducted with participants at the beginning, and the result of the research is best viewed by the participants. However, there are other ethical dilemmas in doing and writing research with biographical narratives and life-history data (Goodson and Sikes, 2001). Tensions or dilemmas, such as presenting teachers disclosing their thinking and working life, the relationship between anonymity, or confidentiality, and visibility, are conflicting and sensitive (Miles and Huberman, 1994). The level of disclosure should follow ethical codes and virtues. This is a rule of a life-history study.

In my doing research with a life-history method, my practical solution is that, whatever the participant mentioned as a secret in the telling, I keep it to myself. Also, the issue regarding how research can be conducted, in a way that I could get good data, and so that the participants' voices would not be buried is considered with common sense and lessons from others. For instance, why life-history narrative is employed, what and how it can be appropriately analyzed, and how it is represented to maximize their voices and interpretation, resulted from a critical and creative reading of the literature of life-history and narrative perspectives. For example, in dealing with the power relationship between the researcher and the researched, I gained a lot from a piece of literature which says that the interviewee:

"...takes over the control of the interview situation as to where and when to meet the researcher, and talks freely." (Bertaux, 1981: 39).

From the outset, power or turn-taking issues were taken into consideration, bearing in mind that the purpose of such studies is giving voice to the teachers and to empower them to improve their own practice (see Goodson and Sikes, 2001). As Cortazzi (1993: 28) noted, a narrative gives its teller a "long turn", and "strong rights", to hold the floor for the maximum time, exercising power to attend to the points they want to talk about. How the participants are represented should be agreeable to the participants, meanwhile respecting the truth and reality, which demands a high level of professional competence.

Other dynamics in research into narrative of life experience demands the balance of fictionalization and authenticity (see Sikes, 2005). For instance, a question I came across in practice is: Should I fictionalize the name of the city of the fieldwork, or keep it real? The researcher has to use his/her own sense. My solution is that I should keep the real name, for the sake of the audience, in case they have the curiosity to know where on earth it is, while, in doing so, I have to anticipate that there will be no negative impact on any participants or schools. The participant's names, and the names of the schools, are fictionalized in my own work.

However, what might be criteria that are meaningful within interpretive or qualitative inquiries, particularly, with life-history or biographical research? Some writers, such as Guba and Lincoln (1989), Silverman (2001) and Agar (1986) believe that the criteria for the quality and power to elicit belief in qualitative analysis in general should be different from that in quantitative analysis. Following a similar line, Silverman (2001) addresses the credibility of qualitative research and proposes different criteria for measuring the quality and credibility in qualitative research from validity and reliability, two of them are:

• The values of the researcher.
• The truth status of a respondents' account.

Other researchers, such as Sparkes (2001), suggest that validity and reliability have multiple meanings and can be adapted to look at qualitative research. It requires interpretation and differentiated understanding though, when applied to qualitative research work, such as biographical data, otherwise it is problematic (see also Kirk and Miller, 1986; Sikes, 2004). It is the researcher's responsibility to be able to provide an account of considerations and actions of quality and credibility.

I continue to consider and address the matter of validity and reliability, dependent on my understanding of the matters and the meanings of the two words from my experience of doing research with a life-history narrative perspective, and tell what action has been taken to assure the quality, with assistance of knowledge from the literature. This is consistent with what Sparkes (2001: 542, 2002: 201) called the "diversification of meanings perspective", in responding to the issue of validity and reliability in research in general, and in life-history research in particular. By this, I mean, as a researcher, I need to know the meaning and the alternative approach to the important matter concerning "validity" and "reliability", in order to address and account for the matter appropriately.

According to Henerson, Morris and Fitz-Gibbon (1989: 133, in Zhao, 2008b), validity is to answer the question: Is the instrument or the method an appropriate one to study what the researcher wants to know? The researcher needs to build validity into research through consideration and action by including a wide range of evidence of teachers' educational experiences and knowledge, in my case of research with Chinese teachers, through life-history and the biographical method, and observation. By using the biographical narrative method, and prolonged engagement in field observation, which involved real persons and their lived experiences as data, as a result, I have captured a unique case of three teachers of three successive generations. In addition, the biographical narrative data is verified, and interacts with authentic fieldwork observation recordings, by getting into close contact with the participants. Life-history, or biographical narrative data, and observation, have recognized the participants as persons, and maintained their integral characters and relations to their culture and history.

Validity might mean different things to different researchers. In general, validity means the quality of being authentic: authenticity, genuineness, realness, truthfulness, which is in line with what some qualitative researchers and scholars, such as Sparkes (2001, 2002: 201, 208), and Lincoln and Guba (1985), have advocated: "authenticity" and "truth" to be the measures of quality for qualitative research. Also, Neuman (2002: 171) says "validity means truthful". Life-history study has good reason to pursue this form of quality, because researchers who take a life-history narrative perspective, their research as part of their life experience (e.g. Goodson, 2007). In my case, first of all, I want to be truthful to myself, so that then it can be so to others.

More specific to studies with narrative theory and methods, scholars (Sparkes, 2002: 216; Blumenfeld-Jones, 1995: 27; Clandinin and Connelly, 2000; Denison, 2003; Markula and Denison, 2005) suggest additional quality indicators. In particular, "fidelity" is illuminating in understanding this type of study. Blumenfeld-Jones (1995: 27) summarizes a few points of the meaning of this quality, including "adherence to truth or fact" and "exactness of reproduction of detail". Given this form of study is about the life-history of the participant, and under a cross-cultural communication, the "exactness" is very important. In a way, people write truthfully about what researchers have been doing and thinking which provide research testimony, and this is a way of being responsible to the audience. The appropriate interpretation of data is a way of being responsible to the participants, in the way it is faithful to the "data" – their own accounts. The researcher's interpretation is based on what it means to the participant/teller – fidelity (Goodson and Sikes, 2001; Sparkes, 2002: 216; Blumenfeld-Jones, 1995; Denison, 2003) – which is the core of studies of this kind. There is also the matter of accuracy. Therefore, the presence of an "other" – the participant – in biographical research reports means that:

> "...they are always written with at least double perspective in mind: the author's and the 'other's'." (Elbaz, 1987: 14, in Denzin, 1989: 18)

The eye of the other directs the eye of the writer. I hope this elaboration can give rise to resonance. Research should try to be truthful at least to the audience, the participants, and the researcher, so that the study is plausible and believable.

As a rule, life-history narrative researchers do not normally intend to over-generalize with their study, for the reason that every life-history is unique as well as relational; life experiences are not inter-exchangeable. This has been realized, and pointed out by others as well, for example, Carter (1993: 10) maintains that the narratives of teachers make the issue of generalization especially problematic, one reason being that narrative, by its nature, resists singular interpretation. Therefore, individual life-history is not subject to generalization, but is for interpretation and understanding. Every life-history in study is a living book, full of human knowledge and feelings, as well as educational experience, in the way that every individual human may have a differentiated understanding of education, for instance, and of teaching and learning. Even the same teacher may have different insights into their work at different stages, and ages, or when in different contexts (see also Goodson and Sikes, 2001). Nevertheless, the cumulative effect of narrative reasoning is a collection of individual cases, in which thought moves from case to case, instead of from case to generalization (Polkinghorne, 1995; Markula and Denison, 2005). From this, certain common contextual factors emerge as themes, which have had strong influences on the participant's practice and understanding, and these are discussed later.

Trustworthiness

Reliability as criteria to look at research has synonyms such as "consistency" and "trustworthiness". In qualitative research, they are pursued and valued (e.g. Goodson and Sikes, 2001; Sparkes, 2002). According to Henerson, Morris and Fitz-Gibbon (1989: 133, in Zhao, 2008b), reliability indicators answer the question concerning whether the instrument yields consistent results. This can be understood in various ways (e.g. Sparkes, 2001). My understanding of reliability or consistency in research with a life-history perspective is that scholars do what they say, and say what they do.

As a researcher, to address validity and reliability issues appropriately, it is worthwhile using one's common sense and learning from others. As a rule, many life-history studies are committed to justice and trustworthiness. As always, not everybody is fully trustworthy and trust must be placed with care, but without trust, we cannot stand (O'Neill, 2002; Sikes, 2000). In doing research, a trusting relationship is crucial to get valid biographical data. When I was doing research of people such as teachers, the participants are real persons and, I chose to trust them. That is why I went to listen to them for their knowledge of teaching, and watched them teaching in the field for observation. They trusted me and regarded me as a critical friend. This dialogical relationship is inherently ethical and makes it possible to draw close to their reality and enhance the true status of a respondent's account (Miller, 1996; Silverman 2001; Sikes, 2004). Individual teachers shared with me their insights and genuine understandings, I listened to them sincerely. Sometimes I was touched by their stories. At times, they asked me for my opinions and to comment on their work. This can be discerned in the excerpts of notes I kept along the way during data-collection and analysis:

> "The narrative approach also led to improvisations in which the researcher must answer many questions the participant had. It has been my principle that the research should be useful and meaningful in whatever way it could be, at whatever scale…"

Often, as a researcher, I was regarded as an expert and as an "expert" present at fieldwork, I accepted the invitation to make a comment on the event as a guest speaker, I told them my opinions truly and honestly. For instance, when I was asked to comment on a teaching competition, I acknowledged that a teaching competition could be a communication for sharing and achieving good practice, from which teachers could learn from each other, and it was helpful for establishing a sense of professional community for educators, and for communication. However, I also pointed out that:

> "I personally do not like teaching competition at all, because teaching, or education, is not a race through which the athletes can compete for speed and strength, so what is a teaching competition for? It can be a performance or demonstration of how a teacher interprets the textbook, or applies new methodology, or new technology."

Yet consistency, truth(s), or being truthful, mean different things to different people. In what the follows, I continue to illustrate this perspective with an empirical research study.

Chapter Four

Diachronic Analysis

From this chapter, I apply the life-history narrative to research on Chinese teachers' experience in the Chinese culture. In this chapter, I discuss about the characteristics of biographical narrative data and introduce the framework of diachronic and synchronic analysis, illustrating the diachronic analysis with an intergenerational case.

Understanding Life-history Narrative as Data

Most research-oriented narrative of life-history is produced through dialogues, purposeful conversations, and ethnographical observation, which is a chorus of voices, for instance, of researched and researchers, in a way that what the narrator says is inevitably influenced, or oriented, by his/her own way of telling or observing (Goodson and Sikes, 2001), as well as the listener's interactions or responses, or the purposes of the research, even when the listener/researcher is trying to minimize his/her input (Riessman, 1993). My project of life-history narrative research was conducted with 17 participant teachers from different schools in a middle-sized city in China. To collect biographical narrative data and observation notes of teachers' work in context, I spent half a year with them in their schools and constantly interacted with them. That is to say, data produced through biographical narrative interviews or other modes, as a matter of fact, is a product of collaboration by the researched and the researcher.

Narrative accounts are full of conflicts and contradictions, with which the researcher must make peace rather than just ignore or silence (Josselson, 1996a). However, this is not just simply difficult to analyse. In contrast, it brings the dynamics and complications of teachers' real lives into sight in research

(Polkinghorne, 1988; Sparkes, 2002; Josselson, 1996b, c; Thomas, 1995; Jackson, 1995, Markula and Denison, 2005). This is where, and how, scientific rigour is exercised and respected in the study of social sciences and humanities. For example, in the project in discussion, when a probationary teacher, Miss Zheng, talking about her feeling, said "this job gives me bitter joy"; a veteran teacher, Mr. Cheng summarized his teaching life as "painfully happy", which contains dualities. It would be inappropriate to categorize it as satisfaction or bitterness. What is obviously conveyed in these expressions is they have paradoxical feelings toward their job. The researcher has to be responsible with correct interpretation and representation, by making this point transparent, leaving space for readers to decide their own interpretations.

Therefore, to preserve the features of this kind of data, in analysis and re-presentation, stands out as a challenge, which requires an alternative analysis, rather than a straightforward categorical method (Polkinghorne, 1995; Riessman, 1993; Woods, 1987; Cortazzi, 1993; Sparkes, 2005), because it is different from the data obtained through surveys, or through some very structured interviews, whose categories are often selected prior to the data collection. Narrative is a collaborative construct by both the researched and the researcher, or a wider community, as described earlier in various ways, because clarifications and meanings are constantly negotiated through dialogues and conversations. This could be detected in many narrative dialogues, with probing questions or remarks, such as "Could you elaborate more on…", "What do you mean?", "That is to say…" or by response markers like "Yes" or "Not exactly". For example, the following excerpt from a biographical narrative in my study can validate this point:

Annie (researcher): Are you satisfied with being a teacher?
Li: I am not dissatisfied; it is so-so. I am a little passive about this.
Annie: Why passive?
Li: Personally, I think only when a person is interested in his/her work, can he/she achieve success. I am not interested in the current job any more. I have many puzzles about it, about my own teaching, so I feel I won't make a big success of it. So I passively accept.
Annie: What does success mean to you in being a teacher?
Li: One should love the job to produce better effect.

Annie: From the conversation, I can see there is a process of change; you seemed to have loved it, and now have become a bit passive.

Li: Yes. I did love it, it was new to me, but the newness has gone.

Annie: Do you think you need a professional development in teaching?

Li: I don't want to learn about it any more.

Annie: Why not?

Li: Because I don't want to be a teacher any more.

Annie: What do you want to do then?

Li: Something else with English.

From this narrative conversation, in some way, the researcher acted as a participant in keeping the dialogue flowing, constantly showing understanding and interpretation toward what the participant said. In turn, the teacher's response may confirm, or reject, or modify, the interpretation. This actually becomes a procedure of validation in teachers' narrative studies (Cortazzi, 1993). As shown in the above fragment, when the teacher was asked if she was satisfied with her work, she said "I am not dissatisfied", and she went on to say that she was "passive" about it. Then, the reason for her being passive about her work was probed, and the interpretation of a shift from loving teaching to wanting to drop out of it was confirmed. When conducting analysis with participant's narrative accounts, the analyst, actually, understands the person, to some extent, through the data, from what they said and did.

When listening to the voice of the narrative conversations, and reading the narrative texts, people's life experience is flowing like a river, and I felt it cannot just be cut off. I found myself in a situation that echoed Riessman's (1993) experience of her turning to alternatives to looking at the narratives as data. This mirrors my state during a moment looking for appropriate approaches to meaningful analysis, as she says:

"I searched the texts for common thematic elements. But some individuals
knitted together several themes into long accounts that had coherence
and sequence, defying easy categorization. I found myself not wanting
to fragment the long accounts into distinct thematic categories… As I
have thought about it since, it was a 'click moment' in my biography
of doing research as a narrative researcher." (Riessman, 1993: vi)

Biographical narrative as data calls for alternative ways of analysis to that of categorical breakdown, in order to be fruitful in representing narrative accounts of life-history. Wittgenstein (1953, in Huberman, 1995: 142-143) has convincingly demonstrated that when we analyse meanings, we rarely obtain clearly demarcated boundaries and "essential" defining properties with the data. Wittgenstein's useful alternative justification is that

"...concepts resemble each other as family members do; they possess certain overlapping features but do not necessarily share one feature in common. If the themes in the study had possessed clearly defined boundaries, then it would have been an indication that the data set had been oversimplified by the analysis."

Narratives are accounts of life experiences, and comprehension of them, that present forms of human living, ways of conducting education and knowing about the world. It requires narrative analysis, which resists a temptation to be rigidly categorical (Geertz, 1988: 75-76; Riessman, 1993; Cortazzi, 1993; Bruner, 1996; Clandinin and Connelly, 2000; Smith and Sparkes, 2005). This points up that analysis involving categorization should be used in a way that narrative data can be appropriately treated and meaningfully interpreted.

Diachronic and Synchronic Framework

In order to make greater use of qualitative data in educational studies on life-history, Stables (2002) suggests an analytical framework of diachronic and synchronic analysis of educational biographical narrative data which is imported from structural linguistics. He (ibid) points to the current emphasis on forms of synchronic analysis of data at one point in time, which involves examination of the data synchronically (i.e. at the same time), to identify the general issues and categorization of themes that emerged across all the participants. Synchronic analysis presents themes, for example, concerning teachers. However, it is not sufficient to evaluate the educational practice, and Stables (2002) argues that when such synchronic analysis is supplemented with forms of diachronic analysis, in the context of life-history, it can help generate an important evidence-base over a long time can enhance educational studies with greater validity. Therefore, the biographical data is better analyzed and presented along both diachronic and synchronic dimensions. My specific process of analysis along both dimensions involves constructing life stories, identifying and interpreting metaphors and critical incidents as demonstrated in Diagram 2 below.

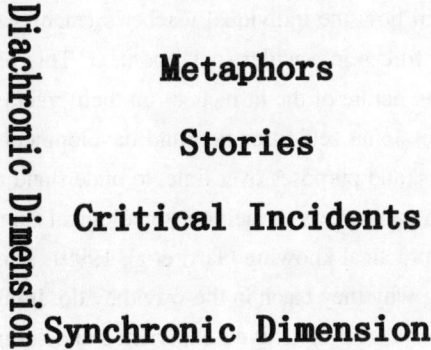

Metaphors

Stories

Critical Incidents

Synchronic Dimension

(Diachronic Dimension — shown vertically on the left)

Diagram 2: Diachronic and synchronic analysis with metaphor,
life-story and critical incident

The horizontal dimension of analysis involved examination of the data synchronically (at the same time), to identify the general issues and themes that emerged across all the individual participants, also through the constructing of life stories, such as of leading to becoming and being a teacher, interpreting metaphors and critical incidents. This dimension was termed the synchronic analysis. Some examples of analysis along this dimension across individual teachers are presented in Chapter Five.

Along the vertical dimension, the first step was to examine the data over time, diachronically, looking at the development of the teacher's knowledge of teaching with the individual teacher, and more generally within the sample cohort. I have termed this aspect of the analytic framework the diachronic dimension of analysis which will be further illustrated and discussed. It examined the developments of teachers' knowledge over a time span in their life-history. It enabled the research with teachers to make connections between individuals' lives and personal histories, and the wider socio-historical developments in China mediated by the key metaphors, and critical incidents that participants used to describe their experience and understanding.

The diachronic scheme laid out the structural framework to reorganize their narrative accounts that emerged naturally, reflecting the life-history sequences from a holistic perspective. As personal dimensions of teaching are often interwoven with, and embedded in, social ones, this level of analysis tended to describe and explain how the individual teacher's teaching is directed by, and embraced in, other forces in a wider social context. This provides an arena to trace the sources and nature of the influences on their practices. It also aimed to examine their professional self-formation and development through their own actions, expectations, and purposes over time, to understand them as the persons they are, in order to gain access to their epistemological stance that guides their understanding and practical knowing (Tirri et al, 1999). This also gives insight into comprehending why they teach in the way they do. It takes the readers into the participant's world, and their lived experience and future aspirations. This may point to a route for teachers' professional development, with a starting point of understanding their situated knowledge, by being friends with their minds (Greene, 1991, in Witherell et al, 1995: 41). This is penetrated through detailed analysis, with critical incidents, life stories and metaphors from their narratives. Specifically, the in-depth diachronic analyses give a view on what is the core of the participant's professional self, how his/her knowledge was shaped, what happened in his or her life-history secondary-school learning experience, their university life, current teaching, as well as future plans, and how those things proceeded, and why things occurred as they did.

The diachronic dimension of analysis is particularly illustrated with a case of three teachers of three successive generations.

A Case of Intergenerational Analysis of Three Teachers

In a significant sense, in the diachronic dimension, the biographic-narrative interview and observation in the field has fortuitously captured a case of three teachers of three successive generations as participants (Zhao and Poulson, 2006). This intergenerational phenomenon occurred in the data without prior planning on my part in selecting the sample. It is identified during the fieldwork and decided. This case of intergenerational analysis enabled the study to set the development in individual professional lives within the wider social, economic and political developments in China, between the late 1960s and up to now, and to examine in more detail the interplay between structure (i.e. wider political and economic context affecting individuals' choices and decisions) and agency (i.e. what an individual did in particular socio-political contexts, and how they came to the choices they made – often in restricted circumstances) and how this shaped their professional lives. For instance, how the outburst and the aftermath of the "Cultural Revolution" redirected some teachers' life-history. It also enabled me to identify the generational differences between teachers in China – for example, those who started their careers during the period of the "Cultural Revolution", and those who had begun teaching in more recent times, as China has begun to move towards a free-market economy.

Ms. Tang (aged 55) represents the first generation, a senior teacher coming up to retirement, who has actually retired by the time of follow-up fieldwork. Mr. Cheng, a middle-career teacher (aged 46), who has just become the English subject coordinator of the schools in the district, is a former student of Ms. Tang, and represents the second generation. Ms. Xu, a younger teacher (aged 31), a former student of the middle teacher (Mr. Cheng), represents the third generation. The analysis is mainly based on the biographical narrative interview data, and observation notes. This part of the analysis focuses on the changes and continuities of the teaching practice in the given place, over a time period of more than three decades, in the context of social transition in China. Part of this analysis has also been published elsewhere (see Zhao and Poulson, 2006). I will start with a brief introduction to the three individual teachers, drawing on the information from their own narratives.

Ms. Tang is a senior teacher of English who had taught for more than 30 years across junior and senior secondary levels. Humorously, she used a metaphor, calling herself as "teacher^3" – teacher "cubed", by which she means that, she is a teacher who has taught a lot of students, over several generations, including Mr. Cheng (the senior, middle-career teacher, representing the second generation of the intergenerational analysis), two former students now lecturing at the university in the town, as well as a couple of students pursuing studies overseas. She is also the deputy head-teacher of the senior secondary school. She has "apprentices" – new teachers – to mentor at the school. She retired when soon after the interview. She had loved teaching all her working life, particularly because being with students makes her feel "forever young". Her early learning experience reflected the schooling situation of China in the 1960s. She started to teach English without having completed secondary education, because of the political campaigns. In particular, the historical "Cultural Revolution" was a turning point in her life, redirecting her life-history, which can be seen in her story of how she became a teacher:

"Born soon after the establishment of the People's Republic of China, in 1950, I had a childhood at the time that China was reconstructing from the ruin of war. During this period of time, relations between China and the Soviet Union were good, and China duplicated the 10-year school system of the Soviet Union. In 1958, the same year that the 'Great-Leap-Forward' and the 'Anti-Rightist Campaign' started, and the terrible beginning of the Chinese famine of 1958-1960, I entered 10-year school, and then learned Russian as a foreign language in primary school. I was the only one among 36 students selected to go to a junior secondary school in 1965. Doing well at the school, I started to learn English and had an English teacher who worked with American prisoners-of-war in the Korean War [known as the 'Anti-America, Aid-Korea War' in Chinese history]. Because the teacher had an American accent and emphasized oral English, I learned American English. I was interested in English because the teachers used symbolic gestures, had dulcet-toned voices, and had materials in the original language. I was attentive and made a lot of oratorical speeches at school activities. I was supposed to graduate from secondary school in 1968. However, the 'Cultural Revolution' had already begun in 1966. Some teachers were treated as 'Capitalist-Roaders' during the 'Cultural Revolution'. Instead, some senior students took over some of the classes in the school. I was one of those students. I was then settled in a rural village. The children in the rural area were more disadvantaged, and there was a great lack of teachers. As I did well in my 'personal revolution', I was put forward to be a teacher in a rural school. I taught various subjects, including English. In the 'university of life', I was later recruited to be a worker in a Project (a multi-purpose water control and power generation project). I had been through the 'university classroom' of the open air and the workshop, plus I had previous experience of teaching English, so I was again picked out to be forwarded to teach English in the project school."

The start of the 10 years of the "Cultural Revolution" interrupted her schooling, and carried away her opportunity of going to study at a university. A senior secondary school leaver, she did well in her "personal revolution" to become part of "the proletariat", and she was eager to change "down to the bone", so as to really be a part of the working class. One's class status was important and the workers held a relatively high political status as members of "the proletarian" occupations, at a time (1966-1976) when intellectuals were politically vulnerable, and many were harassed. The aftermath of that period of history resulted in her thirsting for knowledge, and an endless struggle for a university degree. She eventually achieved the degree. The process of learning presents itself throughout her long life:

"In 1972, university admission was partially resumed, after the 5 years of closure from 1966 to 1971. The universities opened the door to workers, peasants and soldiers, without any entrance examinations. However, entrance more or less was determined by class status, working class enjoying more privilege then. I did not get a recommendation to go to study at university, because my class origin was not 'proletarian'. Nevertheless, I did get an opportunity for professional development, with a year studying at a teachers' university with undergraduate students. After the 'Cultural Revolution', intellectuals gradually regained better status. The system radically changed to become 'the meritocracy', in which status was given according to the level of academic degree. In this time of paucity of teachers, I trained some of my students, and some workers, to be teachers, and later they got their degrees. I felt it ironic that the students I trained were given the status of scholar, but I remained 'unscholarly', because I did not have any university degree. In the 1980s, I continued to study for a degree, and I had an opportunity to study with a Television University program, where I studied for an associated degree along an open-university model. This was like a long-awaited drink for my thirst for learning, and later I studied at a teacher university, from 1993, and a few years later I was eventually rewarded with a BA degree. My pursuit of the degree was truly like the long war."

For many people, and for society, the beginning of the "Cultural Revolution" was a watershed. The "Cultural Revolution" was the most wrenching and complex mass movement in modern Chinese history. It had tremendous impact on people in the midst of it, emotionally and mentally (Sheringham, 1984). Many years later, Ms. Tang felt bitter about not being treated as a scholar because of her lack of a university degree, as reflected in her narrative:

> "I was not given the status of an intellectual, like other teachers, for many years. My colleagues told me, 'You've taught so many excellent intellectuals; it's the greatest irony that you were not regarded as an intellectual.' So I feel I was a handicapped person."

This rings true. Near retirement, Ms. Tang felt pressured, and less adaptable, compared to her young colleagues. Ms. Tang does not like teaching to be merely transmission; she thinks that, if teaching is, then it is dead. She holds a great assurance that language is for communication. She wanted to enliven her class and let the students learn through play, and practice, and use of the language. She believes teaching is open ended, and does not believe in blind imitation. On the other hand, she believes students should learn something from the teacher – in other words, teacher is the knowledge provider and model for students. She requires her students to memorize English textbooks, and trains her students to take dictation – the characteristic of teaching by transmission and learning by rote. In this study, the Chinese EFL teachers' narratives contain such bi-polarities as transmission/communication, causing paradoxical feelings, showing the multifaceted nature and rigour of teacher knowledge.

Mr. Cheng is Ms. Tang's former student. He has just become an English teaching coordinator for the district, and is still missing the classroom. As an English teacher of more than 20 years, Mr. Cheng has taught junior and senior secondary levels. On the one hand, he acknowledges the high rhetorical status given to teaching, which has been nationally regarded to be the most glorious occupation under the sun – in China a teacher is called 'the engineer of the human soul'. On the other hand, he has also realized teaching is a tedious job, which has no boundaries of personal and occupational self. According to his narrative, the pay of secondary teachers in China is relatively low, and has remained almost unchanged for a decade. He is aware that, in China, at the senior secondary level, teachers are working long hours every day, usually for six-and-a-half days a week. Having worked at secondary school level for more than 20 years, he wanted a change in his life, so that he could do something for himself – for instance, working on his MA dissertation, or editing a book. He has accepted the position of coordinator of the English subject, and has just left a job as the head of English subject at the senior secondary school. Even though the pay is less, he has greater opportunity to pursue his other interests, he said. Working among the schools, he organizes activities and teacher's professional development. However, he still misses the classroom.

Mr. Cheng entered EFL teaching in the early 1980s. He shared a similar story in becoming a teacher as Ms. Tang did. Mr. Cheng was a devoted English teacher, attentive to English education in China, longing for experience of an English-speaking country. Having taught English for more than 20 years, he is aware of the change in tendency, in that teachers should not be the provider of knowledge, but a facilitator of learning:

"Teachers don't have to have a great bucket of knowledge in order to give a student a drop; teachers should use a drop of knowledge to facilitate a bucket of learning for the student. As the quality of secondary teaching is under exploration, I believe teaching is the most important part of a teacher's life; they spend their professional life in the classroom, and the value of a teacher is reflected in his or her teaching. In terms of effectiveness, the classroom is the battlefield and university entrance examinations are the final battles."

As an English teacher, he still feels regret at having not been given any chance to study in an English-speaking country, even though he knew a few others had been given that chance. When a chance came to him, he was asked to pay part of the expenses, which was too much for him. He could see that some leaders in the system are hesitant to make investment in teachers' professional development:

"Some leaders may perceive that if a certain amount of money was spent on hardware, they could purchase something that is visible, for instance, they would like to spend the money on a building, if it were spent on a staff member doing professional development, he may come back still as a person, and the value is not so visible."

He is interested in Chinese English teachers' school-based professional development. He has been reading the work of several main commentators, and knows about the development of the curriculum and of textbooks in the EFL field in China. He thinks the main achievement of education in the recent two decades in China is the new curriculum standards, and he believes Chinese education is changing for the better. Having seen through the welter of flattering platitudes, and feeling teaching to be a tedious job, he realized teachers, to a large extent, remain as "burning candles" in the culture of China at large, and he used the metaphor of a "ferryman" for himself:

"Year after year, taking people (students) from one side to the other, the teacher remains forever on the river, without any sense of high achievement. I am worried that the secondary-school teaching occupation cannot attract intelligent people, and China should adjust its educational policies, increasing investment in compulsory education."

He was planning to give a lecture on the preparation for English composition to the students taking university entrance examination. It has been part of his plan to compile an English reading book about the Three Gorges Project, to draw English learning closer to the local life and culture of the school students.

Ms. Xu feels the current style and amount of teaching assessment limits the enjoyment of English teaching and learning. She is in her 12th year of teaching EFL at junior secondary level. She is currently head of English at her school. She knows that English holds an important status in the curriculum and is one of the compulsory subjects (like maths and Chinese) examined for senior school entrance and university entrance, in her school as in other schools. English is allocated more sessions than the actual curriculum requires. She also perceives that English is not treated as a language at all, but a subject for examinations. Generally speaking, she feels teaching English can be complete, in particular, when putting aside the aspect of teaching toward the examination. The wider socio-political climate in China has been undergoing radical transition, which has had clear influence on individual teachers' personal and occupational experiences, and therefore on their knowledge of teaching. Of the younger generation, Ms. Xu's story of becoming a teacher bears a different character from those of Ms. Tang and Mr. Cheng:

"When we started to study English at junior secondary school, we had an English teacher who could speak English with good pronunciation and intonation. I think it is a good start for learning English. I gained interest in studying English from the beginning, and I felt it easy. Though the early textbooks were organized according to the mechanism of grammar with reading texts, teachers gave students some opportunities to speak and practice using English, so they could speak better English, avoiding being 'English dumb'. For instance, some English teachers in the school conducted a programme for students to perform an English song at the New Year party. And another teacher let students role-play drama with English texts in class. When Mr. Cheng was my English teacher in Senior 2, he took a few of the students to an 'English corner' to practice speaking English, which reinforced my interest in English and my confidence in using English. However, the dominant way of teaching was to explain grammar items and other language points, and write example sentences on the blackboard, with students taking notes. In 1993, I went to a teachers college with my parents' support, and it was my own choice to major in English Education, and thus I became an English teacher at a secondary school."

On a typical day, she goes to school at 7:15 in the morning, works until midday, spends two hours' lunch break at home, then returns to school until 6:30 in the evening. In addition to the normal teaching sessions allocated explicitly, maths teachers and English teachers usually fill students' free study time in the afternoon, commenting on the homework, testing on certain material, or doing dictation and recitation. It is really difficult to calculate exactly how much time any one of them spends working, including the time spent on marking homework. She feels her teaching load is heavy. She said she felt like a "robot" when correcting students' homework, and she felt correction is useless; but if correction isn't done, students would not take it seriously. After working like this for 12 years, she felt herself like a "skilled worker" in this field:

"Putting the aspect of examinations aside, teaching English can be complete and enjoyable, teaching with games and singing English songs, etc. However, when teaching and learning English is connected with examinations, all decision-making is associated with what and how English might be examined, in order to get high marks. English is then not treated as a language at all. I often switch to Chinese when teaching grammar. Teachers teach what might be examined. Teacher appraisal is conducted, and the schools are ranked, according to the examination scores. I feel I am fighting against the students' boredom and depression, caused by the current examination system."

Ms. Xu's narrative account of her working situation is very much in line with Hargreaves' (2003) comment that Socrates said that the unexamined life is not worth living. For teachers, it is the over-examined life that is the problem. Teachers with over-examined professional lives complain of eroded autonomy, lost creativity, restricted flexibility, and constrained capacity to exercise their professional judgment. Teaching toward various examinations sacrifices the human emotions of teachers in favour of clinical efficiency, removing any meaningful sense of learning as human growth (Hargreaves, 1994). They are fighting against the boredom and stress of "What is measured is what is taught". This is part of the reality of most Chinese secondary teachers' work.

Ms. Xu has a strong feeling that students are more difficult to teach now, compared with when she started teaching. Society is developing in response to the improvement in the economy. Relations between people are changing. Education is easier to get, and not the only way to make a living. Students today are not so attentive to education as students of previous generations.

Though all the three teachers have a special interpersonal relationship, as three successive generations, differences and changes among them are notable, through observations and in-depth analysis. They are at different career stages, with years of varied experience in teaching. Consistent with Huberman's (1989) study of teachers' career cycles, Ms. Xu is at the stabilization phase in her occupational life, she has been gaining independence and mastering pedagogical maturity. She is affirmative about her career choice to be an EFL teacher: "With my experience in this field, I want to stay on." While Mr. Cheng is at a mid-career pivotal moment, having obtained confidence and flexibility in teaching, and leading his colleagues in the senior secondary school. He has just undergone a reassessment of his life and work, considering multiple scenarios. He has turned down the tempting offer of a further promotion at his former school, and decided to experiment with a new role as coordinator, working across schools, with other EFL teachers, to increase his impact on classroom teaching and learning, beyond the boundaries of just one school. Ms. Tang, at the moment of her early retirement, with the added responsibility as a deputy-head of the senior school, has been willingly engaged in classroom teaching all her career life. Ms. Tang's narratives revealed her feelings of greater confidence, serenity, and self-assurance, as a veteran teacher. Of the three teachers of three generations, Ms. Tang has just had her early retirement and is making a tour around China; Mr. Cheng has started his new role as a coordinator and achieved his MA degree in English education; Ms. Xu stays in the classroom.

The intergenerational analysis along the diachronic dimension has looked at the three participant teachers' educational experience and their development across a period of more than three decades which entails a picture of change, and continuity, of educational practice and individuals' interaction, within the context in China over the past three decades.

Change and Continuity

Change and continuity in the educational practice, or in wider society, does not hold distinct boundaries, nor take place linearly, or alternatively. They are a process, rather than a successive series, which coexist and interweave as the practice evolves over time.

Changes in education can be radical, while continuity persists. For instance, the structure of the school system, pathways to becoming a teacher, syllabus, and versions of textbooks, have all been changing over time, while components such as transmission teaching, and large class sizes, remained comparatively stable for decades. Though the three teachers of three different generations, and the two individual life histories, have become teachers under different historical circumstances, they all lead, and participate in, their occupations in their own institutions.

Take, for example, the pathway to becoming a secondary English teacher in

China, in particular – the qualification requirement has undergone a rapid change over recent decades. When the senior teachers, such as Ms. Tang and Mr. Cheng, started to teach English during, and soon after, the "Cultural Revolution", there was no demand for a degree at all, during that chaotic period in Chinese history. The third generation, represented by Ms. Xu, and other novice teachers in study, had their education in a "Post-Cultural Revolution" era, and so have no awareness of the impact of the "Cultural Revolution". A historical view of pathways to becoming an EFL teacher, and the change across a time of more than 30 years seems to lead to a pattern as demonstrated below (see also Zhao 2008a):

No Degree⟹Vocational Secondary⟹Associate Degree⟹BA Degree…

It is widely perceived that teaching English for mainstream schools requires a Bachelor's Degree, and a degree from a teachers' college or university is preferred.

Other changes are obvious in participants' pedagogical practice, ambitions, expectations, and awareness of teachers' status in society, and in their views on teaching and textbooks. They unconsciously use the metaphors they live and teach by as tools, to help make sense of their lived experiences, and the reality of their work. As elaborated in the literature review and data analysis chapters, a metaphor, as a tool of thinking, can well illustrate their deeper conceptual systems, grounded in their experience and social-cultural world (Lakoff and Johnson, 1980; Miles and Huberman, 1994). The Diagram below summarizes metaphors from the different generations of the three teachers:

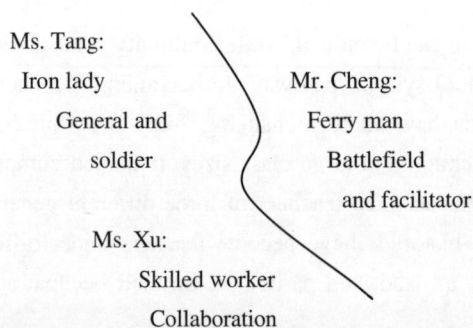

Ms. Tang:
Iron lady
General and
soldier

Mr. Cheng:
Ferry man
Battlefield
and facilitator

Ms. Xu:
Skilled worker
Collaboration

Diagram 3: A chart of key metaphors of the three generational teachers

In the case of the three teachers of three generations, the first generation, Ms. Tang, described the image of herself as an "iron lady", after having experienced various hardships in adapting to life in the countryside, and as a construction worker during the "Cultural Revolution". This means she could do the work of a man. Despite this, she felt herself "handicapped", in the same way as society, living through the time of turmoil of the "Cultural Revolution" and its aftermath, which resulted in a "revolutionary mind-set", as mentioned earlier. That particular period of history had a tremendous impact on her. She saw herself as participating in an important period of social change. This is also reflected in her other use of metaphors, such as the expectations for a student to be a "general" rather than only a "soldier". She encourages her students to be outstanding:

> "Those who don't want to be a general are less likely to be an excellent soldier."

On the other hand, it also reflects the competitive situation of education in Chinese culture. This is just one side of Ms. Tang's image as a teacher and person. Her pluralistic narrative also demonstrated her assertion of pedagogical innovation, eagerness to learn, and pursuit of reform.

The second generation, Mr. Cheng, believes teaching is the most important part of a teacher's life; because he spends their professional life in the classroom, and the value of a teacher is reflected in their teaching. In terms of effectiveness, he used the revolutionary metaphor of the classroom as the "battlefield", and university entrance examinations are the "final battles" for teachers and their students. He also used post-revolutionary professional terms; he is aware of the change in the trend of English teaching, in that teachers should not be the provider of knowledge, but a "facilitator" of learning;

> "Teachers don't have to have a great bucket of knowledge in order to give a student a drop; teachers should use a drop of knowledge to facilitate a bucket of learning for the student."

He perceives that the quality of secondary teaching is under exploration. However, in the culture of China, the pay of secondary teachers in China has remained "almost unchanged" in recent years, while the salary of people working in higher education has increased a lot. He is conscious of these dilemmas of education. He used the metaphor of a "ferryman" for himself.

It seems that teaching in the classroom, covering the given content, does not live up to his ambition, or his ideal life style (see Giddens, 1991). He has taken action to distance himself from the traditional image of the cynical or disenchanted teacher resisting change (Huberman, 1993). He has undertaken a change in his life with a normal two-day weekend, and so has just become an English education coordinator. Though the pay is less, he can have some time for his other interests, while he can still sustain his commitment to EFL teaching. He seems sure of what he is doing. His tone, in telling of his life and educational experience, sounds a little bitter – and he is concerned that the current educational system cannot attract more talented people to become teachers. He is still looking forward to an opportunity to experience life in an English-speaking country.

The representative of the third generation did not use any revolutionary vocabulary in her narrative. Ms. Xu used different metaphors, which reflect the current process of industrialization in China. She said she felt like a "robot" when correcting student homework, and she felt the correction is useless; but if the teacher does not correct homework, students would not take it seriously. She seems half-consciously aware that she is becoming concerned about the routine and monotony of the current teaching. Her view of students indicates a wider change in Chinese people's financial and social life, and ideology, which consequently has had an impact on her teaching, as can be seen through Ms. Xu's narrative about her feeling of difficulty in adapting to the new generation of students:

"I have a strong feeling that students are more difficult to teach, compared to when I started teaching. Society is developing, along with the economic improvement. The relationships between people are becoming indifferent. Education is easier to get, and not the only way to make a living. Students from One-Child-Policy families take for granted what they get without hard work. Students are not so attentive to education as previous students were. They care too much about themselves, and pay less attention to others, the collective concerns and public interest."

Ms. Xu is fighting against the boredom of the students, and their depressive feelings caused by the current assessment situation, and she is irked by the tiresome and repetitive work of correcting student exercise books, and having to teach the mandated textbook like a "skilled worker".

Other aspects of changes can be envisaged through their narratives, knowing the context they live in. One recurring theme is the example of textbooks, which have undergone three rounds of changes. Content is added and changed with time, requiring a more communicative view of teaching. When Ms. Tang started to teach English in the rural school during the "Cultural Revolution", she seemed to have enjoyed much more freedom and autonomy at that time, and academic learning and examinations did not appear to be so important:

> "When I started to teach in the rural school, I did not let the children call me 'teacher', instead I had them call me 'aunt'. I composed materials myself, copied using a mimeograph. And it was full of politically coloured and revolutionary language, with slogans, and everyday-life elements: 'Wheat, rice, field'. The teaching course contained my enthusiastic love for the Communist Party and the nation, as well as my reflections on learning. As not many people knew about teaching in a rural place, I had the freedom to teach as I liked. I sometimes let the students be teachers. When I was recruited as a worker in the project back to an urban posting as a worker and became an English teacher at the project later, my students could take over the teaching in the rural school."

The teaching described in this episode of narrative seems very different from the teaching at the current time in China. The system is becoming more centralized, and bureaucratically controlled, teachers teaching to mandated textbooks. The teaching resources are richer, and more available in the market now; however, teachers do not have the freedom to choose for classroom teaching, because they have to deliver the prescribed curriculum, from given textbooks and materials. More recently, the national curriculum was issued in 2001, which is perceived by Mr. Cheng as one of the greatest achievements of educational development in the recent two decades in China. Teachers work toward examinations and clinical accountability. This may deprive teachers of a sense of enjoyment, and the worth of their work (Hargreaves 1994, 2003), which, therefore, impedes teachers in catering to the individual student's need, motivation, and interest. The dilemmas of education always exist, but with different substantive variables at different historical moment, and stage of career.

However, teaching EFL has continuously produced a narrative in the teacher, with contradictory and paradoxical emotions and understandings of their work. In Cortazzi's (1993) words, teachers' narratives are full of polarities. For example, Ms. Tang thinks that she has been poor financially, yet rich spiritually. She thinks it to be a glory, and to be respected, to be a teacher, and she feels contented. While Mr. Cheng describes his feeling as "I am painfully happy with this occupation", and Ms. Xu's feeling about teaching is one of satisfaction, only leaving aside the aspect of examination. In this aspect, there is no exception. Even a novice teacher in study has encountered the "bitter joy" of teaching, during her first few weeks of real teaching.

The social environment has a similar impact on the three generations' work, in terms of the over-imposition of examination, as can be seen in Ms. Xu's narrative. It shows her to be a teacher feeling that the current assessment regime delimits her enjoyment of English teaching and learning.

The ideal situation, for Mr. Cheng, is to abolish the university entrance examinations, which are unfair to some students, because, in China, if a student fails this important examination, he or she, without a university degree, is deprived of many life opportunities and chances. Across more than three decades of teaching practice, teaching EFL has remained virtually unaltered, consisting of instructional formats of teaching from the book, teacher-fronted instruction, and learning by rote; the high social expectations of education, the administrative hierarchy, norms and working arrangements, which are known as part of the: "...traditional Chinese culture of learning" (Cortazzi and Jin, 1996a; Jin and Cortazzi, 1998, in Hu, 2003: 306).

The continuity is adequately demonstrated and explained with the interrelation in the cross-generation narratives. Ms. Xu, as the representative of the third generation, has given a vivid narrative about how her English teacher (Mr. Cheng) taught English to them:

"In senior secondary school year 2, we had a new English teacher, Mr. Cheng, who could speak good English. He usually explained grammar in the textbook in tremendous details, with many example sentences. He could write four sections of blackboard full up, and we took notes from it."

People are historical beings, retaining as part of themselves their previous experiences (Polkinghorne, 1995). This is also reflected in the "apprenticeship of observation" perspective, in terms that the teachers' previous learning experience has a significant impact on the way they teach (Calderhead, 1988). This type of a folkway of learning to teach, and teaching, however, cannot be fully understood without considering the environment of poor input of the target language. Buchmann (1989, 1987) contends that these folkways are teaching knowledge, the light teachers live by, which is profoundly culturally and contextually situated, and interpersonally influential. Ways and knowledge of teaching are known by acquaintance, through participation, and as common sense. It is a kind of natural tendency for teachers, for they have been immersed in that culture of teaching. What is more, this type of teaching is not unique to China. Research has shown that in other countries, such as in the UK, teachers are still, to some extent, dominant in classroom learning; they are still seeking a more dialogical dialogue of pedagogy (see Skidmore, 2000).

Narrative accounts provides us with a historical view of teachers' knowledge and its development, articulated through their own voices, illustrated with condensed life stories, along with critical incidents and metaphors. The locality, and interpersonal relationship, reveals their folkways of learning to teach, teaching, and expertise, which is deeply situated in the cultural context, and influenced by the social provision and personal aspirations. Working histories, the context, and the content, the students and the demands of teaching have changed profoundly over a period of more than three decades. A folk culture of teaching, such as belief in the value of education, in memorization, transmission of knowledge from textbooks, and teaching under the pressure of reforms, and of mandated and public examinations, has continued, and remains, with a high level of stability, at the heart of teachers' work. The emerging reality is becoming more complex, as China transforms into an industrialized and complex state, at rapid speed.

Life-history as Learning to Teach

In the study, the people of interest are teachers who are immersed in the educational situations of their teaching environment. They are also involved in their own past, current and possible future interactions with their students, colleagues, school administrators and family members. They are within their milieu of traditions, customs, purposes and beliefs (Feldman, 1997). Teachers' professional and personal experiences are interwoven with each other. Therefore, the use of life-history narrative research into their biographies has given the time and space for the participant teachers to relate their backgrounds to the way they approach teaching now, and position them in a historical context and a wider landscape as a knowledgeable being. This effort has arrived at the area in education that a person's education never stops as long as he or she lives through this study. The development of a teachers' knowledge, as learning to teach, pervades their life-history, as Elbaz (1991) argued, that authentic teachers' knowledge is grounded in their biographical story.

All the experience of life educates people. During their school days, she or he is understanding education by way of their contact with life, by what she or he does or endures. This education is transferring to him or her the mores and ways of life (Sumner, 1960; Yuan 2003), which makes a human being or a person. Teachers' learning to teach and knowledge development actually goes on by minute steps, often repeated without knowing the exact starting or ending point. For instance, their own learning in schools may constitute their early development of teaching knowledge by observing their own teachers and immersion in the environment. They often draw on that experience in their first few years of teaching, as a participant teachers, Mr. Guo said, he could "copy" how his teachers taught him at the beginning of his teaching. In their teaching career, they contact their fellows, which are all the time transmitting the lore of teaching, for instance through observing and listening to what their fellow teachers are talking about, and collaborating in research and teaching activities. Now they take part in professional development activities, and other open-show classes. The significant events in professional development, such as going abroad and doing a degree, can expand their views and update their knowledge. All this regulates the teacher education as knowledge accumulation, through which they develop their folkways of teaching.

That is to say, teachers' knowledge and its development do not exist in isolation. Teachers' development in understanding teaching is more a social and cultural interaction, in addition to personal experience and aspirations. As Dewey (1929) asserts, knowledge, like the growth of a plant and the movement of the earth, is a mode of interaction. Specifically, Kennedy (1988, cited in Zhao, 2008b) suggests that multiple social, cultural and political systems potentially interact to impede or facilitate classroom practices, including teachers' attitude and beliefs, and other skills. According to Kennedy (1988, in Zhao 2008b), culturally-colourful values are the most powerful ingredients in participants' beliefs and practices, which are manifested through the critical incidents and metaphors in this study. For instance, some Chinese teachers value collective learning and covering curriculum over individual learning in order to make the whole class learn. Teaching by transmission or learning by rote to memorize vocabulary and grammar points is a considerable element of everyday classroom practice in this group of teachers in study, which is observed as part of the culture of education in China (Cortazzi and Jin, 1996; Hu, 2002b). This can further explain why part of the characteristics of their knowledge appears to be grammar pedagogy. The teaching of students from the generations of the one-child policy, and teaching competitions, is becoming the new cultural and pedagogical practice across the country.

The challenges Chinese EFL education faces, in terms of teachers' inadequate language proficiency, obsession with textbooks and teaching to examinations with a grammar pedagogy, teaching to students growing up under the one-child policy, are historical results, culturally significant and contextually influenced (Hu, 2002a, 2002b; Leng, 1997). The cultural and professional contexts and discourses influence not just the way teachers describe their experiences but the way they live, to some extent explaining why they teach in the way they do (Rosiek and Atkinson, 2005). These aspects of teaching and learning are ever-changing and evolving.

Chapter Five

Synchronic Analysis

Synchronic analysis examines the general issues and themes that emerged across all the individual participants, also through the constructing of life stories, such as of leading to becoming and being a teacher, interpreting metaphors and critical incidents, to provide consistency, and a means of comparison, with the diachronic analysis. Across individual teachers, I categorized the teachers into three sub-groups, according to their years of experience in teaching. This chapter presents a few examples including two novice teachers, five experienced teachers and one veteran teacher.

The concepts such as novice teachers, or beginning teachers, experienced teachers, and veteran teachers, are drawn from the existing literature of teachers' life and work studies, as well as teacher education and development (e.g. Goodson, 1997; Huberman, 1989, 1993, 1995; Calderhead, 1988, 1997; Knowles, 1992; Bullough, Jr, 1989 etc.). For example, in Bullough, Jr's (1989) case study of a new teacher, Kerrie, his conception of a new teacher, or of beginning teaching, encompasses Kerrie's first year and part of her second year experiences, while the first phase or stage, in Huberman's (e.g. 1989) larger scale research into teachers' life cycle or career stages in Switzerland includes the first 3 years' experience. In this study, the novice teachers and beginning teachers refer to teachers who have 1-2 years experience. Sometimes, when it is referred to a wider experience, I use the first few years of teaching. Teachers of more than 3 years and less than 10 years experience are referred to as newly-experienced teachers. There is no consensus as to exactly how many years should constitute a "new" teacher, an "experienced" teacher, or a "veteran" teacher in the literature, the meanings of which names are also dependent on the cultural context. The teachers are categorized according to the years of experience and the expertise of the participants in this analysis.

The participants' narrative accounts are presented, along with my analysis and commentary, which can be viewed as my response to the extracted narratives of their life-histories. The participants' narrative accounts are distinguished by italics, while the metaphors are in bold.

Narrative Accounts of Two Novice Teachers

Two novice teachers are Miss Wang and Mr. Xia. The context of becoming a teacher, key metaphors and significant narrative episodes, such as critical incidents from their life-history narratives, are analysed and presented below.

■Miss Wang is 24. She is in her second year of teaching, at senior secondary level at a key school.

The Context of Becoming a Teacher
According to Miss Wang's accounts, she did not graduate from a teacher education course, but majored in Technological English for her BA degree. She realized that a degree in English actually gave quite limited job options, when she started thinking about what she could do with the degree, during the senior year of her BA course. After drawing on the experiences of previous graduates from this course, she found many of them had become teachers. Then she started preparing, on her part, for the occupation of teaching. As she said in her narrative, she applied for a position of teaching under the pressure to find employment, and she guessed the reason why, even without a background in teacher education, she has been given this job – she said: *"Mr. Zhu (one of the participants in this study) interviewed me; he gave me this job probably because I have a good track record in my BA course, and sound like a courageous and dynamic person."*

Key Metaphors
Lacking the experience, or background, or qualification, in teacher education, she felt slightly weak. She used metaphor to describe this situation as: *"I feel like a **slow bird**."* By this she means *"I have a different starting point compared to my peer group and other colleagues, that is to say, I am very aware that I did not have any teacher training experience, so I have to catch up by working*

harder." As she said "*I am a diligent person.*" Her metaphor as a "slow bird" is associated with working harder than usual to familiarize herself with her job as a teacher because she realized that her absence of experience of a teacher education course is a weakness for her, while her peers had that experience.

When she recalled her first year of teaching, she described, "*Last year I was nervous in class, I tried hard to recall how my teachers taught me. At the beginning, I relied heavily on my memory of how my senior secondary school teacher taught me. Anyway, my senior school was six years ago; I cannot rely it on any more.*" Now, she has to rely on her own sense and sensibility in learning to teach, and said, "**Classroom management is like grasping sand in your hand, if you squeeze too tight, it hurts your hand, if you loosen your grip, the sand slips through your fingers.**" Classroom management seems to be a prominent issue for novice teachers. Miss Wang wrestles between tightening, and loosening, her grip – she felt control hurt both sides, and the relationship between students and teacher. There is still some distance between "reach" and "grasp" in relation to students. She was learning to reach students by reading books on pedagogy, and learning, as she settles down in her second year of teaching.

She also talked in a metaphorical way about the discontinuity in curriculum transition that she perceives; she said "*the new textbook for senior secondary level is widely perceived to be difficult. **The students feel like they are climbing up a steep hill** when transferring from junior secondary to senior secondary in terms of the change of the level of difficulty in the textbooks*".

Her conceptualization of teaching English is that "*Teaching English is different from teaching history or politics – listing facts and events and summarizing from them*". Probably that is how she was taught in these subjects, or what she knows about how these subjects were, or are, taught, according to her knowledge. She continues, "*English consists of live sentences; it is like abstracting things out of real life. English learning is like **picking up shells, one has to keep them well in the basket. Keeping them in the basket is about memorizing. As for where do the shells come from, they are brought in by the waves, or the teacher gives them, one at a time, to the students and asks them to keep them well and then use them. The teacher can teach them how to pick up shells and make use of them.***" This may reflect one side of her philosophy of "learning to use" rather than "learning by using", in EFL education in China, and a model of teaching that views students as "empty vessels" (see Hu, 2002b: 98, 99).

Critical Incident: Early Mastery of Pedagogy

"I have to learn from the teachers around; I watched others' teaching as well as learning about how to deal with requirements, classroom management and emergency handling. A small incident happened in the pre-sessional morning reading today. I teach two classes, one is class 5, and the other is class 8, which is upstairs. I move between the two classes to maintain discipline and watch them read. When I went downstairs from class 8 to 5, even from far away, I could hear some noise, I spoke to myself, 'Please don't let it be my class 5!' When I went over, I found it was, indeed, class 5. Standing at the door, I could see some students had moved from the back to the front, some had remained in their seats; all of them had ceased reading. They were screaming and laughing. I stood at the door for at least 10 seconds. I did not know what they were doing; I thought they might be collecting money, or exercise books. At first, I did not lose my temper, I wanted to wait and have a look. Then I asked, 'What's wrong?' When the students saw me, they went back to their seats one after another. I asked again, 'What's the matter?' Some students said there was a centipede under the stool. I thought: 'They even made a fuss about a centipede!' I was unhappy. Then I turned to the student who seemed to attract the crowd, 'Zhong Xin, can you tell me what happened?' He stood up and murmured something, I couldn't hear. I raised my voice to say, 'Imagine when you are taking the university entrance exams, if there is a centipede on your question paper, would you jump up from your seat? You are supposed to have some self-control.' Then they calmed down. I was aware that the advice is not to criticize the whole class for the sake of a few. Then I left the classroom. Before the class was over, I went back quietly and saw they were reading, and then I did not say anything. When I came back to the office, I asked the teachers what they would do under such a circumstance. The teachers said it was enough to say a few words, to criticise just slightly. After all, you have to be tolerant with this age group, if you blamed the whole class for the sake of a minority, you would have made the whole class unhappy. Students might think you were overexerting your authority. If you found that some individual student aroused that situation, you could talk to that student individually. I thought about it carefully, and felt my colleagues' advice was reasonable."

This incident anchored in Miss Wang's narrative renders a vivid and authentic description of the classroom incident in terms of the context, such as the time and location of what happened, in detail, a distraction caused by a centipede in the morning reading session in the classroom, including her mental reactions. Cortazzi (1993: 129) uses "disaster story" for this kind of goings-on in teachers' narratives. Prior to Miss Wang's telling of the incident, she had given the orientation. She said: *"I try to teach the way that is acceptable to the students, what I can do is to learn from the colleagues around, including learning to handle an emergency situation, setting up expectations and fulfilling them. I ask any of my colleagues around."* This echoes the literature, as Cortazzi (1993: 55) contends that narratives are "contextually self-contained" in a way tellers give context, sequences and reflection on events and incidents in their narratives, as Brunner (1996) assert that narrative has sequences and meanings. Tellers provide their own personal interpretations. The conclusion I draw from this incident is that the protagonist, Miss Wang, is learning to deal with unexpected situations in classroom management, which is based on the teller's interpretation. The criticality of this incident is it happened the same day as when the conversation took place, which captures a snapshot of the commonplaces in a new teachers' everyday working life. Through another lens, it captures a reflective and mindful self-image, of who is concerned in classroom management in the first years of teaching. Because of the evaluation, her reflection on this incident is explicit, as she managed to handle this incident without making the whole class unhappy, which indicates a sense of achievement and makes it part of the learning experience in her early mastery of pedagogy. The critical incident also depicts the mental activity in a decision-making process, regarding how to handle potential classroom chaos, marking a significant point in her memory. She seemed to be satisfied and confident with the solution. As a result, she could maintain her image as a reflective and learning novice teacher, which seems to be a great achievement for her at that point in her life. This image is further reinforced by her beautiful metaphor of classroom management as *"grasping sand"* in terms of level of control.

Understanding of Students

Miss Wang feels that the students are becoming increasingly difficult to handle, they do not care about going to university so much. Her explanation for this is: *"It is easier to go to university now. Students have lost the ethos of studying with all their might. The value system has changed as well. Some students paid 30,000 – 50,000 Yuan extra to come to study in this school due to not reaching the grade of admission. My former secondary classmates felt ashamed to pay extra money to go to a key senior high school. They studied extremely hard. But now those students feel differently. Probably the wider environment has changed; the school ethos has changed as well.*"

■Mr. Xia, is 24 years old, in his first year of teaching at senior secondary school. He worked in TV media for one year before he started teaching.

The Context of Becoming a Teacher

Like Miss Wang presented above, having majored for 4 years in Technological English in a university, he then worked in a TV station in advertising for a year, and then got a teaching position in the school. Though becoming a teacher is not a purely personal decision, he did not expect to become a secondary teacher when in university. He perceives that *"it is determined by the society as well, because teaching is, at least, a proper job available to me, as employment in China is not optimistic"*. His ideal job is to do TV media and advertising.

Key Metaphors

Mr. Xia is typical of early idealism at the beginning of teaching. His comments on education in China and the comparison with that of America indicates he is an idealist, and ambitious, as well as altruistic, in becoming a teacher. This account includes a few metaphors that express his view, indications of his assumptions about the educational system in Western countries. He said: *"I always think Chinese education is disadvantaged, in a way that students follow a narrow road of knowledge. Their knowledge structure is like a **well, deep and narrow**. Comparatively, American students' knowledge structure is like a **pond, broad and shallow**. [He did a comparative study on personality between Chinese and American people for his BA dissertation.] This is an issue of the educational system. This is about grasping the educational principles as well. And they should not train children to be tractable."* His metaphor may reflect the situation in China where students spend most of their time at schoolwork, preparing for going to a good university for a bright future, sacrificing the developing of hobbies at school.

Critical Incident

"In my first class, my very first class, on September 1, I said to students, we are all equal, anyway, we are all young people, you are younger people; I am young as well. Anything can be said between you and me, anything, if it is relevant to the class. Anything can be said after class; in class it should be relevant to the class. That is to say you can let your hair down if you want, break down the barriers and obstacles. That is exactly what I told them, I always hate hypocrisy."

The position drawn from this incident is: Mr. Xia appeared to be an idealist in his first class, and made a strong attempt to try to establish a democratic or equal student-teacher relationship. This resulted in some difficulty in his classroom management in terms of disciplining students and getting through his lesson plans.

Views on Chinese Children

*"Chinese children were trained to be 'a good child'. 'A good child' is a typical term; a tractable child is regarded to be a good child. When I was a child, I felt this word is a compliment. People label children as 'a tractable child' or 'an intractable child'. After I entered university, I hated people saying I was tractable. When they said that, I felt I was easily led, taught, or controlled or easily handled. I did not have my own volition. Even right up to now, I get upset when people say I am tractable. Children are over-protected in China; the older generation has had a hard life, they think that now it is great for the younger generation to have everything, and they do anything for the child. However, the tragic consequence is that children are deprived of their experiences. The other thing that makes my **heart ache** is that children have lost their intrinsic nature of being a child, they say and do what adults teach and tell them to say or to do. They don't even consider speaking their own opinion. Since birth, or since they can speak, children follow and repeat others. Students used to bury themselves in books, and did what the teacher told them to do. They accepted what the teacher taught. But nowadays students are not like us when we were students – they are physically bigger, independent and lively, but immature; they have their own individual needs, and they like fresh ideas. Now they look at the teacher with sceptical eyes – they have their own opinions and they make their own judgments."*

Narrative Accounts of Five Experienced Teachers

The four newly experienced teachers are Ms. Mary, Ms. Tao, Mr. Guo and Ms. Xiong, plus one very experienced teacher, Mr. Zhu.

■ **Ms. Mary is 29. She has worked for 1 year in administration, and she has taught for 8 years (4 years at junior secondary level, 4 years at senior secondary level).**

The Context of Becoming a Teacher

Ms. Mary regarded herself as a person who is not ambitious. She went to an English course at a teacher's college for several reasons. First, she thought an English-related course gave better employment prospects, and that it is not a bad idea to become a teacher. Her parents suggested that it is good for a girl to live a steady life by becoming a teacher.

Key Metaphors

Ms. Mary told about her early years of learning to teach through trial-and-error: *"To be honest, at the early stage of teaching, I could not realize what problems I had. But now, when looking back, I can see I have come through in a **roundabout** way"*, by which she modestly means that she was not able to teach effectively in her first years of teaching, but improved a lot through practice. *"I needed somebody to point out my mistakes and give suggestions."*

Ms. Mary has undertaken a month's professional development in the UK, and some native English-speakers are teaching at her school. She made an interesting comparison of the styles of Chinese teachers in comparison with native English-speaking teachers: *"Generally, Chinese teachers teach in a **gentle** and **mild** way. Teaching is seldom seen to be lively and active, or passionate. It has little of genuine communication... The majority of the students may listen when teachers teach in this gentle and mild way, but not actively. Students sitting at the back of the classroom don't follow; they even fall asleep. If the teacher were to teach with passion, the students will become interested and concentrate better."*

Ms. Mary was very thoughtful and aware of developing her pedagogical content knowledge – making the content teachable and acceptable to students, making efforts to avoid making her students learn by mere memorization, which shows how, in her learning about teaching, she is struggling to move away from mere transmission. *"Students think **English is something far away from them**. So sometimes I try various different ways in my teaching. A few days ago, when I was preparing to teach phonetics, I read some books about how others teach it. But these ways don't seem very good to me. I was anxious to find other ways; I talked about it with my colleague who used to teach Chinese, the way of teaching Chinese Pin-Yin sounds similar to teaching English phonetics. I talked to him about my plans. He negated all my ideas and asked why **I would bother to do it in a nonlinear way**, why not just do it in a direct way, presenting the phonetics and let them repeat for memorization. He said I did not need to **beat around the bush**. Sometimes I also examine my ways. **Probably, the content is something I have to give to them directly,** and then they should memorize it through effort. I often ask myself how I can get them to grasp it with little effort. Perhaps, students should just make the effort to memorize it, nothing is easy. But now, my idea is to make students master it effortlessly. Though, it might be impossible for me to make lots of variations of everything for them."* This above incident of discussing with her colleague about teaching phonetics also indicates that she has doubt about teaching *"by giving it to them directly"*, and she was uncertain and cautious when experimenting with new ways in incorporating student construction for learning, probably, because it has not yet become common practice in the school, or beyond, in the city. She is recognized as an excellent teacher and has won first prize in various teaching competitions, and she has been newly appointed as the head of English at the school.

Critical Incident

"I went to the University of Wales and studied there for a month as well. Particularly, I was impressed by the trip to Wales – the teachers taught very well there. I felt a big difference, and thought I should study hard and teach better. However, in reality, when we were in the UK, the class we were in had only 9 students; and the English teacher, in general, was relaxed in teaching. He asked us to role-play a job interview – one of us was the interviewee and others were the interviewer, then we sat down and started. The whole session was doing the activity. In our own context, we have more students in the class."

Ms. Mary responded to my question concerning what it is that inspires her to keep on in the teaching profession, with this above incident. Continuing professional development activities extended teachers' views of teaching, and may create a goal for their growth, as Ms. Mary reflects on that experience: *"I think the ideal teaching and learning is the kind I came across in Wales: teachers and students are engaged in learning. We had three hours of lessons a day, but we did not feel it was three hours, time passed very fast; I wanted to learn more. The teacher only taught us half a day, everybody enjoyed it as a process. The teacher enjoyed teaching too. I cannot reach that level yet."* In addition, continuing professional development events and activities may generate more interest in teaching, as it is implied in Ms. Mary's narrative about her future plans: *"I still want to **recharge myself** by going out and studying more, but we don't have many opportunities. I would like to study more about education; I have not found any other things that interest me, so far."*

Subjects Matter and Students

As has been demonstrated, her relations to students frequently link to the subject she is teaching. According to her narrative, at the beginning of her teaching she was often made to cry by her students. *"In the first year, I was made to cry almost every week. The biggest weakness I had, and I still have it now, was **I did not put myself in the student's shoes**, for example, when teaching about the alphabet, 26 letters, I thought it so easy that it could be mastered in a few minutes. However, to students, it could be very difficult."* Owing to her *"own learning experience"* she acknowledges that she thinks differently now: *"I did French as my second foreign language when preparing for my postgraduate exams. When I did it in the college, I felt it easy. I tried to pick it up last year. It was so difficult. Then I had a realisation that students learning English felt similar to my learning French – they study it and forget; it needs reinforcing. It had been a mistake that I had not understood until then."*

However, her relation to her students is quite emotional. *"Sometimes, I felt **a loss** from working with students, because I devoted a lot without reward, which left me feeling badly about that. I want goodness for them; I could not just let them drift on their own."* ... *"In the first class of this semester, I wanted to discuss a question to the students about 'What is the purpose of studying English?' and 'How can we study English well?' I think it is a meaningful topic. Some students said 'we were given a book and asked to study it'. Well, within less than* *ten minutes, a boy student spoke up, 'Stop talking about that; let's start our lesson.' I have ideas, but sometimes..."* She continues: *"When I come to the classroom with passion, seeing the students uninterested, **I feel drenched with cold-water,** feeling very disappointed. I feel very frustrated when a good idea cannot be realized in the classroom. Putting aside the examination marks, every single student is lovely. My last year-group very much celebrated my birthday, from year 1 to year 3. My heart would not allow me to ignore them. I thought I should **look after** them."*

■ **Ms. Tao is at age 27. She had worked as a civil servant in a local government department. She is in the 4th year at teaching junior secondary level.**

The Context of Becoming a Teacher
Her undergraduate degree is in International Finance. But half of that course was dealing with English. After graduation, she worked in a Science and Technology Association, part of the local government. She said: *"It is like a place for retirement, I was 21 then. I was afraid I would lose ambition if I stayed there longer. It was a comfortable place; I needed to go to work for just half a day, either morning or afternoon. But I did not like it. Then I became a teacher, through my mother's arrangement. The course of my life was controlled and changed by my mother."*

Key Metaphors
*"At the start of my teaching, I followed the textbook rigidly. It was pointed out that it **was like flogging a dead horse.** Gradually, I learned to use the textbook and exercise book flexibly."*

She had an interesting comment on the teaching occupation and the pay for it: *"I read some comment on the teaching occupation, and teachers, on the Internet. It is said **they get up earlier than roosters, go to bed later than servant girls, and earn less than peasant workers.** It is sad if people have such an image about the teaching occupation...Though there has been some increase in teachers' salary in recent years. That is still **modest.** My husband was often kidding me about it. 'You get up so early in the morning, come home late in the evening, now we don't have a child, you hardly do any housework. Before I married you, I was told your salary was high. Yes your salary is higher than mine, but your* *income is less than mine.' "*

Critical Incident
I met Ms. Tao at a teaching competition and I invited her to participate in the study. She talked about this experience, and what she learned through it, which is viewed as a critical incident in her recent teaching experience.

"What I learned from taking part in the teaching competition this year is that we should not set a fixed answer for students' views. Since the teaching competition, when I teach now, I always allow students to express their own view, for instance, I've just taught a lesson which was a drill about comparatives 'What do you like best, chickens or ducks?' Many students say 'I like chickens', 'because they are lovely'. I encouraged students say their view instead of repeating the sentence in the text. When a student said 'I like chicken best because it is delicious', many students burst into laughter, but I praised him and said 'A very good answer.' This way, students will learn to express their own ideas rather than repeat the text. Later on, when the students were asked: 'Where do you like better, the countryside or the city?' a student said 'I like cities better, because I can play computer games in the city, but I can't in the country.' "

Teaching competition is a phenomenon in the fieldwork. It is a way of communicating teaching through demonstrating practise as a kind of work-based professional development. Ms. Tao explicitly expressed its positive impact on her teaching with concrete evidence, which can be further seen in her progress in teaching, moving from adherence to, or obsession with, the textbook, to incorporating more authentic practise in English.

"Yesterday, I asked a student to describe an animal, and then let other students guess what he was describing. Students were interested and engaged. If the students are encouraged to express their own ideas, students do so. It seemed that I did not cover the material I needed to, but I believe students achieved more than just following the text. I used to be faster in pace, but now I give more time to students to practice, spend less time dealing with the textbook, and the students learn faster. If allowed, wouldn't more and more students speak out their own ideas rather than rigidly follow what is said in the textbook? I think teaching English is not about teaching a few words or language points – they can do that

with tapes and books bought from bookshops at home. I am not sure how other people would look at this." However, she does not feel very certain whether any progress in her practise has happened recently.

Motivating Students

Ms. Tao seems to be good at motivating students, as she knows what to discourage and encourage in teaching, in relation to the students' cognitive development and the content of the lesson. *"When studying dialogues or text, I discourage them from reading or memorizing exactly what is said in the book. I would be very happy to see them replace some words in the sentence, or make the dialogue more varied. For instance, if the sentence in the book is 'Is this a map?' I would like to hear them say something different from 'map' when they are practicing. I would like to make the learning, even in the classroom, more real/authentic. For example, we are doing comparison now, I encourage then to compare things in the room, or things they are familiar with. They have just had a sports meeting; they can use the context to do adverb comparatives, such as who runs faster? In general, in junior 1, students were interested in acting-out things, due to their limited knowledge of the target language; in junior 2, they prefer talking about ideas, as they've studied English for more than one year, and they can say a lot in English.*

■Mr. Guo is 34. He has taught English in primary and secondary schools for 10 years.

The Context of Becoming a Teacher
Critical Incident

To Mr. Guo, one of the turning points in his life experience is an injury which redirected his career from sports to becoming an English teacher.

"I was admitted to the sports department in a physical education course at a teachers' college. I had to change my course because my eyes were injured when playing football, and had an operation because of a detached retina in one of my eyes. I missed college for a year after the operation. For this reason, I was not supposed to do physical sports and was advised to change. I felt English was interesting, and in addition, my English was not bad." So he passed the test and changed to the English education course. There are some other reasons for him to choose English, first he felt it was easier to find a job with English; he also

perceived that English teachers were esteemed in society.

Key Metaphors
According to his memory of his English learning experience at secondary level, his English teacher taught him to learn English as:

*"At that time, **the teacher often said that studying English was like having steamed bread, the dry steamed bread, just swallowing it, without thinking too much. If one could endure the mother of all hardships, he could become one of the crème de la crème.** The most unforgettable thing is about learning English. China was closed off, we did not encounter English initially until we entered secondary school. There were no tape recorders in the school; we studied English merely in class, 45 minutes a session a day... In senior secondary school, **there was so much stuff. It was transmitted into us; we contained it and did not know how to use it. It was a real sense of pouring it into us. I was in a boarding school. I was under great pressure; it was a life of three stations – dorm, classroom and canteen."***

Mr. Guo talked about his learning English in comparison to learning maths this way:

"When I was in senior secondary school, I could use various ways to work out a mathematics question, a few hours passed before I solved it. It was great fun doing maths. Another issue about learning English is that it involves mouth, eyes and thinking at the same time. When doing maths, it is just deep thinking."

Inevitably, his experience and expertise of sports appeared in his cognition of English learning, as he made a joke of it:

"I cannot get away from sports."... "Learning English through drill-and-practice is like training people in playing football – if it is not to train them to be football or basketball players, it is fun. Otherwise, it is boring to do the repetitive physical training."

The conflict between teaching for ability development and for high examination marks *is* perceived as a "***dilemma***", by Mr. Guo, *"On one side, we have to give* *students space and freedom to develop them in all rounds. On the other, **the measure of examination scores, the benchmark, is there. High scores speak.**"*

About the Curriculum

Mr. Guo talked about the change in curriculum of EFL in relation to other subjects. This extract from the conversation is taken as evidence, with concrete details.

Guo: *In a broad sense, the system has called for reducing the load on students.*

Annie: *Has it been reduced substantially or not?*

Guo: *It has been reduced substantially in some subjects. In contrast, the standard has been raised in terms of English. For instance, the text about Karl Max which we used to study in Senior 1 now has been placed in the textbook of Junior 3. The size of vocabulary used to be 800 for junior leavers, 200 words for two-musts; 600 for four-musts. Now 1,000 words are required for four-musts; 200 for two-musts.*

Annie: *What are four-musts?*

Guo: *The "four-musts" are that a student must be able to use the words in terms of listening, speaking, reading and writing – in particular. Examinations will focus on those words required in the curriculum.*

Annie: *What kind of curriculum?*

Guo: *It is a book, or two books.*

Annie: *Is it entitled as Curriculum?*

Guo: *It seems to be "New Curriculum Standard".*

Annie: *New Curriculum Standard. Is it the one that sets up the objectives for each year group? Does it integrate junior and senior year grades?*

Guo: *No...It seems to target junior year grades, oh, it does not mention grade years... but for example, the foreign-language elementary school leavers should reach a prescribed level...*

The understanding of the Curriculum may vary from teacher to teacher. Change in Curriculum regarding content and time. In a broad context, the country has advocated not raising the standard in compulsory education against ever-rising expectations for schooling, in the sense that the difficulty level of certain subjects should be lowered, and children should have some play-time instead of always being involved in school work over a long time after normal hours or at home. This has been long advocated, but many schools had not implemented it. Recently, the local government of Hubei province has taken the initiative and made it illegal for schools to require their students to be at school earlier than 8:20 in the morning, or on Saturdays and Sundays for extra lessons. By implication, for teachers, the contact time should be reduced. However, the standard of English has been substantially raised.

Children Growing up under the One-child Policy

Mr. Guo has a wide and historical view when talking about his students: *"Seeing through a teacher's perspective, I can see some issues related to school, family and society. When I was a child, parents stood firm on their feet with their authority; children were afraid of parents. Now, in one way, children negotiate with parents, to show that they are right. They want to let the parents know whether what the parents say makes sense or not, or whether it is convincing to them. They would not listen to the parents just because parents have the right to hit them. What's more, there are broad channels that children can get information from, such as TV, real life, movies, or from society outside, or from the world outside. They have absorbed a lot. Therefore, if parents don't have qualities for children to admire or respect, and only shout at or hit them, they would not listen to them. In addition, the child is the single child; many parents have talked to me about this issue. When verbal criticism or talk does not work, parents tend to hit them, and then the child rebels in their own ways. The child knows he/she is the one and only child, the single baby; as a result, they sometimes can threaten parents. There are some students like this in the class. When they feel like it, they hand in homework – and they don't hand in homework when they don't feel like it. They behave wilfully. What can a teacher do with this? It is useless for a teacher to talk to them. Talking to them does not produce any effect. I made a home visit to explore why a child behaves this way. There are many better ones; they study very hard and they seem to be very understanding. In addition to listening to the teachers, discussing with the teachers, they take extra classes outside school. Private tuition is common now. In general, children now are better-informed, and the language learning environment has improved too, as English language has become more readily accessible, and, in particular, foreign teachers come directly to teach here."*

■**Ms. Xiong is 34 years old, and has 9 year-experience of teaching senior secondary level and 5 years junior secondary level for all together 14 years.**

She is now a deputy-head of a junior secondary school.

The Context of Becoming a Teacher

I did not ask her how she became a teacher; instead, I asked her whether she is satisfied being a teacher. She earnestly addressed this point with *"satisfied as in four characters – Ying yu jiao shi [Chinese, means English teacher]"*. She meant she felt satisfied with it only when "English" was attached to "teacher" – "English teacher".

Key Metaphors

Ms. Xiong's way of telling about her experience is very metaphorical. When she is elaborating on the relationship between teaching to, and beyond, the textbook, which is another polarity in this group of Chinese teachers' curriculum narratives, she said: *"If they [the students] don't take in the basic material included in the textbook, **then output [mainly speaking or writing] is like an inaccessible pinnacle.** They have to memorize it. **Even an intelligent house-wife cannot make a meal without basic ingredients.** That's my personal view."* This can also be interpreted as her understanding of the relationship of input and output in language learning.

Ms. Xiong compared her current state of being a teacher and that of the past, which demonstrated a path of development as, *"I have some general feeling that **I did not feel the flow to manage teaching to some extent. I could only teach the textbook to students. The class was not so lively. I feel a process of growth. I feel flow and I am walking on a smooth path now."***

Her desire to be excellent, and her love of knowledge and competence at being an English teacher has taken her to her position as a deputy head and a bright future, which is adequately evident: *"Other people, including my family, **say that I sit in my position firmly without any threat. There is no looming crisis of being laid-off for me.** I do not want to be out of practice with English teaching. I cannot stay in this position as deputy-head forever, but I can be a life-long English teacher. **People can take away my position as a deputy head, but my professional knowledge is always with me. I want to look ahead.** In this environment, I feel compelled to be outstanding among my peers, putting pressure on myself. **I just look further. I want to deserve the title as an English teacher.***

Otherwise, other people may say what an English teacher is. She doesn't even know this word."

Her expectations of her students shows her understanding of her role as a teacher: *"I learn first and then teach.* **Learning should go beyond certain boundaries and so should teaching – students should go beyond the teacher. The teacher is just a bridge, and the teacher is not the equivalent of English at all. The students should not see what the teacher demonstrates to them as the whole world of English.** *I have been telling students like this. I told them they must be much abler than me."*

According to her knowledge, the current system is not flexible enough for teachers to undertake long-term professional development. For example, there is no supply teacher scheme yet: *"We **have a fixed structure.** If I leave for professional development, who comes to teach my classes? If somebody is arranged to teach the classes, where can I stay when I come back? For example, if I leave for two years for a study, somebody else will be arranged to teach my classes. Where can I fit in when I come back?"*

Critical Incident – Looking beyond the Textbook
As a deputy-head, she is very reflective on her own learning, every experience is enlightening and a force of learning to her which is illustrated in this critical incident: *"To handle junior secondary teaching, the basic need is to study the new textbook, we don't have to urge ourselves to do systematic learning or adapt to a new model. Even the advance of teaching methods is not very challenging to teachers. This is just my personal view.* **The reform of teaching methods is not a big challenge either.** *To be honest, I have the desire to learn. To improve my oral English ability, basically, I require myself to watch English TV programmes every day, and speak English every day, even if it is speaking to myself. I must learn.* **I want to look beyond;** *I am teaching junior secondary level; I can do it even if I don't learn further. I think I have embarked on a job with English and I realized it in life that there is a large amount of vocabulary, when I listen to simple English news, is not included in the textbook at all, or in the books available for us to use. Then we must learn from the books that are not used for teaching. So I exert all my efforts to find other books to learn from, then I can find a better connection with textbooks and real-life use. We once had a foreigner,*

a Canadian, come to work in this school for about three and half months. I found that what she said could not be found in the textbook we teach to students. What is used widely by native-speakers in real life could not be found in our textbooks. **We laboriously teach our students something not being used by native-speakers on an everyday life basis,** *which indicates that there are many drawbacks in our education.*

I was enlightened by this experience. **I felt we have learned English for so many years in vain,** *and we continue to teach the students in the old way. For instance, I was most impressed by the word 'contact'. We don't use it with our colleagues, and I have never seen it in our textbooks either. When it appeared in utterance, I could guess what it means. I really had never known the word. Then I urged her to explain the word 'contact' to me. When people say good-bye, they say 'I'll contact you'.* **This stirred me up. I understood at least our teaching stuff was not comprehensive. This experience was stimulating.** *At least I learned some words and they made me think we just learned partially.* **Students may learn from the textbook; teachers must go beyond that."**

Ms. Xiong has professional confidence, sensibility and judgment to decide when to stick to the textbook and how to go beyond it. She has to help the students achieve examinations while cater for other interests. This above critical incident gives evidence to her capacity of direction and leading her colleagues by learning and looking beyond.

■**Mr. Zhu, aged 38, has been teaching English as a foreign language in a key senior secondary school in a city in central China for 17 years, since he graduated from a teacher university. He is the head of the department of English at his school.**

Early Experience of Learning English
"I liked the teacher, I liked English."
"I started to study English from junior secondary, about 1979. The teaching force was not strong. I remember, at the end of first semester, the final examination was to write the 26 letters from memory. I could not do it, because those letters did not make sense to me. I later became interested in English, because we had a very nice teacher, who was very cordial. I still remember her first lesson. She asked 'How old are you?' to every individual student. We answered according

to our real age, as 'I am twelve', or 'I am thirteen'. I was extremely proud that I could speak English, and after the first two lessons, I started to like English. I liked the teacher. I loved to study English well. Later on, I learned English with ease, without having to spend much time on it. In 1981, I went to senior secondary school. My English had been very good. I enjoyed it. In 1983, the system decided to change senior secondary from two years to three years. Some schools implemented this policy from 1984, some schools from 1983. My school put it off one year, implementing the policy in 1984. We had only two years, while the same year-group in other schools in the same city had three years for senior secondary."

The Context of Becoming an English Teacher
Two critical incidents in the above life story can be identified: one is in junior secondary, where he had a very "nice" English teacher, which prompted the click moment for him to become interested in English; the second is the change of the system, as part of the reform, changing the senior secondary from two to three years, which redirected the whole situation of the entrance to university. Some students of his year-group did not graduate, and took university entrance examinations in other schools. Both critical incidents demonstrated the external and contextual influence on Mr. Zhu – he gained an interest in English, then he was admitted to the English course in the Teachers' University (the name is fictionalized) in the last choice of five, but not admitted to Peking University to study to be an ambassador, as his first choice. It resulted in his "deep disappointment". Mr. Zhu graduated from the Teachers' University, and started teaching in 1987.

"At graduation, there were two high-prestige job opportunities – one was to work for the Foreign Ministry, and the other was to be a journalist for the Xinhua News Press Bureau. The prerequisite for both jobs required the candidates to be a Communist Party member... So, I was assigned to teach in this school. It was determined by the way I am, as a person. The head teacher of the school had several talks with me when I came, saying that he hoped that I could be a model teacher. In my early twenties, I was playful, I could not figure out the profound implications in those talks."

In the 1980s, university graduates were "assigned" to a job by the university.

The operation was very complicated, under the planned economy at that time in China, in which the allocation of resources to key sectors, and the movement of products in the market, were centrally directed (see also Yang and Wu, 1999). Normally, there was a quota for government departments, or state-run companies, or enterprises, to take university graduates, and then the university assigned the jobs to the graduates according to the quota. It appeared to be that the graduate took up a job according to the university allocation. Mr. Zhu knew very well that ...

He missed his goal of becoming an ambassador. Consequently, he felt "in low spirit" for the first three years of his teaching. Perhaps that is why he felt it was tragic (see also Polkinghorne, 1995). This, nevertheless, demonstrates that he held on to his own way of being a person, and, in a sense, he does write his own life-history (Denzin, 1989; Sparkes, 1999).

Professional Judgement

China has been changing in recent years. The transformation from a planned economy to a market economy has been impacting on, and changing, the society – for instance, the job market is opening up. The state-sanctioned employment quota is being replaced by the actual market demand. Graduates can meet up with employers in a two-way choice. In the most recent few years, Mr. Zhu has recruited English teachers, and teachers of other art subjects, for the school. When asked what his criteria were in making a professional judgement, when choosing teachers for the school, his rule, or standard, is: "Personality. Personality is the key." The reason is *"Because teaching is working with people – an unsociable, unresponsive or over-proud person is not really welcome. Personality is very important in a teacher. Simply put, he or she needs to be open-minded, easygoing, listening, and accommodating. So, after I have seen that the qualifications are OK, I will interview the candidates. I interviewed many, but few lived up to my standard. Some graduates, after four years' study of English, could not speak English naturally, or fluently, and they were reciting their CV from memory. I normally ask the candidate to introduce him/herself for two minutes, freely in English. I would have a general impression of their English proficiency. Then I ask questions such as: 'Why do you want to be a secondary school teacher? What sort of problems do you think you will confront in teaching in a key secondary school?'; 'When students do not listen in class, what might be the reasons and how you would respond to that?' After the interview, I can draw half a conclusion as to whether the candidate will make a 'good enough' teacher. Of course, I sometimes make mistakes.*"

It seems that, to Mr. Zhu, a "good enough" teacher has both nature and nurture elements, in a way that combines personality as part of the natural upbringing of the person, and professional competence, as merits of dedicated efforts through academic education, or training. He also emphasizes the "nature" part: *"I have never had a session, or a lecture, on how to teach a lesson, it depends very much on a personal gift."* He seems to take the view that teaching has the characteristics of art, as he said:

"I hate following a textbook rigidly, I do believe in inspiration in teaching." In consequence, it affects his decision when recruiting teachers for the school. According to Mr. Zhu, the will to become a teacher comes first, relative to a qualification from a teacher education course. He is aware that few university graduates would consider teaching as their first choice of a career, in the current China. To some extent, in China: *"...being a teacher means high responsibility, high pressure, and low pay"*. However, teaching is a reasonably stable occupation, and things are changing. He said: *"The status of teachers has notably improved in recent years, including the pay."*

When people are at different stages in their life and career, they see different things and set different goals. At the moment, Mr. Zhu is looking at **"measure"**:

*"Education needs **measure**. The key lies in the criteria. Teaching cannot be measured simply with numerical methods. It is subjective. **Anyway, I think the effectiveness of a school lies in the hands of the head teacher.** The innovation and learning of the head teacher direct and **shape** the development of the school. There are narrow-minded competitions among schools. Some schools get better results for university entrance exams, one point that should not be neglected is that they are privileged to select better students."*

The growing competition among schools in the city, and in other parts of China, does not obscure his view that the key school does better at university entrance examinations, in large part owing to the fact that they have the privilege of taking high-achiever students, relative to other schools.

On Teachers' Learning and Professional Sensitivity

In addition to teaching English in the classroom and recruiting English academic staff, taking care of, and making decisions on, professional development opportunities, and activities, is part of his current responsibility and duty, which is present in his thinking, his discussion, and his practice. In the fieldwork, I participated in one of the routine weekly Teaching and Research Activity meetings chaired by Mr. Zhu, in a meeting room at the school, which is regarded by him as: "...a self-regulated and school-based teachers' learning activity." This is a kind of weekly get-together of all the English teachers in the school, to discuss routines and learning. Part of this kind of activity can be, in part, pictured through an episode noted in my research diary:

"...There were 18 EFL teachers present at the meeting. At the start, the chair [Mr. Zhu] delivered a notice about the students' English competition. The meeting proceeded on to the activity of sharing information, and recent learning. A few teachers shared what they found interesting on some websites, including phrases or vocabulary they found useful from their recent reading of English news articles, for example, they mentioned, and explained, phrases such as 'to do one's part', 'to learn the ins and outs', and 'Red sky at night, sealer's delight'... this is followed by theory study. Mr. Zhu pointed out the importance of relating theory to practise; he shared what he has been reading about, and introduced the theory of the 'bottom-up, top-down' interactive model of teaching reading skills... This form of learning activity quite impressed me. In my observation of other teaching competitions, I was aware that teachers' vocabulary is very limited, and it may even be difficult for them to express themselves in English. How can this be connected to the vocabulary-learning and sharing among teachers at this meeting, and at this school? ..."

This critical incident captured a mode of school-based professional development activity, or teacher's learning. Under this circumstance, leading, and sharing learning, is learning. Mr. Zhu's view on teacher's learning, including his own learning, is condensed as:

"There are internal and external demands for the teachers to continue to learn.

Students at this school are excellent; they have high expectations of teachers. Teachers have to take this seriously. Horizontal competition among colleagues is strong. The system of appointment also demands good practice from teachers. Teachers have to develop their professional sensitivity. I think that learning is a life-long activity, particularly for the subject of English. English is not, in any way, a science subject. When teachers of physics, chemistry, and mathematics have learnt the core knowledge of their curriculum, and know how to teach it, they can get along for their whole career, and just become more experienced as time goes on. It is not the case that a teacher, at the age 50, would know everything about English. Learning is not confined by one's age. A few years ago, there were no specific requirements for teachers to learn for the regular teaching and research activities. Younger teachers may think that I, as a head leading the group, have enjoyed various advantages and titles. I model the professional learning, giving them tasks. They may feel compelled to learn. If they don't continue to learn, they will feel they lag behind. That is to say, sometimes, learning is an external demand; sometimes, it is subtle influence from others. It is a kind of pressure too. When they have the habit, they may convert it to an autonomous behaviour, rather than it being imposed by others. People influence each other. It will gradually become a collective behaviour. When a new member joins the group, he/she will be socialized into the learning culture."

Mr. Zhu is leading the group through learning. Given that the wider world is changing radically, learning becomes compelling, according to his view. The current economic development enables individuals to become more mobile, travelling around the country to find a position in teaching, or in another walk of life. Mr. Zhu is making an effort to nourish the learning culture among his colleagues in this community, by leading the learning in his group, and conducting learning as practice, which contributes to the well-being, and the capacity, of the school (see Knight, 2002). Mr. Zhu knows well what he needs to learn, which is reflected in this extract from the interview:

Annie: *Regarding your own learning, what do you think you need to learn?*

Zhu: *Well, I think what I need most to learn is systematic theories. It is better that some experts could make it easier to understand. If I study it by myself, I may not be able to understand a theory by just reading about it. Unfortunately, there is little opportunity to attend that kind of lecture.*

I am disappointed with the messy domestic forums and conferences here in China. I always stress the concept that we should have the professional sensitivity to know what we need to learn, and, also, what we are not good at. For instance, when one feels inadequate in teaching reading, he/she should work on this particular weakness. This is related to professional sensitivity.

The Image of a Teacher and Teaching

By leading the EFL group in the school. The repertoire of his experience base is full of insights into education in China. His narrative account demonstrated a bright professional image, and his voice of, and for, education is strong, which is integrated with his way of being a person, under the constraint of the system. His early learning experience of English: His image and understanding of teaching – **"Education is a life-long course."** – has been evolving and deepening along the way of teaching, expressed through the following metaphorical thinking, which is highly philosophical and theoretical:

*"I think teaching should not be **an experiment**, but **a life course**. This is recognized through experience, because when a person is looking for a job, he/she has some initial understanding about the job, which is to make a living at that job. Then this understanding may be gradually enhanced to look at it as an occupation, or even a profession. Now teaching is promoted to become professionalized. If one is recognized as a professional teacher, he/she will pursue professional skills and knowledge. However, **education is very different from other occupations, in the way it deals with living human beings, rather than objects or products.** When there is something wrong with some product, people can make it again. **However, it is difficult to remedy a human defect caused by education.** Therefore, I think **education is a life-long course. It is a sacred course.** We have to constantly adjust ourselves and renew our understanding and knowledge to face new challenges."*

Mis-education of living people is not remediable, according to Mr. Zhu's understanding and experience. He has understood the world by recognizing others as persons, and continuous experience as education (e.g. Dewey, 1938; Pring, 2000). He thinks old and fixed teaching patterns can be constraining. Experienced as he is now, he has flexibility, like Ms. Tang in the three-generational analysis, and he has a teaching plan too, but not just copying what is in the lesson plan to the blackboard. He said, *"I don't teach with a textbook in my hand, everything is in my brain. My students know that I don't copy stuff from the textbook."*

His image of a teacher is not *"the kind with a facade of chalk-and-talk, holding a book in one hand, a chalk in the other, **copying** from the textbook to the blackboard"*. He answered my question concerning what, for him, are new ways of teaching. He responded to me by asking more questions:

"Are chalks necessary in teaching? Do we have to depend on a book? What is the core knowledge of a subject?"

Of course, he perceives that there is an issue of *"cultural heritage"*. For example, his students think it is not necessary for them to learn traditional Chinese characters and Chinese classics. They are using language in innovative ways when they chat on the Internet. His students are debating with him on these issues. He strongly rejects media reports on teaching by using an unchanged image of the teacher as a *"**burning candles**"*:

"Candles have nothing left after they burnt themselves; they cannot light up for more people. It is said that teachers should be able to stand wear-and-tear. I was discussing with another Chinese teacher about a new metaphor for the image of the teacher, that has the meaning that when teachers light up for others' path, they should enjoy their work, and enrich their experience; they should learn and grow with their students. He came up with a proper metaphor, but I forget the exact word at the moment, I will check with him. Some teachers think reform has nothing to do with them, and teaching in their eyes involves only a chalk and a book, and other attempts are fanfares, plus fancy ideas."

Mr. Zhu is actually critical about the political use in the media of teachers' life stories using a fixed image: *"...some teachers are not recognized until they are nearly dying of cancer."*

This is an example of what Goodson (1995: 89-98) has reminded us of, in his work, "The story so far: personal knowledge and the political", in the study of teachers' personal practical knowledge – teachers and researchers should have a

critical mind about the purpose of the "storytelling". Goodson also (see also
Conle, 2000a, b) points out that some frozen "storytelling" is not for empowering,
but for reinforcing stereotypes, which is not helpful for improvement, or change,
of practice. Mr. Zhu does have an image of a teacher; it is sort of a *"designer"*.
In his words, to plan a lesson is to *"design a lesson"*, which includes the "three
Ps" – prepare students, prepare with textbooks, and prepare teaching methods
which leave space for inspiration.

By his account, the current reform of education is an advance. He said that,
according to Mr. Li Lanqing's proposition, the reform aims at drawing close to
the level of developed countries; we used to just follow other countries, now we
intend to make a great leap to catch up – however, many teachers cannot follow.
According to his knowledge, many Chinese teachers make the assumption that
Western systems of education are better developed. His reason why Chinese
students should learn English is:

*"Teachers should know how to preserve our heritage. What do foreign people
want to see when they come to China? They want to see something they don't
have in their own countries, such as Tang-dynasty customs, Beijing Opera. We
should preserve these cultural essences. We have to make it clear that Chinese
people learn English not for rejecting our own culture but for communicating
with others about our culture. Language is a kind of tool. It has an economic
point as well."*

Relating to his earlier account, his notion of learning English as a foreign
language is to open students' minds to appreciate other cultures, and to preserve
the Chinese cultural heritage. This reflects a wide, contemporary and urgent
view about the need for universal peace, so that people of different races and
religious and cultural origins should learn about how to live together, and make
a contribution to diversity in society, and strengthening world peace (see also
Stoll et al, 2003; Stables, 2003). English has become a desirable commodity in
China, and this has impact on EFL teachers' life. For example, English teachers
are not easily made redundant, because of the demand from society and the
market. Therefore, this can be understood in his personal theory of his teaching,
his reason why people in China study English, which is derived from his
experience and expertise.

Narrative Accounts of a Veteran Teacher

■Mr. Qu is 47 and has taught English for 24 years after having taught Chemistry for two years. She is the head of the English group in a junior secondary school.

The context of becoming a teacher

Mr. Qu had some English education just prior to the "Cultural Revolution". An excerpt of the biographical narrative interview below tells of her experience of entering into teaching EFL:

Qu: *...I had taught Chemistry for 2 years at a farm school. ...when I transferred to Jian Li, I was told only English teaching positions available. English teaching had just resumed; there were no English lessons during the "Cultural Revolution" in many schools. Those who taught English then were not officially trained English teachers.*

Annie: *Did they do self-study [studying English without a teacher]?*

Qu: *Yes. ...The English coordinator of the county happened to be one of my teachers in senior secondary school, who taught music to my class... His English was good. When he knew I was teaching English and I had not studied it before, he gave me English lessons every evening so that I could go to teach the next day. That's it.*

Annie: *Oh...*

Qu: *Yes. He taught me in the previous evening, I went to teach the next day. I studied by myself, by listening to the radio. At that time, there were no TV sets, and tape-recorders were unaffordable. We could only afford to buy a radio.*

Annie: *When was it?*

Qu: *1978, 1980. ... I was admitted to an associate degree course after the first semester. I did it for two years when I was off-service. There were no teachers for the course, we just watched videos and we watched them repeatedly every day for about two years before I came back to teach. It made a big difference in my teaching after that, I felt **easier** in teaching. I continued to teach this way up to 1992. **I was drafted into Yichang as Talented Manpower.***

Key Metaphors

As her education was stunted by the "Cultural Revolution" in the same way as Mr. Cheng and Ms. Tang, she has kept learning. She does not feel adequate to teach in English freely. *"To be an English teacher, it is ideal if we have more knowledge about the English language; however, **knowledge structure is important.**"* For this reason, she is very hesitant to teach her daughter English: *"I dare not teach my daughter English myself because she is at the beginning stage of studying English. **It is like a piece of white paper.** I am afraid of teaching her something wrong. I pay a native speaker for English tuition."*

Critical Incident

(Researcher's note) Mr. Qu is keen on learning more to improve her English. *"I don't feel free when using English. I want to learn natural English rather than recite from books. Once, I invited an American teacher who used to be my daughter's English tutor for a meal at home. When he came over, I asked him to speak out all the household items in English which were seldom included in the textbooks. I just want to communicate something 'real' with them."*

The environment lacking genuine use of English language plays an important role in how people think about and teach English and why they do it that way. Like many Chinese teachers of English, she has never stopped looking for real occasions to practice English. During the biographical narrative interview, she asked me a lot of questions, in particular about a few important words such as "curriculum" which was known as "teaching outline" in China. She was going to be accompanying her colleagues to a provincial teaching competition, but was not quite sure about the native way of greeting in English. I told her, to me, "Hello, everybody" or "Good morning", etc., would be fine. I said to her, *"You have a strong love of speaking English."* She responded, *"I am an English teacher, if I don't want to speak English, what do I want to speak then?"*

Chapter Six

Pedagogy as Caring

The overall strength of analyzing biographical data along both diachronic and synchronic dimensions lies in the in-depth examination of the life-history cases over time while taking every life-history into account at the same time. The analysis of teachers' biographical narrative along diachronic and synchronic dimensions created a comprehensive view to hear teachers' voice and look at their practice from both vertical and horizontal perspectives. Therefore this made it possible to further discuss layers of meanings emerged from the narrative of individual cases and accordingly, which is "lifted up from" its particulars (Doyle, in Carter, 1993: 10).

Caring and Grammar Teaching

The initial idea of teacher's voices of their educational experience has preserved their ways of recounting, and, in general, the characteristics of their understanding, which is jargon-free, authentic, and this, to some extent, draws closest to their life world. Using teachers' life-history narrative has recognized their ever-enriching knowledge, and ever-changing relations with the other constituents of the system. Hence, this endorses that teachers' life-world, and experience, is the source of their knowledge (Carter, 1993), as Wu (2002: 173) explored in his study of teachers' stories of curriculum change in China, and he states:

> " 'Teachers' knowledge' is not only derived from their life world in the first instance in terms of concrete experience, but also included in the latter. Knowledge, so to speak, is not something that we can move around from one person to another, but is deeply rooted in the fundamental

mode of teachers' being in understanding."

In other words, teachers' understanding and knowledge is unique to, and not quite interchangeable between, teachers. It is not quite quantifiable either; instead, it is relational to specific situations and others (See Stodolsky, 1984; Poulson, 2003) and shares some characteristics. According to Bernstein's (1990) view, pedagogy nevertheless can be conceptualized in terms of: visible and invisible. The visible aspect appears to be the manifestation of the teacher and their students' performance, the external product the teacher is producing, such as examination scores. The invisible component part lies in the competence or capacity rather than the performance, which puts emphasis on the procedure and contextual conditions they create for themselves to change and adapt, and enable the student to develop and grow intellectually.

Drawing on the analyses along diachronic and synchronic dimensions of biographical data has revealed that the teachers' knowledge is a complexity and a plurality, interwoven from subject matter, moral virtues, caring, and emotional intelligence. This is characterized as a culture of pedagogy as humanistic caring which is not quite obvious to perceive but noticeable to feel. This aspect of pedagogy is essential to entail learning among students and themselves. Paradoxically, what is observable of teachers' daily practices and accounts of their classroom experiences additionally indicate that the other side of their pedagogy is largely associated with, and manifested in, grammar teaching and rote learning, with memorisation of vocabulary and grammar rules. This can be termed as grammar pedagogy (see e.g. Gu, 2003; Hu, 2002a, b; Cortazzi and Jin, 1996; Zhao, 2008a, b).

These most significant characteristics, the visible grammar teaching and invisible caring of the participants pedagogy can be visualized in Diagram 4 below, derived from the analysis of their understanding of teaching and learning, showing how the participants' pedagogy has caring and grammar teaching intertwined in a dynamic balance, which is constantly shifting and moving towards finding the ideal combination as conditions in society also shift and change.

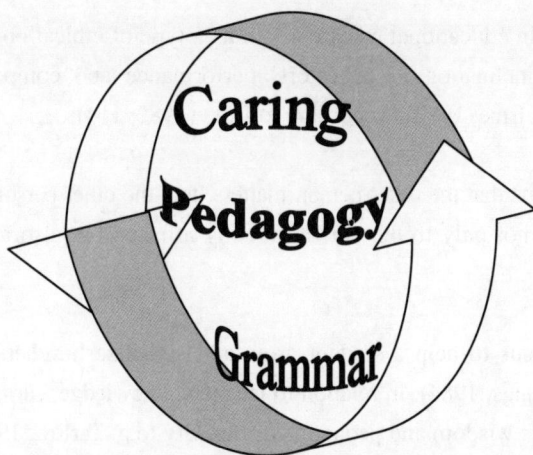

Diagram 4: Pedagogy intertwined with caring and grammar teaching

Such is the nature of their caring, and the grammarian teaching of their pedagogy is so prominent, that they impinge on the teachers' day-to-day conduct of their teaching in a uniform way. This notion is supported by all the participants' accounts and my own observation. For example, while most teachers hold the belief that learning involves memorizing rules of grammar in a caring manner. This can be illustrated by the novice teacher, Miss Zheng's, class, when Miss Zheng taught a word for the students to memorize:

> "When I was teaching the word 'family', I asked whether any student knew any special way to remember this word. Many students knew 'Father and mother I love you'. The initials of this sentence form this word, so it is easier for them to remember better."

This kind of caring and loving atmosphere, embracing memorization, which generates meanings such as reasons why they teach, the striving to improve and adapt, interplays and wrestles through their whole pedagogical life with other feelings, such as the feeling of pervading stagnation, lack of knowledge and skills to change at the same time. Overall, the humanistic caring pedagogy in practice is largely manifested in forms of their humanity, their time, and their empathic feelings.

Caring is noted in educational research both as a type of ethical obligation and natural human inclination in educators' performance and competence (e.g. Noddings, 1984; Irme, 1982). According to Irme (1982: 114):

> "Caring means that the other person matters, that the other person makes
> a difference not only to the person directly affected but also to others
> who care."

Foremost, it means to help a student grow and actualize him/herself through education (Noddings, 1984). In relation to teachers' knowledge, caring is viewed as teachers' crafts wisdom and pedagogical capacity (e.g. Tarlow, 1996; Dewey, 1929).

Caring is recognized as the most noteworthy characteristic of Chinese teachers' knowledge and understanding of teaching. My research found that teachers' teaching appeared to be teacher-dominated, which is in fact that they put the student first in the way they care for students as human beings, and for their welfare, such as learning to achieve. In their narrative, the "significant others" and moments, in many cases, are their students, who took up a lot of their accounts, and this turned out to be a good place to behold the teachers' understanding and knowledge of learners and their learning. It indicates their professional characteristics of their pedagogy. For example, Ms. Li's preparation for lessons is actually to "prepare students for the lesson". An extract from her narrative account can further illustrate a caring humanistic pedagogy grapples through grammar teaching:

> "At the current stage (students at the age of 12-15 years), students want
> to know everything clearly. Therefore, I think there is difficulty in student
> English learning. Language is not easy to teach either. I have a student in
> the class, who is good at science. He always uses the logic of science as
> rules of learning English, asking a lot of questions. On the one hand, I
> have to protect his interest in questioning, on the other hand, I have to
> explain and gain his trust. Oh, it is just too difficult. But it is not that I
> don't welcome questions; on the contrary, I encourage them to ask
> questions and think. The teacher-student relationship has suffered too.

First, it is related to subject matter, because English is a language, there are rules that are helpful for people to learn it, but there are exceptions too. When I teach about English grammar rules students always can find exceptions; the student may be confused with the rule, and then distrusts the rule. Sometimes it can influence students' trust in the teacher – this is one aspect. The second, in many cases about learning a language, is that it sometimes relies on the learner's sense of the language or the knowledge about the target culture, the customs, or the idioms. Not all of them are explainable; students have to understand that so that they would not be confused."

To them, English is regarded as a language rather than a set of knowledge, but with rules to grasp. But, to them, student development is infinitely more important than the subject matter. Their care is charged with and committed to the protection of students' learning interest and curiosity, maintenance of the student-teacher relationship and students as people. Caring is sometimes associated with a kind of anxiety and commitment, which is actually defined in dictionaries. To some extent, this is described by Noddings (1984: 9) as a state of mental engrossment:

> "...to care is to be in a burdened mental state, one of anxiety, fear, or solicitude about something or someone. Alternatively, one cares for something or someone if one has a regard for or inclination toward that something or someone."

That is to say, some teachers care about students' learning and students themselves out of natural inclination, and with obligation. One of the participant teachers, Mr. Zhu's notion that teaching should not be an "experiment" but a "life course" expressed what teaching might mean to him and how he is committed to his work. On the other side, grammar teaching affects teachers and impedes teachers' feeling of the meaning of their work, which can be transformed into a more meaningful and constructive mode of practice demands on-going analysis in future research.

The role of caring, in relation to teachers' knowing, in education, has been gradually recognized for its importance in relation to students' learning and personal growth (e.g. Acker, 1995; Noblit, 1993; Zembylas, 2003; Webb and

Blond, 1995; Goodson and Hargreaves, 1996; Perez, 2000). For instance, in Noblit's (1993) ethnographical case study, he observed how a school teacher constructed caring using her power as a teacher in her classroom, and then recognized that a really powerful teacher rests in her moral authority of caring. This may explain why some teachers can win genuine respect from students. For instance, Mr. Zhu's metaphorical cognition of education indicates his worry about the ultimate effect of education on students:

> "Education is very different from other occupations, in the way it is dealing with living human beings, not objects or products. When there is something wrong with a product, people can make it again."

By implication mis-education of students as human beings is irremediable. A respect for humanity that centres on humans and their values, capacities, and worth, and concern with their interests, needs, and welfare, has long been the highest of goals, as well as the most basic conduct of education, regardless of the difference between cultures, and the boundaries between countries (Dewey, 1938; Noddings, 1984; Stoll et all, 2003; Bullock and Wikeley, 2004; Tarc, 2005). Many teachers recognize that they are working with human beings and toward their development; quite often they call their students "children". For instance, Ms. Mary's English teaching is directed with:

> "I want goodness for the children (her students)... My heart does not allow me to ignore them." "I want them to be able to learn English even after they leave school."

Her responsibility is bound up with treating the student as a whole person, aiming towards their capacity of "all-round development" and how English learning and education can contribute to students' lifelong learning and goodness.

As well as conducted in practice, caring about humanity in teaching is necessitated in the nature of the task of teaching English as a subject in the national curriculum. "In the basic education level, (before tertiary education) the task of English subject is:

> "...to stimulate and build up student's interest in English, imbue students

with confidence; form a good learning habit and effective learning strategy; develop autonomous learning capacity and collaborative spirit; enable students to master a certain level of English language in the skills of listening, reading, speaking, and writing, and a certain level of comprehensive ability to use the language; develop students' spirit of observation, memorization, thinking, imagination and creative conduct; help students understand the world and cultural differences, expand student horizontal view and patriotism; shape a healthy worldview and lay a base for students' life-long learning." (Ministry of Education, 2001: 1-2)."

Caring for human interest and life-long learning is, in fact, described in the curriculum document as probably a necessary condition for teaching a subject in China. From teachers' narrative accounts and teaching, there is no way for them, or for me, to segregate this humanistic caring from their practice. This common caring character in both curriculum description and day-to-day practice can perhaps shed light on the mores and lore of their teaching. This, then, can contribute to understanding the participants' knowledge and apprehending their pedagogy in terms of ways of being a teacher and ways of teaching – as caring.

Conversations about a "typical day" and the early phase of their teaching have brought out their commitment to their work in terms of time, both from the requirement of the job and from their own willingness to invest as discussed earlier in diachronic and synchronic analysis. Mr. Xia found out soon after he embarked on this job of teaching that teaching is the kind of job where the day's work does not end at the end of the day, he had to take work home and work at night. Another novice teacher Miss Wang gave a similar account on her understanding of teaching in terms of time commitment:

"When I was a student, I did not realize how much time it took for the teacher to keep students behind for recitation or dictation. Now, I realized that it requires the teacher to have a willingness to invest time to do so. I used to think that was of a teacher's job. But, now, I understand better."

Teachers spend time talking, acting in the best interest of their students, spend time talking to their students, which serves as both the means and the end in both mundane and serious matters. Actions taken today were often seen as enabling and empowering a student to live a more successful life in the future, for instance, helping students go to university. Mr. Zhu has endlessly talked heart-to-heart and debated with his students about why students should study English, and the relationship of new variations of Chinese language used on the Internet, and in mobile messages, and "Chinese classics" and "Chinese cultural heritage".

Care about Those Who Care

What caring can reward a teacher with varies, though, for instance, when Miss Liu realized her "verbal communication" was notably improved through a lot of talking to students, one of her students pointed out to her that he felt she treated him impatiently. Therefore, Miss Liu learned that even talking with student needs sensitivity. Miss Zheng found that her talking to a student brought her a "big smile" from that student. Ms. Mary's confession that she could not "put herself in students' shoes" at the early stage in her teaching, indicates she can, and does so, now, which makes her think nothing else can catch her interest except education as a career, which can be understood. She gradually has begun to flow in teaching, and is coming to terms with her work. When they care for students, they learn from caring. Therefore, caring is relational, and reciprocal, beneficial to both those who care and those who are cared-for (Noddings, 1984).

Likewise, scholars such as Goodson and Hargreaves (1996), and Webb and Blond (1995), thus argue for an epistemological status for caring in teacher knowledge as discussed in the literature review. In Webb and Blond's work (1995: 611) "Teacher knowledge: the relationship between caring and knowing", they studied a teacher's narratives and contend that the teacher in their study knows from caring and being in a relationship with her students. They call that "relational knowing". I would like to endorse that caring can be legitimated as part of the condition to make learning happen and part of the purpose of education, as Noddings (1992, in Acker, 1995: 22) argues that caring should be what school education is for:

> "The first job of schools is to care for our children. We should educate all our children not only for competence but also for caring. Our aim should be to encourage the growth of competent, caring, loving, and lovable people."

Novice teachers such as Miss Liu confessed that "I am not tough enough to be a teacher yet" and she realized that her strength is her "loving heart". This could be understood as she is actually an outcome of such caring education in one way; in another way, she probably has not realized yet, that, as a teacher, she does not need to be "tough", the strength of her tender and "loving heart" is mighty enough for her to carry on her work, because the ultimate job is working with people, not just subjects. In order to do this well, we must help children to integrate what they are learning into their own lives – to make content meaningful and personally relevant (Zehm and Kottler, 1993).

A caring feature of the participant teachers' knowledge is also shown in the teachers' emotional ties to their work and their students, which is indicated by the strong feelings related in their narratives. This has been recognized by Hargreaves (1998: 835) as "the emotional practice of teaching". He (ibid: 835) claims that "emotions are at the heart of teaching" which "comprise its most dynamic qualities", and literally, "for emotions are fundamentally about movement", which also indicates that people who teach are movable and touchable. Teachers' narratives have captured this aspect of teaching practice as paradoxical feelings, as floating in both diachronic and synchronic analysis. For example, a veteran teacher, Mr. Cheng feels he is "painfully happy" with teaching; he missed his classroom after he became a coordinator; while novice teacher, Miss Zheng, perceives her new job, teaching, gives her "joy", yet is also "bitter". Their stories are highlighted with emotional products such as "tears", "smiles" and times of "low spirit", depending on how well their students learn and make progress, which further illustrates how their knowing and feelings are related to, and nested with, their students in their context. The negative side of the paradoxical feelings, on the other hand, is recognized, by Acker (1995: 33), as the difficulty that stems from the high expectations teachers hold of themselves, which sometimes result in their pains and bitterness, when they do care about their work.

By implication, Zembylas (2003: 104) has drawn attention to, and realized that, teacher emotions and feelings and realized that they are the product of the cultural, the social, and the political, in relation to teachers' burn-out, stress, joy, happiness and continuing commitment, in addition to their personal aspirations and autonomy. However, such phenomena were not fully recognized and accepted among researchers, who tended to emphasize teaching practice as primarily a cognitive activity. These soft human dimensions of teaching or learning deserve more discussion (Zehm and Kottler, 1993: 3). Other researchers are convinced that emotion and reason can be linked through narratives, for instance, Bateson (1991, in Emihovich, 1995: 40) offered a succinct comment:

"There is no need to drain intelligence out of situations where emotions are important."

because both cognitive and affective factors co-exist and impact on teaching practice and the person who does it (see also Calderhead, 1996; Hargreaves, 1998). After all, cognition and emotion are all intellectual.

Zembylas (2003: 106) continues to point to the "neglect of a topic" and the lack of caring about teacher emotion, and advocates caring for those who care and who know. Thus, attention should be drawn to the fact that teachers are not just well-oiled machines (Hargreaves, 1995, 1998), their feelings and well-being are part of their quality of teaching, but are human beings, because we do not want teachers to feel like a "robot" or "skilled worker" while they work, taking care of learning in educating our new generations. Therefore, the discussion in this direction can create a new dynamic, and encourage a missing conversation in the area of caring about emotions and feelings in teaching. Perhaps, paradoxically, policy-makers or school leaders should attempt to do the impossible, to give strong impetus to the development of a caring, supportive teachers' workplace (Acker, 1995). New research, perhaps, is needed to explore further the ideas concerning how social-political and cultural aspects define the experience of teacher emotion, in order to generate emotional rules that reduce negative feelings, such as of pain, bitterness and passiveness, and enhance the kind of positive emotions such as happiness, goodness, success, pride and satisfaction. As Hargreaves (1996) acknowledges, the context that inflects teachers' voices in particular ways might be the subject department of which the teacher is a member, or the district in which she or he works; these contexts of teaching shape not only what teachers can do, but also the knowledge and experience that guide their teaching.

Chapter Seven

Post-epiphany

In this chapter, I intend to conclude by reflecting on the impact of doing research with a life-history perspective on myself which encouraged me to share some of my personal experience and the understanding of teachers and research. I also picture the image of a teacher using the language from the participant teachers from the research.

At the macro level, first of all, teachers' life-history study gives voice to the participant teachers' own narrative accounts, and lets the story tell about the teachers – who they are, where they come from, how they were educated, and how they educate. This study has captured both the "big picture" of the educational story with cultural colour, along with a form of folk pedagogy, focused on crystallising incidents and conceptual metaphors from the teachers. At the micro level, it has tremendous impact on me.

At the outset, I wished to develop knowledge for the understanding of teachers, and extend my own horizons of education. The telling of teachers' stories has opened my mind to reflect on my own story of teaching and learning, to capture the authentic process of how the pedagogical self is shaped in a certain mode of culture and then transformed through the force of learning, broadly, from life. As a result, what is also really expanded in the end, I feel, is my heart through the journey of doing research with life-history perspective. I view this as very valuable to me as the outcome of this work; because the heart is found to be a right and boundless place that I can, and do, keep things, rather than grasp them in my hands. In a sense, I may do research with my hands, such as when I need to type, and when writing, and to hold a book when reading, however, what is written, and chosen to read, depends on what comes from my brain and whether my heart allows me to put it down. In terms of classroom management, for example, as one of the participants Miss Wang expressed, when a teacher grasps students like sand in her hands, when tightening the grip, it hurts both sides, as happens when there is tight control, when there is no space for the students to develop toward their potential; when loosening the grip, it produces distance, and there is loss of touch, so it may appear to be that they do not care about, or do not pay attention to each other. The solution for getting a balance in this situation may lie in the teacher taking the students to heart, rather than grasping them in a grip. The teacher-student relationship, and learning, might be made easier and result in a long-turn effect and a pleasant memory for both sides. The point to make here is not that Miss Wang did not put students in the right place, on the contrary, she was learning, with a "beating heart", which refers to the situation that she was very nervous in the first year of teaching, and sensed with her whole body the situation, and was caring to survive it.

One epiphany that happened in my early years of teaching can illustrate a case of grasping students with my hand and how it affected me. I seem to recall that I was in my second year of teaching. I used to give homework to students after each class, ether in an oral or written form. At the beginning of the next lesson, I normally checked by asking students to read a text, or gathered their homework exercise-books. One student, several times, did not hand in homework. Then one day it came to me to use my power as a teacher, by telling him, "Do not come to the classroom without your homework next time." However, he still came to the classroom without any effort to do the homework. I felt I could not keep my face without taking any step to confront the behaviour of this student. Then, I excessively exerted the power inherent in my role, and said to him, "Please leave the classroom now, don't come back to the classroom without your homework." I insisted, and he left without saying anything. Consequently, it left me in a sort of anxiety, struggling with self-doubt for the whole of the class time, wondering: Am I doing this right? What would happen to him if he went out of school when he should be in a classroom? I felt regret, and wished I had not let him leave the classroom at all. I understood this kind of "power struggle" as non-productive pedagogically, taking away choice, and leaving both the student and myself, as the teacher, unhappy. From then on, I set up a rule to limit myself – I had neither right nor power to keep students out of their classroom or deprive them of their class time as a teacher.

This rule broke down years later – a student from one of my classes came to me and demanded to study in the library for his English class time, while all other students stayed in the classroom with the teacher. He claimed that it was quieter in the library for him. I felt lost, and did not know what to do with this kind of request from a student, because I had never came across this before. Many other university students would simply absent themselves from class without notifying anybody. In my experience up to that point, 5 years into my career, this was very unusual. I felt myself in a quandary, having no hint to guide me, but also somewhat pleased with the honesty of his demand, and his straightforwardness. So, I trusted my instinct to allow him the freedom of his choice. I wondered that, if he thought he could learn better on his own in the library than sitting in my class, then probably I should let him study the way as he liked. After all, he is a university student and should know what would work better for him. It was not, at all, a question of losing face. Then I said to him, "If you think you will go over the textbook and you will be studying for at least the amount of the class time. I have no problem with this. You can come to the class when you feel like you want to, or if you have questions, you can come to me." Then he studied in the library for the English class time for the whole semester, while I met him on campus I was checking if he was doing well with his English study. But he did very well in the examination. I felt I did right in this case because I allowed him to study the way that he thought is better for him. In the end, both of us were happy with the situation. The power of a teacher can be exercised in different ways, which produces different results in students, and in the teacher-student relationship. This result was, to me, a success, and a pleasant memory.

However, as a teacher I did not always know how to use and share the power that I had. With years of learning, I feel quite empowered and improved in a way I can talk about the power of "power", and about which, some time ago, I thought I would not mention it at all, except that "knowledge is the real power" as I said elsewhere. In fact, now I think that power is actually very useful and strong when it is used for empowerment and enabling, and that control is not a bad thing at all; it depends on how people control and with what kind of power. In the case of a classroom situation, children can be controlled, for instance, by care and love which make them feel safe and comfortable, and for many children that is the only way they can be controlled – other ways of control may make them "problematic". Care and love may, in many ways, appear to be an indulgence on the part of the teacher, "giving too much, while challenging two little". Please do not worry, children will not be spoilt with love and care, instead, I feel it can make them become very strong and inspired in learning and life. In my view, everybody has power in their own right as a human being and in relation to others. Infants, for instance, are the most powerful creatures, they cry for care when they need it, and this generates caring attention and actions from adults.

Therefore, the real power of a teacher lies in how they exercise their power, and toward what purpose as a teacher when taking care of their students, which depends entirely on the make of the person as a teacher, on their understanding of teaching, learners and learning. Researching into what makes a teacher, through teachers' knowledge perspective, sometimes goes beyond science, and we have to understand it in the wider human context, which needs the integration of scientific insights into the broader and richer setting of the person's life (J. Polkinghorne, 1996; Goodson, 1994). We seldom can learn from a textbook as to how to teach a class of students. Quite often we rely on commonsense knowledge, and a feel for what is better for students, or how can we make learning happen, and then make a difference for them in order to contribute to their growth. As a life long learner, it is yet hard for me to tell what makes a best teacher. According to Zehm and Kottler (1993: 5-15), who have been teachers and teacher educators, the attributes of a great teacher lies in a collection of some human characteristics such as charisma, compassion, egalitarianism, sense of humour and being personally effective, which are common in teachers who produce durable ideal practice. All great teachers who share those properties – from Socrates and Confucius to Dewey and Tyler, have been really influential and inspirational.

A Chinese saying says that interest is the best teacher. Then, in a sense, planting and maintaining an interest in learning, in students, may produce a long-standing effect, rather than directly transmitting knowledge to them. Transmission itself, however, is not a problem at all; it depends on what knowledge is transmitted, and how and why it is transmitted. For instance, if teachers communicate and grow knowledge as generic skills for survival and for excellence, or knowledge of, and interest in, caring and loving for people and nature, it would be more empowering to the receivers, such as students, and make a greater contribution to a more democratic society and the individual's life. What matters most to students is the style in which such knowledge and wisdom is imparted. A model of a best and ideal teacher can be tentatively portrayed and crafted from the inspiration generated by this research into Chinese life-history in relation to teaching English as a foreign language. The quality of the model played a useful and important role for all the participants to develop their knowledge of teaching, and its further development. It is tentatively conceptualized as an image of a model teacher based on this research into Chinese teachers and their knowledge of education, as well as my life experience as learner.

The image of this model is built and composed of the following main components using the participants' language:

The model image has a brain which is open-minded and it is the central nervous system for imagining and remembering, judging and interpreting, as well as aspects of caring and feeling. This image teaches in order to appreciate its cultural heritage and other cultures. Sometimes students are its ears and eyes. It conducts face-to-face teaching, or distance communication, it has ears to listen to others, and mouth to offer opinions. It cares for, and has, students at heart and in mind, and students' growth can give it happiness and can keep its heart young. It shoulders the responsibility of education and of developing students as whole persons. It writes its own life-history and shapes school effectiveness. It walks and talks as a teacher. That the student benefits from its work gives it a sense of achievement and makes it feel the work is worthwhile and meaningful. It searches its soul and knows what it is that it does, and hopes its work will be adequately recognized and appreciated. It copes with wear-and-tear, and other constraints, and would like to learn and grow with students. It wonders and wants to know more about what the purpose and quality of education is, and desires to move forward to get to where it wants to go. Interest in, and a habit of, learning, are planted in students, which can contribute to their continuing learning for a bright future. It wants to keep a balance between its personal and professional life. Experience is the base of its knowledge.

This model can serve as an ideal teacher theory and the base for developing knowledge that is necessary for teaching or education. It has an image that grows and is always capable of reflecting, adapting to, and leading changes and development as part of the wider society, which can significantly contribute to the existing knowledge of teaching and teachers. It provides a vision, and facilitates action and understanding for teacher education and school communities to foster a practice and theory of creating the teaching force, toward the whole model or part of its specific qualities. It is applicable to human beings in the world regardless of the difference in religion, race, culture and geography. The characteristics of the participants' knowledge of teaching and the image of the model teacher can be taken as the major contribution that this work generated, created and added to human knowledge and the understanding of education.

There are times when I have problems with some divisions, dichotomies, and definitions in doing research, such as qualitative and quantitative research, positivist and post-positivist, realist and relativist, and the gaps, such as between theory and practice. In particular, definitional issues in research are problematic and controversial, because traditions and approaches, such as positivism, post-positivism, post-post-positivism (Denzin and Lincoln, 2005) are present in one another and hardly hold clear-cut boundaries; their existence relies on each other. It is clear that it mirrors a process of change and they are not exactly the same.

After years of immersion in the academic world, to my cognition and gratitude, some divisions are, in fact, just different sides, or components, of the same thing. In a sense, many big dichotomies are united and rested in one thing, for instance, in terms of gender, man and woman are actually just human beings; spirit and material constitute the universe; love and hate is just a position we take as an action, as reflected in a prologue of a Chinese story (Cao, 1991):

"If you love her, take her to New York, because it is heaven; if you hate her, take her to New York, because it is hell."

However, from a different position we take may create a different world with the same people and the same place. For instance, when we take the position to love, we may create and make a paradise in our own feeling. Yet we cannot, consequently, assume that receivers would take it as a heaven at all. As to what people would make of it, or would perceive it to be, all depends on such as whether people know about it, in the first instance.

I still feel it hard to accept that the research world should be completely separated into quantitative and qualitative paradigms; nevertheless, I think there is a difference between qualitative and quantitative data, which appears to consist of the use of words and numbers. There is no absolute qualitative or quantitative research; no research could be communicated very well with mere numbers or without any sense of numbers.

Yet, I would not like to identify myself with any labels such as realist or relativist or feminist or life-history narrative researcher, sometimes I feel I am all of them, while at other times, none of them. In a way, when I was trying to present the research exactly as it is and hope that this constitutes the truthful reality, this may sound like a realist. However, this is driven by the intent to give the audience full space for their interpretation and understanding, because whatever analysis I provide is just my understanding of the meanings and values derived from the research. In this sense, I may act like a relativist. When I am aiming at presenting teachers through their voices, it may sound like a feminist approach. Yet, I am just a researcher. All the epistemological streams are just ways of cognising the world, and expressions of emphasis in doing research, which are available to all of us for situated and actual purposes. Thus, without ascribing to a fixed way, I can act flexibly in serving the purpose of the study. The power of flexibility can entitle and free the researcher to draw on the collective strength of different perspectives in the net of the research field, and the world of philosophy, and to be able to respond to the unexpected in order to serve and fulfil the purpose of research better.

I feel it is a privilege to explore and discover the relationships between meaning, knowledge, human interest and truth, starting from any point; it is inescapable to confront many others. When my research interest started with knowledge about teachers, I feel I need to keep to teachers' real life experience which is to collect the knowledge of their teaching through their own voices. When people feel meaningful, then they may have the knowledge and strength to find the truth of life. Therefore, a study in philosophy has engendered in me an interest in searching the layers of meaning of life with a love for knowledge.

When the researcher relates the research to his or her own experience, the reflexivity can generate the intimacy and authentic understanding of the researched by knowing how to get close to them. As Toma (2000) and Denison (2003) have realized, qualitative study is inherently personal, the researcher(s) cannot and should not hide their attachment to the topic and persons they study. This attachment makes the interactive data collection process work. That is to say, good data is the result of a good relationship with the participants, their voices nevertheless are influenced by the researchers' background and the context in which the researched work; furthermore, nothing does better than that the researcher being genuinely interested in the subject – both in terms of the overall phenomenon and the people who can shed light on it, which blend together their academic interest, passion and compassion into practice.

In a word, with the life-history perspective to look at knowledge about teachers by linking up to teachers' knowledge, this study has avoided neglecting the "individuality" of individuals, and has put diversity of human meanings to first concern (Roberts, 2002). It has fulfilled the purpose of giving voice to the participants' understanding through their life-history narrative and contextualized the present within the framework of individuals' lives, wider social and historical context (Sparkes, 1994a, b; Tripp, 1994; Woods, 1985). Therefore, I am able to present their specific qualities through their life stories, critical incidents and metaphors which are powerful tools to articulate their knowledge while keeping their wholeness as a person. This has realized that a teacher's life-history contains a history of their learning to teach, while life experience in the light of social-cultural context and historical events constitutes the base of their knowledge (Carter, 1993).

However, no summary is adequate to demonstrate people's life and working knowledge, what is represented is much less than what can be presented in any research. With life-history perspective, it has focused more broadly on the teacher's life and work as advocated by Goodson (see 1994; Goodson and Numan, 2002). I hope we can allow, create and invent more methods and languages that do justice to what we have seen and felt. One of the most significant aspect of this study is when I looked into the participants practice, I have captured some specific qualities of their being a teacher while maintaining a holistic view on education, knowledge and experience, as a "monster" or an "elephant" or a "forest", by which I mean the interconnectedness of educational people, the world they live in, can only be partially approached both in scope and depth, in a research report. Limitations exist in all research which requires our ability to be aware of it. Teachers' life-history narrative tells what they know as well as what they do not know with intellectual honesty. As Confucius says:

"Shall I tell you what knowledge is? It is to know what one knows and what one does not know."

Part of the outcomes from doing research with a life-history narrative perspective is that it makes me realise how we are limited by what we know and how we know. In effect, to me, learning is on-going. The art and science of doing research is long, while life is short, but when we regard and live life as art and experiment with creativity into our work, then our life will become of the greatest, and the most everlasting piece of work that we could ever make (Zhao, 2009).

Perhaps, when we see education is part of the experience of being human, then it is not only an event, but also an achievement (Eisner, 1988; Dewey, 1938, 1929). I hope educational research and teacher education can care for and help teachers and students with the knowledge of how to capture the qualities of the world which are there for those who have the skills to take them (Eisner, 1988). It is one of education's most significant purposes and tasks to provide the skills, tools and knowledge through which the participant, both as a teacher and a learner, can create his or her own experience, or "paradigm", rather than being given one.

Therefore, the question asked by one of the participants, Ms. Xu, concerning what is the quality and purpose of education, may vary between individual educators, including all teachers, and students. To me, the quality of education is closely associated with the quality of teachers' knowledge and understanding of teaching and learning, which will realize and fulfil the purpose of education for the society and the individual better. Teachers are the people who dwell in the educational sphere and shape the classroom practice, many of them for all their lifetime. The knowledge, experience, and care, they can reach to, and absorb, will mostly be transmitted to, and breathed in by, their students, our future generations. Many Chinese people see that the purpose of education is to encourage people to do the right and good thing in achieving success, to feel happy. Probably, through education, people in society can learn to live with each other in peace and harmony, supporting and helping each other in creating social prosperity and happiness.

Finally, education for, and care about teachers, should work toward the model with the ideal teacher theory, looking after their heart and soul as well as material matters (see also Palmer, 2003). I know the limitation of this model is the lack of technical jargon and labels when priority is given to the basic conduct of being a teacher. Teachers with the quality of the model will contribute to the equality, social cohesion, and sustainable development, of a more democratic society and common future of China and the world, when they are empowered with knowledge distilled from their teaching and learning experience, and care, because they can pass it on to the new generations.

Appendix I

A Sample of Biographic-narrative Interview

Ms. Xiong, Age: 35
Experience: 14 years of teaching
Student Level: 9 years at senior secondary school and 5 years at junior secondary school
Deputy Head of the school
...

Annie: I would like to know about your experiences of learning English, learning to teach English and teaching English.

Annie: When did you start to learn English?

Xiong: From junior secondary, the teacher in junior secondary then taught with a translation method. The teacher taught, the students listened, but seldom spoke. There were little listening lessons. Probably you learned English this way too. It was "English dumb". We had a good grasp of grammar. Now Yichang is doing well in reform, according to my observation, including watching the public classes at different levels nationwide, and having an overview of the examination papers. The reform in English education is moving forward. Firstly, the teacher quality has improved in various ways; secondly, the teaching methods are advanced. I think English teaching in Yichang is good.

Annie: How do you look at teacher quality?

Xiong: Their English proficiency, their listening, speaking, reading and writing ability in English. Then, their manners, their overview ability, their competence in expressing themselves. I've watched the national public classes – the candidate from Yichang got the first prize. He is a teacher of No. 12 Secondary School. As a reward, he is going to study in England. He is a good representative of Yichang.

Annie: Where was the teaching competition?

Xiong: In Wuhan. Oh, He was the winner of the year before last year. Last year it was somebody from elsewhere.

There are various English language competitions, but there isn't one designed particularly for English teachers. In the school, we can learn from each other. We talk to each other in English and encourage each other. We read English books and watch English TV programmes, trying to use English as much as possible. I personally think we most need to enlarge our vocabulary. As we teach junior secondary level, what we see, listen to and teach are some words. If we just want to loaf on the job, it is easy to just deliver the book to the secondary school students. We may not know much about vocabulary beyond the junior secondary level. Many words are pretty long.

Annie: Nowadays, teaching has changed a lot, do teachers learn by themselves?

Xiong: To handle junior secondary teaching, the basic need is to study the new textbook, they don't have to urge themselves to do systematic learning or adopt a new model. Even the advance in teaching methods is not very challenging to teachers. This is just my personal view, I don't know others' views. The reform of teaching methods is not a big challenge to them. Only when they look ahead, can they feel pressure on themselves. It is easy for them to handle listening or oral classes now.

Annie: Why is it easy?

Xiong: They can understand the listening materials.

Annie: Don't they converse with students?

Xiong: They teach the material. They can understand it.

Annie: Do you have a listening class?

Xiong: It is not a separate class. It is part of the comprehensive English. Some teachers may put the listening material together in one session. They may have a whole session for a reading text. Students read it and the teacher give some instruction. They may have a session for dialogues to practice oral English. We don't have special listening or speaking classes. It is part of the textbook.

Annie: You've just mentioned the teaching method reform, can you tell me more?

Xiong: It is to open students' mouths, and reduce teacher's talk. Teacher should not just talk from the beginning to the end of a class. In the past, teachers could not speak English a lot – they translated everything, and then asked students to memorize it. Now, first of all, teachers should have some oral materials, giving student input and stimulating student output. The teacher gives input and the students produce output. The teacher should have his own language for students to practice with. There are about 50 students in a class, if each of them produces a sentence, they may contribute different input which can enliven the class. Even when students have the same input, they have to open their mouth and speak it out.

Annie: Some teachers used to teach in Chinese.

Xiong: About ten years ago that was the case. It has been changing in the most recent 10 years. It is getting better.

Annie: How do teachers improve their oral English competence?

Xiong: On improving their oral ability, my personal view is that, to be honest, I have the desire to learn. I haven't learnt so much recently, as I have been taking part in composing a book of student's reading materials. Basically, I require myself to watch an English programme every day, and to speak English every day, even if it is speaking to myself. I must learn. I am about to take the Band-6 of College English Test, I will register for it soon, the registration starts today.

Annie: College English Test Band 6?

Xiong: Yeah. I don't have opportunity to take the Band 8.

Annie: Why do you take the Test?

Xiong: Yes, other people, including my own family, say that you are sitting in your position firmly, without any threat. There is no crisis of being laid-off for me. But I want to look beyond; I am teaching junior secondary level; I can do it even I don't learn further. I think I have embarked on a job with English, and I realized that in life there is a large amount of vocabulary, when I listen to simple English news, that is not included in the textbook at all, or in any of the books available for us to use. Then we must learn from the books that not used for teaching. So I exert all my efforts to find other books to learn from, then I can find a better connection with textbooks and real-life use. (CI) We once had a foreigner worked in this school for about three and half months. I found that what she said could not be found in the textbook we teach to students. We are so laborious to teach our students something not being used by the native speakers in life, which indicates that there are many drawbacks to our education. Students may learn to the textbook; teachers must go beyond that.

Annie: Why must teachers go beyond the textbook, students stick to it?

Xiong: The reason for students to stick to the textbook is examinations. Now we are undergoing reform – one curriculum, multiple textbooks. You can choose textbooks to cover curriculum objectives. I heard that foreign countries conduct things this way, I am not sure. It is said that in foreign countries teachers use handouts as teaching materials. It seems impossible in China, as we have examinations.

Annie: Does teaching to textbooks guarantee desirable exam outcomes?

Xiong: Well, I think the basics are in the textbook. In my teaching, including when I talk to my colleagues, the content in the textbook comes first before extending further. They have to cover all the content in the textbook.

Annie: That must be tight with time.

Xiong: Yes. The class I've just taught was tight with time, as I extend at some point; I left a bit in the textbook uncovered.

Annie: Would you just tell me how you taught the class?

Xiong: Well, I thought I would bring along the textbook, but I forgot. I taught lesson 20 in the textbook of junior 3. They were dialogues, two long pieces of dialogues. The second one was labelled with *, which could be ignored. I require myself to cover it and to teach it well. It was about two pamphlets of two hotels, kind of ads for hotels, introducing the rooms and facilities of the hotels. Students were asked to think about which hotel would suits their interest better and why. I allowed them to have a think, and gave them some directions. For instance, if they liked shopping, they might choose the one located downtown, because they might be wealthy and they might choose a well-equipped room; if they wanted to enjoy Western food, they could choose the hotel which offered it; if they liked nightlife, they could choose a hotel with the Internet access 24 hours a day. Then they had to make a decision on which hotel to go to, and gave reasons. They might say I would choose this one because it met my needs for…

Annie: What kind of activity did you use?

Xiong: I gave directions first. I prepared lessons. I would not say: OK, students, look at the two pamphlets and have a think about which hotel you like better. That would not be fine. I would direct, say, if they had money, they could choose a more luxurious one.

Annie: When you asked the students to make a decision, how did they practise it?

Xiong: They did it in pairs. Each student talked about their interests and ideas, they could learn from each other. Maybe one of the students could speak a wonderful sentence. If they shared the interest and made the same choice, they still could talk about it. If they had different ideas, they could have a debate. I mainly used discussion. Junior students have limited language ability, but they did well. The teacher needs to give instructions and input first, otherwise, because students don't have language sources.

Annie: You give instructions first.

Xiong: Yes. Such as if they like shopping, they could choose the one located downtown. If they like swimming, they should consider if the hotel had a swimming pool. If they like both, they would prefer one more than the other, to open their thoughts. Today, they had little debate. Most of them preferred the modern one. The other one was camping in an open place. Few students chose it. Therefore, there was little debate. It would be exciting if they'd had some debate. That's it. Actually this bit is labelled with an asterisk [*]. According to the curriculum, this part of the material is for an extension of students' target language and content of the textbook. It could be passed over.

Annie: What kind of textbook do you use?

Xiong: The one published by the People's Education Press, we are changing to Junior English for China, published by Longman.

Annie: Now there are various versions of textbooks. Can you choose any one for the school?

Xiong: No. The whole city will use the same one, more than that, greater than half of the country will tend to use the same one. We are about to change the textbook. The proposition is from the top. We may add or disregard something to the textbook chosen for us.

Annie: It is not a free choice of materials.

Xiong: It is a free choice for the people at the top.

Annie: Who are they?

Xiong: Probably Ministry of Education or People's Education Press. Anyway, I have no idea. The topmost people say one curriculum, multiple versions of textbook, then they implement it through the layers of the administration. Well, even the province did not give any prescription of what textbook to use. But whatever is to be added must come after the coverage of the textbook. It is like the secondary should not supersede the primary, in case what is taught does not match what is examined.

Annie: Can teachers put aside the textbook, use other alternative materials?

Xiong: At the moment, it is beyond possibility.

Annie: Then the teachers follow after the decisions made by someone in Yichang Education Bureau?

Xiong: That's for sure.

Annie: Even under the notion of one curriculum, multiple textbooks, people tend to use the same textbook, or leave it for another similar new book.

Xiong: Yes. More than half of the country tends to use the same textbook. According to the coordinator for this city, Mr. Xu, you know him, there are 3 or 4 kinds of textbooks currently in use in the whole country. Then you can imagine the coverage of the textbook in the country.

Annie: In such a huge country like China, many places use the same textbook, how can they meet local needs?

Xiong: Probably they want the whole country to make a move forward together, to change. The new textbook is better than the old ones.

Annie: Some students in some remote places may have never seen any hotel?

Xiong: It is beyond their imagination. There are drawbacks to using the same textbook. That's why some bits in the textbook are labelled with *, I guess. They probably have taken this into consideration by marking some material as difficult, with *. Other materials don't need to provoke imagination in the textbook. They just read what is there.

Annie: How many years have you taught English?

Xiong: 13 years. This year is the 14th year.

Annie: When did you graduate from college?

Xiong: In 1991.

Annie: From Yichang Teachers' College?

Xiong: Yeah. The majority of junior secondary teachers in Yichang, and many senior secondary teachers, graduated from that college.

Annie: Is English learning now different from when you were a student?

Xiong: They are more active, have more access to materials. The environment is also better, the whole environment, including both in the classroom and outside classroom language environment; they are more active, and have broader knowledge. When we were students, we just memorized the book.

Annie: Memorization.

Xiong: They have to memorize too, even now. Because they have to access information, take in the information and process it. If they don't take in the basic materials, then output is like an inaccessible pinnacle. They have to memorize it. It is like even an intelligent wife cannot make a meal without rice. That's my opinion.

Annie: Did you think what you learned from the college was adequate for teaching?

Xiong: Not at all – particularly, the vocabulary. I am OK with grammar to handle both old textbooks and the new textbook. The key is the vocabulary; my learning is focused on vocabulary, then reading, and then listening – the three elements.

Annie: Why do you think it is important for yourself to continue to learn?

Xiong: I just look further. I want to deserve the title of "English teacher". Otherwise, other people may say "What an English teacher, she even doesn't know this word!". However, it is impossible to grasp everything.

Annie: Have you ever felt it to be difficult, or had knotty problems in English?

Xiong: It is fine now, because it is simple to just cope with students in the classroom.

Annie: (Laughing.)

Xiong: There is little for them to do outside of classroom in terms of English learning. A Canadian student once stayed in this school for three months. My experience with her made me feel there were many words that we had never seen in our textbooks which she used a lot in everyday life. I was enlightened by this experience. I felt we have learned English for so many years in vain, and we continue to teach the students in the old way. (CI) What is used widely by native speakers in real life could not be found in our textbooks. For instance, I was most impressed by the word "contact". We don't use it with our colleagues, and I have never seen it in our textbooks either. When it appeared in utterance, I could only guess at what it means. I really had never known the word. I urged her to explain the word "contact" to me. When people say goodbye, they say "I'll contact you". This stirred me up. Another word was "garbage" which I had never known about. The Canadian girl once asked me where she could put the "garbage". We did not have a rubbish bin, instead we had a basket. I could not understand what she said. I could read from her body language that she needed to throw away the waste-paper in her hand. Then it made me think how a common word in everyday life could catch me out. I understood that, at the very least, our stuff was not comprehensive. In fact, we had learned "rubbish" and "litter", but not "garbage". This experience was stimulating. At least I learned some words and made me think we just learned partially.

Annie: Do you think you can learn everything, even in this way?

Xiong: No. But it is better than not learning at all. Well, I admire a teacher from Huazhong Teachers' University. He has given a few lectures to us; he is a simultaneous interpreter.

Annie: Did you go to his university, or did he come to Yichang to give lectures?

Xiong: He taught a training class for us. As for translation, we can go around and about and interpret it. He can translate everything simultaneously. Then he trained us to translate what he said. Wow, it was thorny to us. I felt it was so difficult to reach that stage. I was touched again. I want to do better to deserve the title of, and my qualification as, an English teacher. But it is impossible to learn everything. There are many words I have never seen. I am trying to be a bit outstanding among the people around me, but I have a long way to go to be as good as that university teacher.

Annie: University teachers can't necessarily teach secondary school well.

Xiong: That is just a matter of methods. As for English knowledge, the higher level they teach, the more competent they are.

Annie: If you want to deserve the title of English teacher, in addition to the efforts to speak English better, what else in teaching are you trying to improve?

Xiong: Well, I am trying to let student learn from me. When I can speak well, I can make them speak well. If I show that I can do it, they can do it too. They might do even better.

Annie: Have you learned teaching methods, or something like this, in your self-regulated learning?

Xiong: Well, it is mainly about watching others' teaching, or watching some disks of teaching competition, and discussing about it with others. We also had some lectures by others, such as Zhang Xiansheng.

Annie: Who is he?

Xiong: He is from the People's Education Press. I don't know for sure his official position. Anyway, he is somebody responsible for the stream of English teaching and research. He gave a lecture in Yichang. We go to watch provincial public classes too, trying to learn as much as possible from others, for their lively methods which can promote students' learning.

Annie: Basically, you are learning from others' practice.

Xiong: Yes. Yes.

Annie: Regarding teaching, do you have any other forms of learning?

Xiong: Well, I cannot compel myself to read theoretical things. I don't head for theories. I used to subscribe to the *Journal of Primary and Secondary English Teaching*.

It was just too boring for me to watch others' teaching works, engage students to open their mouths and perform something. Now and then, the coordinator also gives us talks.

Annie: What does he talk about?

Xiong: He touches on some theories in a lively way. He went to teach English teachers from 5 provinces last summer. I was about to borrow his notes to have a look. He gives examples to demonstrate theories, the examples may be some teachers' teaching that we know of, or some kind of teaching we have never seen. He throws some light on thoughts. He often talks in English. He has practised his ability. He studied in England for seven months. Sometimes he talks about the situation in England. It is good just to listen to him when we cannot go there.

Annie: How many English teachers do you have in your school?

Xiong: We have more than ten, 14. Each teacher teaches two classes.

Annie: What do you think of the teaching occupation?

Xiong: It is acceptable. I was sort of prepared to accept it. English is something I would choose to do, but being a teacher...

Interrupted...

Annie: How long have you been teaching in this school?

Xiong: I started in No. 13 Secondary School.

Annie: Where is it?

Xiong: It is not far away. It is a senior secondary school. I worked there for 9 years there, and 4 years in this school. I was transferred to this school. In fact, the senior secondary school teachers get higher pay. They have some students pay tuitions fees. But junior secondary is compulsory.

Annie: Is the funding allocated by the government?

Xiong: Yes. It is fixed. Students in compulsory education don't pay a tuition fee. Even immigrant children don't pay extra money. The income is limited.

Annie: How many students are there in a class?

Xiong: About 50. It is OK in urban Yichang.

Annie: How is the student source?

Xiong: Not good. The residents in this area are mostly laid-off workers and peasants. We actually had a look at the student background two years ago. About 2-3 children were from the families of doctors, 5-6 were teachers' children; there are 3 schools in the neighbourhood. All together, less than 10 children were from well-off families.

Annie: You mean in a class?

Xiong: No. The whole school of more 1,000 students, about 10 children's parents are teachers, 2-3 children's parents are doctors. The rest of them are all from families of workers and peasants.

Annie: Because of the location of the school in Wujia District, close to rural areas.

Xiong: The major big factories are in this area. Those workers' have limited education. Some did not have the education up to senior secondary.

Annie: What made you think of students' background?

Xiong: It is very obvious. We don't need to look at any registration, we just know this. I know how many children are from families of doctors or teachers. I am quite familiar with the area.

Annie: How is this school different from other schools in Yichang?

Xiong: There are so many government departments, so many civil organizations, people who work there send their children to other schools, not this school.

Annie: Do they think their child would learn better in other schools?

Xiong: In general, they do. But it is not absolute. For instance, we would pay more attention to our children's education. Those peddlers working in the market all day, delivering coal, or polishing others' shoes in the street, don't look after children's study. They may get up at 3 in the morning, then they may have no idea whether their children are late for school or not. Some night market peddlers work till 10 p.m. They may have no idea whether their children do their homework or not. This is a general situation. Well, not every parent is ignoring their child's learning.

Annie: How are the students themselves?

Xiong: Most of them are not keen on learning. Some are – just a small proportion. The general situation is not optimistic. However, teachers are responsible and hard working. We know about the situation of teachers and students in other schools, we also know about that of this school. It is not easy for our teachers. Some teachers do want to move to a better school, to teach better students. Most of them are doing their job well, not complaining. Well, some complain – they still do their job. They don't loaf on the job because the condition of this school is not good enough.

Annie: The physical environment is not much different from other schools in Yichang.

Xiong: The Education Bureau invests fairly in every school. The buildings, the campus are not different from other schools.

Annie: Hardware is very similar.

Xiong: The Education Bureau puts the same weight on every school. It is the location – the Education Bureau cannot change the student source. The number of students is similar. Schools are different in student quality. We teachers know the situation. Some teachers had trial teaching before they settled down to teach at this school.

Annie: Do all the teachers hold a BA degree in English?

Xiong: It is better now. Most teachers who came in recent years have a BA degree. From 2000, only candidates with a BA degree have been recruited.

Annie: Are you satisfied with the teaching job?

Xiong: Yes. I am happy with the four characters – Ying Yu Lao Shi – English teacher. I cannot do any other job, as I don't know how to. I am used to being a teacher. I even don't know how to start a new job. I don't have to teach classes now, but I required myself to teach in the classroom, though it does not make much difference in pay.

Annie: Why do you still teach?

Xiong: I don not want to be out of practice with English teaching. I cannot stay in this position forever, but I can be a life-long English teacher. People can take away my position as a deputy head, but my professional knowledge is always with me. In this environment, I feel compelled to be outstanding among my peers, putting pressure on myself. But outside of this circle, I don't know who are more competent than me. Within this circle, I am trying to excel. I have this ambition. When I feel I lag behind somebody, I will work hard to catch up. I am not comparing myself to senior secondary or university teachers. After all, I have routine work to do.

Annie: Do you have any other special memory or story about teaching English?

Xiong: I seem to not have any particular special story. I have some general feeling. I used to feel rigid. I did not feel the flow of managing teaching to some extent. I could only teach the textbook to students. The class were not so lively. I feel a process of growth. I feel I am walking on a smooth journey now. I don't have any specific story about this, but, when looking back, I feel progress.

Annie: When you started to teach, did you have difficulties?

Xiong: It seemed OK, because at least I could copy the old tricks – how my teachers taught me.

Annie: Did you use the old ways to teach at the beginning?

Xiong: Yes. It was stale. Reforms had started by the year I commenced teaching, the year before I became a teacher. Yichang started to promote a new textbook from 1990, starting to use the book published by Longman. When I came to teach in 1991, I was not used to it; I used the simplest way to teach with the book, for instance, the first lesson was "Good Morning", I translated it into Chinese and asked them to repeat it after me.

Annie: Translating and reading.

Xiong: Yes. Translating and reading, and then the students memorising – that's it. It was stale. It seems now, ways used to teach junior 1 are simpler than that used for junior 3, but at least the class is more lively. Some students itch to have a go at answering a question. It used to be that students listened and repeated after the teachers, and memorized as the teacher required. They were not eager to have a try. Now you can often see it in class. I think every teacher has a process – it is less likely that they can teach well from the beginning, or they teach worse than when they started. They must be better than they were.

Annie: Would you like to continue to be a teacher?

Xiong: Yes, because I don't know how to do other jobs. At the age of thirty-something, it seems impossible to start over again.

Annie: People in their thirties are still young.

Xiong: Yes, but to start over in a new career is not possible, I think. What's more, there is no opportunity to do so.

Annie: How would you give a definition of "teaching English"?

Xiong: Well, I have never thought about it. I just have some perceptions. Teaching English is, first of all, accumulation of knowledge, and then teach it well to the students, and make students able to use it. Then students become better than the teacher. I learn first and teach. Learning should go beyond certain boundaries, and so should teaching – students should go beyond the teacher. The teacher is just a bridge, and the teacher is not the equivalent of English at all. The students should not see what the teacher demonstrate to them as the whole world of English, I have been telling students this. I told them they must be more able than me. It is possible for them to learn more than I know; I also know something that they don't know. I am not all that English is about. They have to make sense of English from other channels too. I am just a bridge for them to step over to another world, before they can learn on their own and can make better sense of English.

Annie: Teaching is giving.

Xiong: Sure. Many students are better than me. I have worked for more than 10 years. My early students have gone further than me. I remain here, probably being more backward. My first group of students are in their twenties now. Some have established their own families, living a better life than me. I am embarking on a sacrificial job.

Annie: As for learning opportunities, what you engage with now are mainly from watching others' classes. Do you have any special professional development opportunities?

Xiong: Yes, by watching classes, listening to reports. No other special ways of professional development. It is impossible.

Annie: Why is it impossible?

Xiong: It is affected by the personnel system. We have a fixed scheme. If I leave for professional development, who comes to teach my classes? If somebody is arranged to teach your classes, where can you stay when you come back? Say if I leave for two years for a study, somebody else will be arranged to teach my classes. Where can I fit in when I come back?

Annie: You can have a supply teacher.

Xiong: Well…

Annie: Don't some teachers have maternity leave?

Xiong: Some teachers in the school will share the workload then. The long term study seems impossible. Short seems OK. Usually, the short term trainings are on summer vacation. Last summer, I was in a programme aided by Northern American volunteers. Some American and Canadian volunteers come to train Chinese teachers every year. They usually come in summer. It is impossible for us to leave school for a long term.

Annie: You went last summer?

Xiong: Yes. It was an intensive training for English teachers in listening and speaking English. There were totally 42 days, only 10-something students in a class, one teacher taught a class for 42 days.

Annie: Did you pay for that?

Xiong: The school paid for me. There are short trainings like that for some subjects, usually once a year. Some are in term time, for about two weeks.

Annie: What is learnt?

Xiong: There is some theoretical stuff, along with watching classes and lecturers. Longer term trainings are mainly on summer vacations.

Annie: How many times have you been on summer-time trainings?

Xiong: 2-3 times. I remember I did Mandarin in Wuhan.

Annie: Mandarin?

Xiong: Mandarin examiner training.

Annie: Which body organized it?

Xiong: Hubei Province Chinese Language Working Committee.

Annie: How long did that take?

Xiong: About 10 days. Well, the teachers in the school love learning, so they take this kind of opportunity.

Annie: Do other teachers have opportunities too?

Xiong: Almost every subject has opportunities, but not every teacher has the opportunity to go. For instance, last year, I reported what I learned in the programme to other teachers, so that we can learn together and make progress together.

Annie: Is there any standard for teachers to reach in terms of learning?

Xiong: Not exactly. Some teachers would like to learn, some would not.

Annie: How can teachers learn from each other in the school?

Xiong: We have Teaching and Research activities, normally once a week. Every teacher has to participate. Teachers of the same subject get together or watch a public class of each other. However able a teacher is, they can show it in a class. I usually lead in showing a class, demonstrating to teachers what I took in from learning, and showing them. There are various ways to convey what I've learned from various training programmes to other teachers in the school. It's up to themselves to take it on board or not. I can't force them to memorize 10 words, or 5 sentences, in English every day. What I can do is just to lead, giving out information. It depends on themselves whether to take it and make progress.

Annie: Do you give lecturers to your fellow teachers?

Xiong: Haven't yet. I speak at meetings in the school. I talk to them about everything I learned from the programmes paid by the school, without any reservation. I went to study as a representative of this school; I learn for them and help them learn too. It is not individualism, otherwise I should pay for these learning opportunities myself, and I should not have leave from teaching. Anyway, teachers in this school love learning. I can feel the effect from what they say and do. For example, Ms. Huang, you've just seen her, she is head of English. Sometimes her chatting can reflect what she is learning. She sometimes may say "Last night I stayed up late". I would ask why, she would say "I read a book", and so on. I could feel what I say and do could encourage them to learn. I was just reading about some self-report of a teacher's work. She mentioned that in addition to finishing teaching, she also did... We did not give specific tasks for teachers to accomplish in learning. Some do learn.

Annie: What did the teacher say in her report?

Xiong: She said she was monitoring students watching English programmes on CCTV. She required her students to watch it – in order to check the result, she had to watch it too. I can see her love for learning between lines. They have to learn, otherwise, they would be left behind.

Annie: Do you have any senior teachers at the school?

Xiong: Yes, we do. But they are not much older than others, just a little bit older. They are sure to have less English, and their methods are staler. They doubtlessly respect work. Outcomes of teaching are also good. Though there are various reforms undergoing in teaching, in fact, some teachers just slightly modified their teaching, there was not vigorous, or substantial, change in their teaching. The examination results of their teaching are not bad. Well, the examination system remains the same. Well, there are some changes in examinations, but the direction hasn't been changed. So they still can have good examination results. They work hard, so the result is not bad.

Annie: Now the whole nation is learning English, why do you think they are learning English?

Xiong: Speaking from a broad perspective, it is for promoting communications between countries. English is used most widely, and we should master some English knowledge, etc. Well, I haven't thought about it yet. I just like English very much. To students, some may think it useful, some may not. Like maths, we studied maths, but seldom use it now, particularly the advanced maths knowledge. At least I don't think I have used any maths stuff learned at the senior secondary level. It depends what course or profession students would take up later. Whatever other course they would do, if it is not mandated, I think...even it is compulsory for examinations, little English is used. This is my personal view. Now, some students can learn, I teach them. It is sure that many students may not use it a lot. As I said, like some mathematical knowledge, I may not use it at all in my life. If students do another course rather than English, they may think English useless. However, it is a kind of basic knowledge.

...

Annie: Thank you very much.

Appendix II

A Sample Follow-up Conversation

Follow-up conversation with Ms. Zheng

Annie: I've sent you the transcript and translation of the interview via E-mail. Have you had a look at it?

Zheng: Yes, I've read them.

Annie: Any comment? Is there anything that did not present what you meant?

Zheng: I think there are no problems. Oh, I remember one thing, as to the punishment of students. Last time I mentioned to you about one student in my class who could not take the dictation well. When I talked to him, he said he was unable to do it well, even if I were to ask him to copy it 50 times. Actually, I did not punish him by asking him to copy it 20 or 50 times. Usually, when I identify the problems they have, I talk to them, and probe for their own ideas of resolution. Sometimes, they suggest that they should copy it repeatedly many times. It is not my idea to punish them this way.

Annie: I will go back to the data and check. Anything else?

Zheng: Another thing is about planning lessons, regarding aspects taken into consideration when preparing a lesson. Now I've made some improvements. I make efforts to help students understand the Western cultures. I also pay attention to students' emotional competence education. When I do activities, I intend to build up their team spirit and cooperation skills. I changed a bit through gradual exploration.

Annie: Will you please be more specific about this point, for instance, how do you conduct an activity?

Zheng: For example, I did a topic on time. My objective for this topic was to reach an outcome of students making a timetable for themselves, so that they can establish a good habit for their lives and study.

Annie: Does every unit in the textbook have such an implication?

Zheng: The unit is focused simply on language issues. I take it further.

Annie: Is it based on your own understanding? Or do you extend it with your own initiative?

Zheng: Yes.

Annie: It is more than teaching English. Anything else I need to modify in the data?

Zheng: No. Nothing else I think.

Annie: How about the translations?

Zheng: They are fine.

Annie: Has there been any negative impact from this study on you?

Zheng: Some aspects, which you could think of, while I could not, were helpful to me and generated progress in me. It seems there isn't any negative influence.

Annie: The other thing I would like to know is about your work in the first year. So far, you've been a teacher for nearly a year, what is the most significant thing that you could share with others?

Zheng: I've just talked with Miss Liu about it. We feel if we were allowed to do the first year again, I could do much better. I was often asked by friends, when chatting with them, about my experience as a teacher. They think I have a nice temper; they wanted to know what it is like when I am teaching. I think it is about my personality. I was such a person who did not know how to care about others or was not very considerate. But, as a teacher, I should put my feet in my students' shoes, to think for them in their place. I also need to be very patient with them, to treat them as children. Sometimes, when I talk to them, or criticize them, they may not be able to realize that it is good for them. I try to communicate with them about my kind intentions to achieve teaching, and learning, to benefit each other. So the student-teacher relationship will be better and the classroom atmosphere will be easier. I do not want to use the authoritarian power of a teacher to gain their respect. When they like me, they respect me genuinely.

Annie: Last time when I interviewed you, you had been a teacher for just about 20 days. Now you have been a teacher for nearly a year, have you met any specific difficulties, or received support from others?

Zheng: Once something happened between one of my students and me. We were doing countable and uncountable nouns. When studying the noun "rice", I mentioned that "rice" is uncountable, while one of the students pointed out that "rice" was taught as a countable noun by his previous teacher. I thought that perhaps he had studied about it in private classes by another teacher. Then I asked him to check with that teacher after class and come back to tell me about it. He would not. There is another student in the class who likes asking questions. When we were doing the names of countries and their adjectives, such as Canada and Canadian, the student pointed out that Canadian should be pronounced the other way. Then I said it was good that you could find out questions and asked him to look it up. What occurred to me at that moment was if I told him straight away about the right pronunciation, they might forget soon; if I asked them to do something with it, it might produce a better effect. The next day, in the morning reading session, the first thing that I did was to ask him if he had looked it up. The answer I got from him was negative. I said to him in the class how I wished he had looked it up. Then I told them about the right pronunciation of the word. I encouraged them to keep asking questions until they found satisfactory answers. I advocated enquiry. I always try to stir up some change in their thoughts through concrete things.

Annie: In fact, the word "rice" can be countable and uncountable.

Zheng: I checked about it. When it is used as food "rice" is uncountable.

Annie: Any other difficulties?

Zheng: I was kidding with other teachers that I could teach other new teachers with my experiences this year. I could talk about how to be a classroom teacher and classroom teaching. But they said they needed to experience them in person to find out. Miss Liu and I both feel if we were allowed to do the first year again, we would do it differently and better.

Annie: Is there any change in your views on the work of being a teacher, after actually being a teacher for a while?

Zheng: Before I started teaching in a school, I had thought the job of teaching was easy. After I became a teacher, I found this job to be difficult and tiring.

Annie: In what way?

Zheng: In various ways – because I am a class teacher, I come to school early, and I am always the last to leave. I feel tired both physically and emotionally. I always try to use different ways of teaching, so that the students can learn something new. It takes time to prepare lessons and collect information. In addition, I always try to put myself in their shoes, to treat them as children, hoping that they can have a good future. However, whatever I do, they don't seem to care much. When I see my efforts are fruitless, I feel sad, while it also goads me into putting in more efforts.

Annie: Can't you try some other way? If you keep on this way, you might come to feel totally exhausted.

Zheng: For a while, I really felt exhausted. I constantly adjusted my emotions. For instance, when I get frustration from students, I try to talk to others, to change my mood. I try to avoid falling into a negative cycle. I try my best to do well. I watched a programme on TV, in which a writer said encouragement could turn an idiot into a gift. I am trying the method of encouragement, trying to be aware of their progress and good behavior, even a little bit, and letting them know. For example, a few days ago, a student volunteered to clean the blackboard. I saw him do it, and praised him for it in the class. I want to have a try to see whether praise can have such an effect or not.

Annie: Children are different.

Zheng: I've thought about that. I've been thinking about whether a teacher should intend to change a child's personality, or not, by education.

Annie: Probably a personality is influenced by various factors, not only through education.

Zheng: English learning needs their participation. I am trying to engage them and enliven the class. But some students are introvert, and they don't participate. Some subject teachers also have let me know that there are only some students in the class who respond to teachers actively.

Annie: Praise may only result in unintended outcomes, such as students learning in order to be praised, it can be risky.

Zheng: Some parents want the teacher to praise their children rather than criticize them. They let the teacher know that the child takes in good words only. Parents put demands on teachers as to how their children should be treated. They contact the school, then the head teacher may pass the pressure on to the teachers.

Annie: What support have you had from the school?

Zheng: When I have knotty problems, some individual teachers may offer ideas. As for other support, I don't have any special memory about it.

Annie: Are you satisfied with being a teacher?

Zheng: I think being a teacher requires a great sense of responsibility. Since I have chosen to be a teacher, I just try my best to do it well. Whenever my students asked me what it feels as a teacher, I told them it makes me both happy and sad. Every job is two-sided.

Annie: So far, do you have any other comments on being a teacher?

Zheng: I don't have other special feelings about it at the moment. Probably I will feel stronger when I have finished a cycle from junior 1-3.

Annie: How about your working time?

Zheng: I come to school at 7:20 in the morning and leave here at about 6:30 p.m. I usually take the textbook back home, and spend 1-2 hours on preparation. For instance, the day before April Fool's Day, I was considering how to introduce this to the students, and how to design some activities for it.

Annie: Do you feel notable progress in your teaching?

Zheng: Yes, particularly in classroom management.

...

Annie: Thank you very much for your time.

References

[1]   Acker, S. (1995) Carry on Caring: the Work of Women Teachers. *British Journal of Sociology of Education*, 16/1, 21-36.

[2]   Agar, M. (1986) *Speaking of Ethnography*. London: Sage.

[3]   Armstrong, P. (2000) Education for Integrity: Values, Educational Research and the Use of the Life History Method. In R. Gardner, J. Cairns & D. Lawton (eds.). *Morals, Ethics and Citizenship in Contemporary Teaching* (pp. 218-230). London, Sterling: Kogan Page.

[4]   Aspin, D. (1984) Metaphors and Meaning in Educational Discourse, In W. Taylor (ed.). *Metaphors of Education* (pp. 4-21). London: Heinemann Educational Books.

[5]   Atkinson, R. (1998) *The Life Story Interview*. London: Sage.

[6]   Ball, S. (2003) The Teacher's Soul and the Terror of performativity. *Journal of Educational Policy*, 18/2, 215-228.

[7]   Ball, S. (2008) *The education debate*. Bristle: The Policy Press.

[8]   Ball, S. & Goodson, I. (1985) *Teachers' Lives and Careers*. London: Falmer Press.

[9]   Bateson, M. C. (1989) *Composing a Life*. New York: Atlantic Monthly Press.

[10]   Beattie, M. (1995) New Prospects for Teacher Education: Narrative Ways of Knowing, Teaching and Teacher Learning. *Educational Research*, 37/1, 53-70.

[11]   Bennett, D. (2004) *Logic Made Easy*. London: Penguin Books.

[12]   Berliner, D. C. (1990) If the Metaphor Fits, Why not Wear it? The Teacher as Executive. *Theory into Practice*, 29/2, 85-94.

[13]   Bernstein, B. (1990) *The Structure of Pedagogic Discourse, Class, Codes and Control*. London: Routledge.

[14]   Bertaux, D. (1981) From the Life-history Approach to the Transformation of Sociological Practice. In D. Bertaux (ed.). *Biography and Society: the*

Life-history Approach in the Social Sciences (pp. 19-29). California: Sage Publications.

[15]   Bertaux, D. & Bertaux-Wiame, I. (1981) Life Stories in the Baker's Trade. In D. Bertaux (ed.). *Biography and Society: the Life-history Approach in the Social Sciences* (pp. 149-169). California: Sage.

[16]   Bishop, K. (2000) *An Investigation into the Role of Subject Matter Knowledge in the Development of Novice Science Teachers' Pedagogical Content Knowledge* [PhD thesis], Bath University Library.

[17]   Black, A., & Halliwell, G. (2000) Accessing Practical Knowledge: How? Why? *Teaching and Teacher Education*. 16/1, 103-115.

[18]   Blumenfeld-Jones, D. (1995) Fidelity as a Criterion for Practicing and Evaluating Narrative Inquiry. In J. A. Hatch & R. Wisniewski (eds.). *Life-History and Narrative* (pp. 25-37). London: The Falmer Press.

[19]   Brooks, V. & Sikes, P. (1997) *The Good Mentor Guide*. Buckingham: Open University Press.

[20]   Brown, S. & Mcintyre, D. (1988). The Professional Craft Knowledge of Teachers. *Scottish Educational Review* (special issue), 39-45.

[21]   Bruner, J. (1986) *Actual Minds, Possible Worlds*. Cambridge, MA: Harvard University Press.

[22]   Bruner, J. (1996) *Culture of Education*. Cambridge, MA: Harvard University Press

[23]   Bryman, A. (2004) *Social Research Methods*. Oxford: Oxford University Press.

[24]   Buchmann, M. (1987) Teaching Knowledge, the Lights that Teachers Live by. *Oxford Review of Education*, 151-164.

[25]   Buchmann, M. (1988) The Careful Vision: How Practical is Contemplation in Teaching? [On-line document] URL: http://ncrtl.msu.edu/http/ipapers/html/ip891.htm (Last retrieved 03/03/ 2006).

[26]   Buchmann, M. (1989) Making New or Making Do: An Inclusive Argument about Teaching. *Oxford Review of Education*, 15, 181-195.

[27]   Bullock, K. & Wikeley, F. (2004) *Whose Learning?* Buckingham: Open University Press.

[28]   Bullough, Jr. R. V. (1989) *First-year Teaching: A Case Study*. Columbia: Teachers College, Columbia University.

[29]   Bullough, Jr. R. V., Knowles, G. & Crow, N. A. (1991) *Emerging as a Teacher*. London: Routledge.

[30]   Butt, G. & Gunter, H. (2005) Challenging Modernization: Remodelling the Education Workforce. *Educational Review*, 57/2, 131-137.

[31]   Calderhead, J. (1987) *Exploring Teachers' Thinking*. London: Cassell.

[32]   Calderhead, J. (1988) The Development of Knowledge Structures in Learning to Teach. In J. Calderhead (ed.). *Teachers' Professional Learning* (pp. 51-64). London: The Falmer Press.

[33]   Calderhead, J. (1996) Teachers: Beliefs and Knowledge. In Berliner, D. & Calfee, R. (eds.). *Handbook of Educational Psychology* (pp. 709-725) New York: Simon and Shuster Macmillan.

[34]   Calderhead, J. & Shorrock, S. B. (1997) *Understanding Teacher Education: Case-studies in the Professional Development of Beginning Teachers*. London and Washington D.C.: Taylor & Francis, Inc. Pub.

[35]   Cao, G. (1991) *A Native of Beijing in New York*. Beijing: China Literature United Press.

[36]   Carre, C. (1993) The First Year of Teaching. In N. Bennett & C. Carre (eds.). *Learning to Teach* (PP. 191-221). London and New York: Routledge.

[37]   Carter, K. (1990a) Teachers' Knowledge and Learning to Teach. In R. Houston (ed.). *Handbook of Research on Teacher Education* (pp. 291-310). New York: Macmillan.

[38]   Carter, K. (1990b) Meaning and Metaphor: Case Knowledge in Teaching. *Theory into Practice*, 29/2, 109-126.

[39]   Carter, K. (1992) Creating Cases for the Development of Teacher Knowledge. In T. Russell & H. Munby (eds.). *Teachers and Teaching: From Classroom to Reflection* (pp. 109-124). London: The Falmer Press.

[40]   Carter, K. (1993) The Place of Story in Research on Teaching and Teacher Education. *Educational Researcher*, 22/1, 5-12.

[41]   Carter, K. & Doyle, W. (1996) Personal Narrative and Life-history in Learning to Teach. In J. Sikula, T. J. Buttery & E. Guyton (eds.). *Handbook of Research on Teacher Education* (pp. 120-142). New York: Macmillan.

[42]   Cheng, L. X. (2004) *Teachers and the New Curriculum*. Beijing: China Personnel Press.

[43]   Cheng, L., Ren, S. & Wang, H. (2003) Pre-service and In-service Teacher Education of Secondary English Language Teachers in China. [Online Journal], TEFL Web Journal, 2/1, 2003. URL: http://www.teflweb-j.org/index.html, (Last retrieved, 02/03/2006).

[44]   Cheng, L. & Wang, H. (2004) Understanding Professional Challenges

Faced by Chinese Teachers of English. [Online Journal], URL: http://writing. berkeley.edu/tesl-ej/ej28/a2.html, TESL-EJ, 7/4. (Last retrieved, 27/03/2006).

[45] Chomsky, N. (1972) *Language and Mind*. New York: Harcourt Brace Jovanovich.

[46] Chui, B. & Yong, S. (1995) Teacher Trainees' Motives for Entering into a Teaching Career in Brunei Darussalam. *Teaching and Teachers Education*, 11/3, 275-280.

[47] Clandinin, D. J. & Connelly, F. M. (1988) Studying Teachers' Knowledge of Classrooms: Collaborative Research, Ethics, and the Negotiation of Narrative. *The Journal of Educational Thought*, 22/(2A), 269-282.

[48] Clandinin, D. J., & Connelly, F. M. (1996) Teacher's Professional Knowledge Landscape: Teachers Stories – Stories of Teachers – School Stories - Stories of Schools. *Educational Researcher*, 25/3, 24-30.

[49] Clandinin, D. J. & Connelly, F. M. (1994) Personal Experience Methods. In N. K. Denzin & Y. Lincoln (eds.). *The Sage Handbook of Qualitative Research* (pp. 413-427). Thousand Oaks, California: Sage.

[50] Clandinin, D. J. & Connelly, F. M. (2000) *Narrative Inquiry Experience and Story in Qualitative Research*. San Francisco: Jossey-Bass Publishers.

[51] Claxton, G. (1990) *Teaching to Learn*. London: Cassell.

[52] Cleverley, J. (1985) *The Schooling of China: Tradition and Modernity in Chinese Education*. Sydney, London & Boston: George Allen & Unwin.

[53] Cochran-Smith, M. (2003) Sometimes It's Not about the Money: Teaching and Heart. *Journal of Teacher Education*, 54/5, 371-375.

[54] Cochran-Smith, M. & Lytle, S. L. (1990) Research on Teaching and Teacher Research: the Issues That Divide. *Educational Researcher*, 19/2, 2-11.

[55] Conle, C. (2000a) Thesis as Narrative or "What is the Inquiry in Narrative Inquiry?" *Curriculum Inquiry*, 30/2, 189-214.

[56] Conle, C. (2000b) Narrative Inquiry: Research Tool and Medium for Professional Development. *European Journal of Teacher Education*, 23/1, 49-63.

[57] Conle, C. (2001) The Rationality of Narrative Inquiry in Research and Professional Development. *European Journal of Teacher Education*, 24/1, 21-33.

[58] Connelly, F. M., & Clandinin, D. J. (1988) *Curriculum Planners: Narratives of Experience*. New York: Teachers College Press.

[59]   Connelly, F. M. & Clandinin, D. J. (1990) Stories of Experience and Narrative Inquiry. *Educational Researcher*, 19/5, 2-14.

[60]   Connelly, F. M., Clandinin, D. J. & He, M. F. (1997) Teachers' Personal Practical Knowledge on the Professional Knowledge Landscape. *Teaching and Teacher Education*, 13/7, 665-674.

[61]   Connelly, F. M. & Clandinin, D. J. (1999) *Shaping a Professional Identity: Stories of Educational Practice.* London: The Althouse Press.

[62]   Convery, A. (1999) Listening to Teachers' Stories: Are We Sitting Too Comfortably? *Qualitative Studies in Education*, 12/2, 131-146.

[63]   Cook, B. L., & Pang, K. C. (1991) Recent Research on Beginning Teachers: Studies of Trained and Untrained Novices. *Teaching and Teacher Education*, 7/1, 93-110.

[64]   Cortazzi, M. (1993) *Narrative Analysis.* London: Routledge, Falmer.

[65]   Cortazzi, M., & Jin, L. (1996) English Teaching and Learning in China. *Language Teaching*, 29/2, 61-80.

[66]   Creswell, J. W. & Miller, D. L. (2000) Determining Validity in Qualitative Inquiry. *Theory into Practices*, 39/3, 124-130.

[67]   Cuban, L. (1990) Reforming Again, Again and Again. *Educational Researcher*, 19/1, 3-13.

[68]   Day, C. (1999) *Developing Teachers, the Challenges of Lifelong Learning.* London: The Falmer Press.

[69]   Day, C. (1993) The Importance of Learning Biography in Supporting Teacher Development: An Empirical Study. In C. Day, J. Calderhead & P. Denicolo (eds.). *Research on Teacher Thinking, Understanding Professional Development.* London: The Falmer Press.

[70]   Day, C. (1999) *Developing Teachers the Challenges of Lifelong Learning.* London: The Falmer Press.

[71]   Day, C., Fernandez, A., Hauge, T. E. & Møller, J. (2000) (eds.). *The Life and Work of Teachers.* London: The Falmer Press.

[72]   Day, C., Elliot, B. & Kington, A. (2005) Reform, Standards and Teacher Identity: Challenges of Sustaining Commitment. *Teaching and Teacher Education*, 21/5, 563-577.

[73]   DFES (2001) Teacher Workload Study. [Online-Document] URL: http://www.teachernet.gov.uk/wholeschool/remodelling/workloadstudy/ (Last retrieved, 03/03/2006).

[74]   Denison, J. (1998) An Interview with Norman K. Denzin. *Waikato*

Journal of Education, 4, 51-54.

[75] Denison, J. & Rinehart, R. (2000) Introduction: Imagining Sociological Narratives. *Sociology of Sport Journal,* 17/1, 1-4.

[76] Denison, J. (2002) Writing a "True" Sports Story. *Auto/Biography,* 10/(1&2), 131-137.

[77] Denison, J., & Markula, P. (eds.). (2003) *Moving Writing: Crafting Movement in Sport Research.* New York: Peter Lang.

[78] Denison, J. (2003) Movement Practices through Text. In J. Denison & P. Markula (eds.). *Moving Writing Crafting Movement in Sport Research* (pp. 201-213). New York: Peter Lang.

[79] Denison, J. (2006) The Way We Run, Reimaging Research and the Self. *Journal of Sport & Social Issue,* 30/4, 333-339.

[80] Denzin, N. & Lincoln, Y. S. (eds.). (2000) (2nd edition) *The SAGE Handbook of Qualitative Research.* California: Sage.

[81] Denzin, N. & Lincoln, Y. S. (eds.). (2005) (3rd edition) *The SAGE Handbook of Qualitative Research* (3rd edition). California: Sage.

[82] Denzin, N. (1989) *Interpretive Biography.* California: Sage.

[83] Dewey, J. (1929*) Experience and Nature.* Illinois: Open Court.

[84] Dewey, J. (1938) *Experience and Education.* New York: Collier Books.

[85] Dewey, J. & Bentley, A. F. (1949) *Knowing and the Known.* Boston: The Beacon Press.

[86] Doyle, W. (1997) Heard any Really Good Stories Lately? A Critique of the Critics of Narrative in Educational Research. *Teaching and Teacher Education,* 13/1, 93-99.

[87] Doyle, W. & Carter, K. (2003) Narrative and Learning to Teach: Implications for Teacher-education Curriculum. *J. Curriculum Studies,* 35/2, 129-137.

[88] Eisner, E. W. (1988) The Primacy of Experience and the Politics of Method. *Educational Researcher,* 17/5, 15-20.

[89] Elbaz, F. (1983) *Teacher Thinking: A Study of Practical Knowledge.* New York: Nicholls.

[90] Elbaz, F. (1991) Research on Teachers' Knowledge: The Evolution of a Discourse. *Journal of Curriculum Studies,* 23/1, 1-19.

[91] Elbaz-Luwisch, F. (1997) Narrative Research: Political Issues and Implications. *Teaching and Teacher Education,* 13/1, 75-83.

[92] Ellis, C. & Bochner, A. (2000) Autoethnography, Personal Narrative,

Reflexivity. In N. Denzin & Y. Lincoln (eds.). *Handbook of Qualitative Research* (pp. 733-796). London: Sage.

[93]   Emihovich, C. (1995) Distancing Passion: Narratives in Social Science. In J. A. Hatch & R. Wisniewski (eds.). *Life-history and Narrative* (pp. 37-48). London: The Falmer Press.

[94]   Eraut, M. (1994) *Developing Professional Knowledge and Competence*. London: The Falmer Press.

[95]   Eraut, M. (2000) Non-Formal Learning and Tacit Knowledge in Professional Work. *British Journal of Educational Psychology*, 70, 113-136.

[96]   Erlandson, D. A., Harris, E. L., Skipper, B. L. & Allen, S. D. (1993) *Doing Naturalistic Inquiry*. London: Sage Publications.

[97]   Fairclough, N. (1989) *Language and Power*. London and New York: Longman.

[98]   Farrell, T. (2003) Learning to Teach English Language During the First Year: Personal Influences and Challenges. *Teaching and Teacher Education*, 19/1, 95-111.

[99]   Feinberg, W. (1993) *Japan and a Pursuit of a New American Identity: Work and Education in a Multicultural Age*. New York: Routledge.

[100]   Feldman, A. (1997) Varieties of Wisdom in the Practice of Teachers. *Teaching and Teacher Education*, 13/7, 575-773.

[101]   Fenstermacher, G. (1994) The Knower and the Known: The Nature of Knowledge in Research on Teaching. In L. Darling-Hammond (ed.). *Review of Research in Education*, *20* (pp. 3-56) Washington D.C.: American Educational Research Association.

[102]   Fenstermacher, G. (1997) On Narrative. *Teaching and Teacher Education*, 13/1, 119-124.

[103]   Ferrarotti, F. (1981) On the Autonomy of the Biographical Method. In D. Bertaux (ed.). *Biography and Society the Life-History Approach in the Social Sciences* (pp. 5-19). California: Sage.

[104]   Floden, R. E. & Clark. M. C. (1988) Preparing Teachers for Uncertainty. *Teachers College Record*, Summer.

[105]   Foster, B. (2001) Choices: A Dilemma of Woman Agricultural Education Teachers. *Journal of Agricultural Education*, 42/3, 1-9.

[106]   Freeman, D. (1993) Renaming Experience/Reconstructing Practice: Developing New Understandings of Teaching. *Teaching and Teacher Education*, 9/5/6, 485-497.

[107] Freeman, D. (1991) "To Make the Tacit Explicit": Teacher Education, Emerging Discourse, and the Conceptions of Teaching. *Teaching and Teacher Education*, Vol. 7. pp. 439-454.

[108] Freeman, D. (1994) The Use of Language Data in the Study of Teachers' Knowledge. In I. Carlgren, G. Handal & S. Vaage (eds.). *Teachers' Minds and Action* (pp. 93-109). London: The Falmer Press.

[109] Freeman, D. (1996a) "To Take Them at Their Word": Language Data in the Study of Teachers' Knowledge. *Harvard Educational Review*, 66/4, 732-761.

[110] Freeman, D. (1996b) The "Unstudied Problem": Research on Teacher Learning in Language Teaching. In D. Freeman & J. C. Richards (eds.). *Teacher Learning in Language Teaching* (pp. 352-374). Cambridge: Cambridge University Press.

[111] Freeman, D. & Johnson, K. L. (1998). Reconceptualising the Knowledge-Base of Language Teacher Education. *TESOL Quarterly*, 32/3, 397-417.

[112] Freire, P. (1994) (Translated by R. Barr) *Pedagogy of Hope*. London: Continuum.

[113] Fullan, M. (2001) *The New Meaning of Educational Change*. New York: Teachers College Press.

[114] Gardner, H. (1989) *To Open Minds: Chinese Clues to the Dilemma of Contemporary Education*. New York: Basic Books.

[115] Gatbonton, E. (1999) Investigating Experienced ESL Teachers' Pedagogical Knowledge. *The Modern Language Journal*, 83/i, 35-50.

[116] Geertz, C. (1988) *Works and Lives: The Anthropologist as Author*. Stanford: Stanford University Press.

[117] Geertz, C. (1995) *After the Facts: Two Countries Four Decades, One Anthropologist*. Cambridge, MA: Harvard University Press.

[118] Giddens, A. (1991) *Modernity and Self-Identity: Self and Society in Late Modern Age*. CA: Stanford University Press.

[119] Glaser B. G. & Straus A. L. (1967) *The Discovery of Grounded Theory: Strategies for Qualitative Research*. Chicago: Aldine Publishing Co.

[120] Golombek, P. R. (1998) A Study of Language Teachers' Personal Practical Knowledge. *TESOL Quarterly*, 32/3, 447-464.

[121] Golombek, P. R. & Johnson, K. E. (2004) Narrative Inquiry as a Mediational Space: Examining Emotional and Cognitive Dissonance in Second-Language Teachers' Development. *Teachers and Teaching:*

Theory and Practice, 10/3, 307-327.

[122] Goodson, I. (1992) Studying Teachers' Lives: An Emergent Field of Inquiry. In I. Goodson (ed.). *Studying Teachers Lives* (pp. 1-18). London: Routledge.

[123] Goodson, I. (1994) Studying the Teachers' Life and Work. *Teaching and Teacher Education*, 10/1, 29-37.

[124] Goodson, I. & Walker, R. (1995) Telling Tales. In H. McEwan & K. Egan (eds.). *Narrative in Teaching, Learning, and Research* (pp. 184-195). New York: Teachers College Press.

[125] Goodson, I. (1995) The Story so Far: Personal Knowledge and the Political. In J. A. Hatch and R. Wisniewski (eds.). *Life-history and Narrative* (pp. 89-99). London: The Falmer Press.

[126] Goodson, I. (1997) Representing Teachers. *Teaching and Teacher Education*, 13/1, 111-117.

[127] Goodson, I. & Hargreaves, A. (1996) *Teachers' Professional Lives*. London: The Falmer Press.

[128] Goodson, I. (2000) Professional Knowledge and the Teachers' Life and Work. In C. Day, A. Fernandez, T. Hauge & J. Møller (eds.). *The Life and Work of Teachers* (pp. 13-26). London: The Falmer Press.

[129] Goodson, I. (2001) Social Histories of Educational Change. *Journal of Educational Change*, 2/1, 45-63.

[130] Goodson, I. (2003) *Professional Knowledge, Professional Lives: Studies in Education and Change*. Maidenhead: Open University Press.

[131] Goodson, I. (2007) All the Lonely People: the Struggle for Private Meaning and Public Purpose in Education. *Critical Studies in Education*, 48 (1), 131–148.

[132] Goodson, I. (2008) *Investigating the Teacher's Life and Work*. Rotterdam: Sense Publishers.

[133] Goodson, I. & Numan, U. (2002) Teacher's Life Worlds, Agency and Policy. *Teachers and Teaching: Theory and Practices*, 8/3/4, 269-277.

[134] Goodson, I. & Sikes, P. (2001) *Life-history Research in Educational Settings: Learning from Lives*. Buckingham and Philadelphia: Open University Press.

[135] Grbich, C. (1999) *Qualitative Research in Health*. CF: Sage.

[136] Grimshaw, T. (2002) *Discursive Struggle in Chinese Universities: Responses to English and its Associated Discourses* [PhD Thesis].

University of Kent Library.

[137]   Grossman, P. (1990) *The Making of a Teacher: Teacher Knowledge and Teacher Education*. New York: Teachers College Press.

[138]   Gu, Y. Q. (2003) Fine Brush and Freehand: The Vocabulary-Learning Art of Two Successful Chinese EFL Learners. *TESOL Quarterly*, 37/1, 73-101.

[139]   Guba, E. G. & Lincoln, Y. S. (1989) *Fourth Generation Evaluation*. Newbury Park, CA: Sage.

[140]   Guba, E. G., & Lincoln, Y. S. (1994) Competing Paradigms in Qualitative Research. In N. K. Denzin & Y. S. Lincoln (eds.). *Handbook of Qualitative Research* (pp. 105-117). Thousand Oaks, CA: Sage.

[141]   Gudmundsdottir, S. (1990) Curriculum Stories: Four Case Studies of Social Studies Teaching. In C. Day, M. Pope & P. Denicolo (eds.). *Insights into Teachers' Thinking and Practice* (pp. 107-118). London: The Falmer Press.

[142]   Gudmundsdottir, S. (1991) Ways of Seeing are Ways of Learning: The Pedagogical Content Knowledge of an Expert English Teacher. *Journal of Curriculum Studies*, 23/5, 409-423.

[143]   Gudmundsdottir, S. (1995) The Narrative Nature of Pedagogical Knowledge. In H. McEwan & K. Egan (eds.). *Narrative in Teaching, Learning and Research* (pp. 24-39). New York: Teachers College Press.

[144]   Gudmundsdottir, S. (guest ed.). (1997) Introduction to the Theme Issue of "Narrative Perspectives on Research on Teaching and Teacher Education". *Teaching and Teacher Education*, 13/1, 1-3.

[145]   Hammersley, M. & Atkinson, P. (1995) *Ethnography Principles in Practice*. London: Routledge.

[146]   Hargreaves, A. & Woods, P. (1984) *Classrooms and Staff rooms: The Sociology of Teachers and Teaching*. Buckingham: Open University Press.

[147]   Hargreaves, A. (1994) *Changing Teachers, Changing Times*. London: Cassell.

[148]   Hargreaves, A. (1996) Revisiting Voice. *Educational Researcher*, 25/1, 12-19.

[149]   Hargreaves, A. (1998) The Emotional Practice of Teaching. *Teaching and Teacher Education*, 14/8, 835-854.

[150]   Hargreaves, A. (1999) Schooling in the New Millennium: Educational Research for the Post-modern Age. *Discourse: Studies in the Cultural Politics of Education*, 20/3, 333-355.

[151] Hargreaves, A. (2003) *Teaching in the Knowledge Society.* Buckingham: Open University Press and New York: Teachers College Press.

[152] Hatch, J. A. & Wisniewski, R. (1995) Life-history and Narrative: Questions, Issues, and Exemplary Works. In J. A. Hatch & R. Wisniewski (eds.). *Life-History and Narrative* (pp. 113-135). London: The Falmer Press.

[153] Hatch, J. A. (1999) What Pre-service Teachers Can Learn from Studies of Teachers' Work. *Teaching and Teacher Education,* 15, 229-242.

[154] He, M. F. (2002) A Narrative Inquiry of Cross-Cultural Lives: Lives in China. *Journal of Curriculum Studies,* 34/3, 301-321.

[155] Hermans, H. J. M. (2002) The Dialogical Self as a Society of Mind. *Theory and Psychology,* 12/2, 147-160.

[156] Hodkinson, P. & Sparkes, A. C. (1997) Careership: A Sociological Theory of Career Decision Making. *British Journal of Sociology of Education,* 18/1, 29-44.

[157] Howitt, C. (2004) The Use of Critical Incident Vignettes to Share a Pre-Service Primary Teacher's Science Learning Journey. Proceedings of the Western Australian Institute for Educational Research Forum, 2004.

[158] Hu, G. W. (2002a) Recent Important Developments in Secondary English Language Teaching in the People's Republic of China. *Language, Culture and Curriculum,* 15/1, 31-47.

[159] Hu, G. W. (2002b) Potential Cultural Resistance to Pedagogical Import: The Case of Communicative Language Teaching in China. *Language, Culture and Curriculum,* 15/2, 94-105.

[160] Hu, G. W. (2003) English Language Teaching in China: Regional Differences and Contributing Factors. Journal of Multilingual and Multicultural Development, 24/4, 290-318.

[161] Hu, G. W. (2005) Professional Development of Secondary EFL Teachers: Lessons from China. *Teacher College Record,* 107/4, 654-705.

[162] Huberman, M. (1989) The Professional Life Cycle of Teachers. *Teachers College Record,* 91/1, 33-57.

[163] Huberman, M. (1993) *The Lives of Teachers.* Chicago: Teachers College Press.

[164] Huberman, M. (1995) Working with Life-history Narratives. In H. McEwan & K. Egan (eds.). *Narrative in Teaching, Learning and Research* (pp. 127-166). New York: Teachers College Press.

[165] Ing, M. (1978) Theories of Motivation. In D. Lauton et al (eds.). *Theory*

and Practice of Curriculum Studies. London : Routledge.

[166] Irme, R. W. (1982) *Knowing and Caring.* Washington, D.C.: University Press of America.

[167] Jackson, P. W. (1995) On the Place of Narrative in Teaching. In H. McEwan and K. Egan (eds.). *Narrative in Teaching, Learning and Research* (pp. 3-24). New York: Teachers College Press.

[168] Jensen, M, Foster, E & Eddy, M. (1997) Creating a Space Where Teachers Can Locate Their Voice and Develop Their Pedagogical Awareness. *Teaching and Teacher Education,* 13/8, 863-875.

[169] Jin, L. & Cortazzi, M. (1998) Dimensions of Dialogue: Large Classes in China. *International Journal of Educational Research,* 29/8, 739-761.

[170] Johnson, M. (1993) *Moral Imagination: Implications of Cognitive Science for Ethics.* Chicago: University of Chicago Press.

[171] Josselson, R. (1996a) Introduction. In R. Josselson (ed.). *Ethics and Process in the Narrative Study of Lives* (pp. xi-xvii). London: Sage.

[172] Josselson, R. (1996b) Imagining the Real, Empathy, Narrative, and the Dialogic Self. In R. Josselson & A. Lieblich (eds.). *Interpreting Experience, the Narrative Study of Lives* (pp. 27-33). London: Sage.

[173] Josselson, R. (1996c) On Writing Other People's Lives: Self-analytic Reflections of a Narrative Researcher. In R. Josselson (ed.). *Ethics and Process in the Narrative Study of Lives* (pp. 45-60). London: Sage.

[174] Kelchtermans, G. (1994) Biographical Methods in the Study of Teachers' Professional Development. In I. Carlgren, G. Handal & S. Vaage (eds.). *Teachers' Minds and Action: Research on Teachers' Thinking and Practice* (pp. 93-109). London: The Falmer Press.

[175] Kelchtermans, G. (1993) Teachers and Their Career Story: A Biographical Perspective on Professional Development. In C. Day, J. Calderhead & P. Denicolo (eds.). *Research on Teacher Thinking Understanding Professional Development.* London: The Falmer Press.

[176] Kelchtermans, G. (1996) Teacher Vulnerability: Understanding its Moral and Political Roots. *Cambridge Journal of Education,* 26/3, 307-323.

[177] Kelchtermans, G. (2005) Teachers' Emotions in Educational Reforms: Self-understanding, Vulnerable Commitment and Micro-political Literacy. *Teaching and Teacher Education,* 21, 995–1006.

[178] Kelchtermans, G. & Ballet, K. (2002) The Micro-politics of Teacher Induction: A Narrative Biographical Study on Teacher Socialization.

Teaching and Teacher Education, 18, 105-120.

[179] Kirk, J. & Miller. M. (1986) *Reliability and Validity in Qualitative Research*. London: Sage.

[180] Knight, P. (2002) A Systematic Approach to Professional Development: Learning as Practice. *Teaching and Teacher Education*, 18, 229-241.

[181] Knowles, J. G. (1992) Models for Understanding Pre-service and Beginning Teachers'Biographies: Illustrations from Case Studies, In I. Goodson (ed.). *Studying Teachers' Lives* (pp. 99-153). London: Routledge.

[182] Kohl, H. (1986) *On Becoming a Teacher*. London: Methuen.

[183] Kohli, M. (1981) Biography: Account, Text, Method. In. D. Bertaux (ed.). *Biography and Society the Life-history Approach in the Social Sciences* (pp. 61-72). London: Sage.

[184] Koro-Ljungberg, M. (2001) Metaphors as a Way to Explore Qualitative Data. *Qualitative Studies in Education*, 14/3, 367-397.

[185] Kramp, M. K. (2004) Exploring Life and Experience through Narrative Inquiry. In K. de Marrais & S. D. Lapan (eds.). *Foundations for Research: Methods in Education and the Social Sciences* (pp. 103-121). Mahwah, NJ: Erlbaum.

[186] Kwakman, K. (2003) Factors Affecting Teachers' Participation in Professional Learning Activities. *Teaching and Teacher Education*, 19/2, 149-170.

[187] Kyriacou, C., Hultgren, A. & Stephens, P. (1999) Student Teachers' Motivation to Become a Secondary School Teacher in England and Norway. *Teacher Development*, 3/3, 373-381.

[188] Laidlaw, M. (1996) *How Can I Create My Own Living Educational Theory as I Offer You an Account of My Educational Development?* [PhD Thesis] Bath University Library.

[189] Lakoff, G. & Johnson, M. (1980) *Metaphors We Live by*. Chicago: University of Chicago Press.

[190] Lapadat, J. C. & Lindsay, A. C. (1999) Transcription in Research and Practice: From Standardization of Technique to Interpretive Positioning. *Qualitative Inquiry*, 5, 64-86.

[191] Latham, G. (2004) The Bookcase at the End of the Thesis: Revisioning a Literature Review. *Journal of Educational Enquiry*, 5/2, 105-115.

[192] Lather, P. (1986) Research as Praxis. *Harvard Educational Review*, 56, 257-277.

[193] Lather, P. (1991) *Getting Smart*. London: Routledge.

[194] Leinhardt, G. (1988) Situated Knowledge and Expertise in Teaching. In J. Calderhead (ed.). *Teachers' Professional Learning*. London: The Falmer Press.

[195] Leinhardt, G. (1990) Capturing Craft Knowledge in Teaching. *Educational Researcher*, 19/2, 18-25.

[196] Leng, H. (1997). New Bottles, Old Wine, Communicative Language Teaching in China, English Teaching Forum. *A Journal for Teachers of English as a Foreign Language*, 35/4, October-December 1997.

[197] Leung, J. Y. (1991) Curriculum Development in the People's Republic of China. In C. Marsh and P. Morris (eds.). *Curriculum Development in East Asia*. London: The Falmer Press.

[198] Li, M. S. (1999) Discourse and Culture of Learning – Communication Challenges. Paper presented at the Joint AARE-NZARE 1999 conference in Melbourne.

[199] Li, L. Q. (2004) On Education: Interviews with Li Lanqing. Beijing: People's Education Press.

[200] Liao, X. Q. (2000). How Communicative Language Teaching Became Acceptable in Secondary Schools in China, *Internet TESL Journal*, [Online Journal], URL: http://iteslj.org/, Vol. VI, No. 10, October 2000. (Retrieved 22/03/2006).

[201] Lincoln, Y. & Guba, E. (1985) *Naturalistic Inquiry*. London: Sage.

[202] Lincoln, Y. & Denzin, N. (1994) The Fifth Moment. In N. Denzin & Y. Lincoln (eds.). *Handbook of Qualitative Research*. (pp. 575-586). London: Sage.

[203] Liu, J., Ross, H. A. & Kelly, D. P. (2000) *The Ethnographic Eye, An Interpretative Study of Education in China*. London: The Falmer Press.

[204] LoCastro, V. (2001) Teaching English to Large Classes. *TESOL Quarterly*, 35/3, 493-496.

[205] Lortie, D. (1975) *School Teacher: A Sociological Study*. Chicago: University of Chicago Press.

[206] Lyotard, J. F. (1984) *The Postmodern Condition: A Report on Knowledge*. Manchester: Manchester University Press.

[207] MacIntyre, A. (1984) *After Virtue: A Study in Moral Theory*. Notre Dame, Indiana: University of Notre Dame Press.

[208] Mangubhai, F., Marland, P., Dashwood, A. & Son, J. (2004) Teaching

a Foreign Language: One Teacher's Practical Theory. *Teaching and Teacher Education*, 20/3, 291-311.

[209]   Markula, P. & Denison, J. (2005) Sport and the Personal Narrative. In D. L. Andrews, D.S. Mason, & M. L. Silk (eds.). *Qualitative Methods in Sport Studies* (pp. 165-184). London: Berg.

[210]   Martin, J. (1995) Autobiographical Memory, Experiential Understanding, and Knowledge about Teaching. *Teaching and Teacher Education*. 11/4, 421-427.

[211]   Martin, S., Raid, A., Bullock, K. & Bishop, K. (2002) *Voices and Choices in Coursework.* Sheffield: The Geographical Association.

[212]   Martinez, M. A., Sauleda, N. & Guenter, L. H. (2001) Metaphors as Blueprints of Thinking about Teaching and Learning, *Teaching and Teacher Education,* 17(8), 965-977.

[213]   Mead, G. (2001) *Unlatching the Gate: Realizing my Scholarship of Living Inquiry.* [PhD Thesis] Bath University Library.

[214]   Measor, L. (1985) Critical Incidents in the Classroom: Identities, Choices and Careers. In S. Ball & I. Goodson (eds.). *Teachers' Lives and Careers* (pp. 61-78). London: The Falmer Press.

[215]   Measor, L. & Sikes, P. (1992) Visiting Lives: Ethics and Methodology in Life-history. In I. Goodson (ed.). *Studying Teachers' Lives* (pp. 209-234). London: Routledge.

[216]   Meijer, P. C., Verloop, N. & Beijaard, D. (1999) Exploring Language Teachers' Practical Knowledge about Teaching Reading Comprehension. *Teaching and Teacher Education*, 15, 59-84.

[217]   Miles, M. & Huberman, A. (1994) *Qualitative Data Analysis.* London: Sage.

[218]   Miller, M. (1996) Ethics and Understanding Through Interrelationship: I and Thou in Dialogue. In R. Josselson (ed.). *Ethics and Process in the Narrative Study of Lives* (pp. 129-151). London: Sage.

[219]   Ministry of Education, PRC (2001) *English Curriculum.* Beijing: Beijing Teacher University Press.

[220]   Morphy, J. (1994) Principles of Second Language Teacher Education: Integrating Multiple Perspectives. *A Journal of Australian TESOL*, 9/1, 7-28.

[221]   Muchmore, J. (2002) Methods and Ethics in a Life-history Study of Teacher Thinking. *The Qualitative Report*, 7/4. [Online-document] URL:

http://www.nova.edu/ssss/QR/QR7-4/muchmore.html (last retrieved 18/09/2006).

[222] Munby, H. & Russell, H. (1990) Metaphor in the Study of Teachers' Professional Knowledge. *Theory into Practice*, 29/2, 116-122.

[223] Muschamp, Y. M. & Bullock, K. (2006) Learning to Love Learning? – What the Pupils Think. In R. Webb (ed) *Changing Teaching and Learning in the Primary School* (pp. 71-80). Buckingham: Open University Press.

[224] Neuman, W. L. (2000) (4th edition) *Social Research Method Qualitative and Quantitative Approaches*. Boston: Allyn and Bacon.

[225] Neuman, W. L. (2006) (6th edition) *Social Research Method Qualitative and Quantitative Approaches*. Boston: Allyn and Bacon.

[226] Noblit, G. W. (1993) Power and Caring. *American Educational Research Journal*, 30/1, 23-38.

[227] Noddings, N. (1984) *Caring, a Feminine Approach to Ethics and Moral Education*. California: University of California Press.

[228] Noddings, N. (2003) *Education and Happiness*. Cambridge: Cambridge University Press.

[229] Noddings, N. (2005) Caring in Education, the Encyclopedia of Informal Education. [Online document] RUL:http://www.infed.org/biblio/noddings_caring_in_education.htm (Last retrieved: 03/05/2006).

[230] Oliver, P. (2003) *The Students' Guide to Research Ethics*. Buckingham: Open University Press.

[231] Olson, J. (2002a) *Understanding Teaching: Beyond Expertise*. Buckingham: Open University Press.

[232] Olson, J. (2002b) Systematic Change/Teacher Tradition: Legends of Reform Continue. *Journal of Curriculum Studies*, 34/2, 129-137.

[233] Olson, M. R. (1995) Conceptualizing Narrative Authority: Implications for Teacher Education. *Teaching and Teacher Education*, 11/2, 119-135.

[234] Olson, M. R. & Osborne, J. W. (1991) Learning to Teach: The First Year. *Teaching and Teacher Education*, 7/4, 331-343.

[235] O'Neill, O. (2002) A Question of Trust (BBC Reith Lecture 1). http://www.bbc.co.uk/radio4/reith2002/lecture1.shtml (Last time retrieved, March, 2009).

[236] Oosterheert, I. E. & Vermunt, J. D. (2003) Knowledge Construction in Learning to Teach: The Role of Dynamic Sources. *Teachers and Teaching: Theory and Practice*, 9/2, 157-173.

[237] Oxford, R. L., Tomlinson, S., Barcelos, A; Harrington, C., Lavine, R. Z; Saleh, A. & Longhini, A. (1998) Clashing Metaphors about Classroom Teachers: Toward a Systematic Typology for the Language Teaching Field. *System*, 26, 3-50.

[238] Pachler, N. & Field, K. (2001) *Learning to Teach Modern Foreign Languages in the Secondary School*. London and New York: Routledge, Falmer.

[239] Palmer, P. (2003) Teaching with Heart and Soul: Reflections on Spiritualities in Teacher Education. *Journal of Teacher Education*, 54/5, 376-385.

[240] Peoples' Daily. (2003) Teachers Face Big Qualification Tests. [Online Document] URL: http://english.peopledaily.com.cn/200312/26/eng20031226_131265.shtml (last retrieved, 03/04/06).

[241] Perez, S. A. (2000) An Ethic of Caring in Teaching Culturally Diverse Students. *Education*, 121/4, 102-105.

[242] Perkinson, H. J. (1984) *Learning From our Mistakes*. Connecticut: Greenwood Press.

[243] Polanyi, M. (1958) *The Study of Man*. Chicago: The University of Chicago Press.

[244] Polanyi, M. (1962) *Personal Knowledge*. London: Routledge.

[245] Polkinghorne, D. E. (1988) *Narrative Knowing and the Human Sciences*. New York: State University of New York Press.

[246] Polkinghorne, D. E. (1995) Narrative Configuration in Qualitative Analysis. In J. A. Hatch & R. Wisniewski (eds.). *Life-history and Narrative* (pp. 6-23). London: The Falmer Press.

[247] Polkinghorne, J. (1996) *Beyond Science, the Wider Human Context*. Cambridge: Cambridge University Press.

[248] Pomson, A. (2004) Loosening Chronology's Collar: Reframing Teacher Career Narratives as Stories of Life and Work Without End. *International Journal of Qualitative Studies in Education*, 17/5, 647-661.

[249] Poulson, L. (2001) Paradigm Lost? Subject Knowledge, Primary Teachers and Education Policy. *British Journal of Educational Studies*, 49/1, 40-55.

[250] Poulson, L. (2003) The Subject of Literacy: What Kind of Knowledge is Needed to Teach Literacy Successfully? In E. Bearne, H. Dombey & T. Grainger (eds.). *Classroom Interactions in Literacy* (pp. 51-63). Oxford: OUP.

[251]   Poulson, L. & Avramidis (2003) Pathways and Possibilities in Professional
        Development: Case Studies of Effective Teachers of Literacy. *British
        Educational Research Journal*, 29/4, 543-560.

[252]   Poulson, L. & Wallace, M. (2004) Designing and Writing about Research:
        Developing a Critical Frame of Mind. In L. Poulson &M. Wallace (eds.).
        Learning to Read Critically in Teaching and Learning (pp. 37-61).
        London: Sage.

[253]   Pring, R. (2000) *Philosophy of Educational Research*. London, New
        York: Continuum.

[254]   Pui-lan, K., Brown, W., Delamarter, S., Frank, T., Marshell, J., Menn, E.
        & Riggs, M. (2005) Taken with Surprise: Critical Incidents in Teaching.
        Teaching Theology and Religion, 8/1, 35-46.

[255]   Rayner, A. (1997) *Degrees of Freedom – Living in Dynamic Boundaries*.
        London: Imperial College Press.

[256]   Riessman, C. K. (1993) *Narrative Analysis*. London: Sage.

[257]   Riessman, C. K. (2002a) Illness Narratives: Positioned Identities, Invited
        annual Lecture. Health Communication Research Centre, Cardiff University,
        Wales, U.K., May 2002. [Online document] URL: http://www.cardiff.ac.uk/
        encap/hcrc/comet/prog/narratives.pdf, (last retrieved, 06/12/05).

[258]   Riessman, C. K. (2002b) Narrative Analysis. In A. M. Huberman & M.
        B. Miles (eds.). *The Qualitative Researcher's Companion* (pp. 217-270).
        Thousand Oaks, CA: Sage.

[259]   Riessman, C. K. (2002c) Doing Justice: Positioning the Interpreter in
        Narrative Work. In W. Patterson (ed.). *Strategic Narrative: New
        Perspectives on the Power of Personal and Cultural Stories* (pp. 193-214).
        New York, Oxford: Lexington Books.

[260]   Riessman, C. K. (2005) Exporting Ethics: A Narrative about Narrative
        Research in South India. *Health,* 9/4, 473–490.

[261]   Richardson, V. (1994) Conducting Research on Practice. *Educational
        Researcher*, 23/5, 5-10.

[262]   Ritchie, S. (1998) Accessing Science Teachers' Personal Practical
        Theories. Paper presented at the Australian Science Education Research
        Association, Darwin, Australia, 9-12, July, 1998.

[263]   Roberts, B. (2002) *Biographical Research*. Buckingham: Open University
        Press.

[264]   Ronald, C. & Nunan, D. (eds.). (2001) *Teaching English to Speakers of*

Other Languages. Cambridge: Cambridge University Press.

[265] Rosiek, J. & Atkinson, B. (2005) Bridging the Divides: The Need for a Pragmatic Semiotics of Teacher Knowledge Research. *Educational Theory*, 55/4, 421-442.

[266] Ross, H. A. (2000) In the Moment – Discourses of Power, Narratives of Relationship, Framing Ethnography of Chinese Schooling. In J. Liu, H. A. Ross, & D. P. Kelly (eds.). *The Ethnographic Eye: An Interpretive Study of Education in China* (pp. 123-152). New York and London: The Falmer Press.

[267] Ross, J. (1995) From Middle to Senior Management, In J. Bell (ed.). *Teachers Talk about Teaching*. Buckingham: Open University Press.

[268] Rubin, H. J. & Rubin, I. (1995) *Qualitative Interview, the art of Hearing*. London: Sage.

[269] Ryan, K. (1986) *The Induction of New Teacher*. Bloomington: Phi Delta Kappa Education Foundation.

[270] Sabar, N. (2004) From Heaven to Reality through Crisis: Novice Teachers as Migrants. *Teaching and Teacher Education*, 20 (2004), 145-161.

[271] Sarbin, T. R. (1986) The Narrative as a Root Metaphor for Psychology. In T. R. Sarbin (ed.). *Narrative Psychology: The Storied Nature of Human Conduct* (pp. 3-21). New York: Praeger.

[272] Schempp, P., Sparkes, A. & Templin, T. (1998) Identity and Induction: Establishing the Self in the First Year of Teaching, In R. Lipka & T. Brinthaupt (eds.). *The Role of Self in Teacher Development* (pp. 143-160). New York: Sunny Press.

[273] Schön, D. A. (1979) Generative Metaphor: A Perspective on Problem-setting in Social Policy. In A. Ortony (ed.). *Metaphor and Thought* (pp. 254-283). Cambridge: Cambridge University Press.

[274] Schön, D. A. (1983) *The Reflective Practitioner: How Professionals Think in Action*. New York: Basicbooks.

[275] Schön, D. A. (ed.). (1991) *The Reflective Turn Case Studies in and on Educational Practice*. New York: Teachers College Press.

[276] Scott, W. A. H. & Gough, S. R. (eds.). (2003) *Key Issues in Sustainable Development and Learning: A Critical Review*. London, New York: Routledge, Falmer.

[277] Schwab, J. J. (1969). The Practical: A Language for Curriculum. *School Review*, 78, 1–23.

[278] Sheringham, M. (1984) Popularization Policies in Chinese Education From 1950s to 1970s. *Comparative Education*, 20/1, 73-80.

[279] Shulman, L. S. (1986) Those Who Understand: Knowledge Growth in Teaching. *Educational Researcher*, 15/2, 4-14.

[280] Shulman, L. S. (1987) Knowledge and Teaching: Foundations of the New Reform. *Harvard Educational Review*, 15/2, 4-14.

[281] Sikes, P. (2000) "Truth" and "Lies" Revisited. *British Educational Research Journal*, 26/2, 257-269.

[282] Sikes, P. (2004) Methodology, Procedures and Ethical Concerns. In C. Opie (ed.). *Doing Educational Research* (pp. 15-32). London: Sage.

[283] Sikes, P. (2005) Storying Schools: Issues around Attempts to Create a Sense of Feel and Place in Narrative Research Writing. *Qualitative Research*, 5/1, 79-94.

[284] Sikes, P. (2006) Towards Useful and Dangerous Theory. *Discourse: Studies in the Cultural Politics of Education*, 27/1, 43-51.

[285] Sikes, P. & Everington, J. (2001) Becoming an RE Teacher: A Life-history Approach. *British Journal of Religious Education*, 24/1, 8-19.

[286] Sikes, P. & Everington, J. (2004) RE Teachers Do Get Drunk You Know: Becoming an RE Teacher in the Twenty-First Century. *Teachers and Teaching: Theory and Practice*, 10/1, 21-33.

[287] Silverman, D. (2001) *Interpreting Qualitative Data, Methods for Analyzing Talk, Text and Interaction.* London: Sage.

[288] Skidmore, D. (2000) From Pedagogical Dialogue to Dialogical Pedagogy. *Language and Education*, 14/4, 283-296.

[289] Smith, B. & Sparkes, A. (2005) Analyzing Talk in Qualitative Inquiry: Exploring Possibilities, Problems, and Tensions. *Quest*, 57/2, 213-242.

[290] Smyth, J. & Shacklock, G. (1998). *Re-making Teaching: Ideology, Policy and Practice.* London: Routledge.

[291] Sparkes, A. (1994a) Life Histories and the Issue of Voice: Reflection on an Emerging Relationship. *Qualitative Studies in Education*, 7/2, 165-183.

[292] Sparkes, A. (1994b) Self, Silence and Invisibility as a Beginning Teacher: A Life-history of Lesbian Experience. *British Journal of Sociology of Education*, 15/1, 93-118.

[293] Sparkes, A. (1999) Exploring Body Narratives. *Sport, Education and Society*, 4/1, 17-30.

[294] Sparkes, A. (2001) Myth 1994: Qualitative Health Researchers Will

Agree about Validity. *Qualitative Health Research*, 11/4, 538-552.

[295]   Sparkes, A. (2002) *Telling Tales, in Sport and Physical Activity, A Qualitative Journey.* Leeds: Human Kinetics.

[296]   Sparkes, A. (2003) Bodies, Identities, Selves: Autoethnographic Fragments and Reflections. In J. Denison & P. Markula (eds.). *Moving Writing: Crafting Movement in Sport Research* (pp. 51-77). New York: Peter Lang.

[297]   Sparkes, A. (2005) Narrative Analysis: Exploring the Whats and the Hows of Personal Stories. In M. Holloway (ed.). *Qualitative Research in Health Care* (pp. 91-109). Buckingham: Open University Press.

[298]   Spolsky, B. (1989) *Conditions for Second Language Learning.* Oxford: Oxford University Press.

[299]   Stables, A. (2002) Diachronic and Synchronic Analysis of Educational Practice: Taking Account of the Life-history. *Westminster Studies in Education*, 25/1, 59-66.

[300]   Stables, A. (2003) *Education for Diversity: Making Differences.* New York: Ashgate Publishing Company.

[301]   Stodolsky, S. (1984) Teacher Evaluation: The Limits of Looking. *Educational Researcher,* 13/9, 11-18.

[302]   Stofflett, R. (1996) Metaphor Development by Secondary Teachers Enrolled in Graduate Teacher Education. *Teaching and Teacher Education,* 12/6, 577-589.

[303]   Stoll, L., Fink D. & Earl L. (2003) *It's about Learning [and It's about Time] What's in it For Schools?* London: Routledge.

[304]   Strauss, A. (1987) *Qualitative Analysis for Social Scientists.* Cambridge: Cambridge University Press.

[305]   Strauss, S. (2001) Folk Psychology, Folk Pedagogy and Their Relations to Subject Matter Knowledge. In B. Torff & R. J. Sternberg (eds.). *Understanding and Teaching the Intuitive Mind* (pp. 217-242). Mahwah, NJ: Erlbaum.

[306]   Sumner, W. G. (1960) *Folkways.* New York: A Mentor Book.

[307]   Sumner, W. G. (1979) *Folkways and Mores* (E. Sagarin, ed.). New York: Schocken (Original work published 1906).

[308]   Suslu, S. (2006) Motivation of ESL Teachers. *Internet TESL Journal*, Vol. XII, No.1 [On-line document] URL: ttp://iteslj.org/Articles/Suslu-TeacherMotivation.html (Last retrieved, 13/03/2006).

[309]   Tang, X. & Wu, X (2000) Educational Change and Development in the

People's Republic of China: Challenges for the Future. In T. Townsend & Y. Cheng (eds.). *Educational Change and Development in the Asian-Pacific Region* (pp. 133-161). Rotterdam: SWETS & ZEITLINGER Publishers.

[310] Tarc, P. M. (2005) Education as Humanism of the Other. *Educational Philosophy and Theory*, 37/6, 833-849.

[311] Tarlow, B. (1996) Caring: A Negotiated Process that Varies. In S. Gordon, P. Benner & N. Noddings (eds.). *Care Giving: Readings in Knowledge, Practice, Ethics and Politics*. Philadelphia: University of Pennsylvania Press.

[312] Taylor, W. (1984) *Metaphors of Education*. London: Heinemann Educational Books.

[313] Thomas, E. (1997) Developing a Cultural-sensitive Pedagogy: Tackling a Problem of Melding "Global Culture" within Existing Cultural Context. *International Journal of Educational Development*. 17/1, 13-26.

[314] Thomas, D. (1995) Treasonable or Trustworthy Text: Reflections on Teacher Narrative Studies. In D. Thomas (ed.). Teachers' Stories (pp. 1-23). Buckingham: Open University Press.

[315] Tierney, W. G. (2000) Undaunted Courage: Life-history and the Post-modern Challenge. In N. Denzin & Y. S. Lincoln (eds.). *Handbook of Qualitative Research* (pp. 537-555). London: Sage.

[316] Tilley, S. (2003) "Challenging" Research Practices: Turning a Critical Lens on the Work of Transcription. *Qualitative Inquiry*, 9/5, 750-773.

[317] Tirri, K., Husu, J. & Kansanen, P. (1999) The Epistemological Stance between the Knower and the Known. *Teaching and Teacher Education*, 15, 911-922

[318] Tobin, K. (1990) Changing Metaphors and Beliefs: A Master Switch for Teaching? *Theory into Practice*, 29/2, 122-128.

[319] Toma, J. D. (2000) How Getting Closer to Your Subjects Makes Qualitative Data Better. *Theory into Practice*, 39/3, 177-184.

[320] Tripp, D. (1993) *Critical Incidents in Teaching*. London, New York, Routledge, Falmer.

[321] Tripp, D. (1994) Teachers' Lives, Critical Incidents, and Professional Practice. *Qualitative Studies in Education*, 7/1, 65-76.

[322] Turner-Bisset, R. (2001) Expert Teaching: Knowledge and Pedagogy to Lead the Profession. London: Fulton.

[323] Urmston, A. (2003) Learning to Teach English in Hong Kong: The Opinions of Teachers in Training. *Language and Education*, 7/2, 112-137.

[324] Veenman, S. (1984) Perceived Problems of Beginning Teachers. *Review of Educational Research*, 54/2, 143-178.

[325] Vogt, F. (2002) A Caring Teacher: Explorations into Primary School Teachers' Professional Identity and Ethic of Care. *Gender and Education*, 14/3, 251-264.

[326] Wallace, M. & Poulson, L. (2004) Critical Reading for Self-critical Writing. In L. Poulson and M. Wallace (eds.). *Learning to Read Critically in Teaching and Learning*. London: Sage.

[327] Wang , K. (2005) Military Training for College Students – 20 Years On [Online document] URL: http://www.china.org.cn/english/2005/Oct/144153. htm (last retrieved: 20/11/2005).

[328] Wang, J. & Paine. L. (2003) Learning to Teach with Mandated Curriculum and Public Examination of Teaching as Context. *Teaching and Teacher Education*, 19, 75-94.

[329] Weade, R. & Ernest, G. (1990) Pictures of Life in Classrooms, and the Search for Metaphors to Frame Them. *Theory into Practice*, 29/2, 133-141.

[330] Webb, K & Blond, J. (1995) Teacher Knowledge: The Relationship between Caring and Knowing. *Teaching and Teacher Education*, 11/6, 611-625.

[331] Weber, S. & Mitchell, C. (1996) Using Drawings to Investigate Professional Identity and the Popular Culture of Teaching. In I. Goodson & A. Hargreaves (eds.). *Teachers' Professional Lives* (pp. 109-127). London: The Falmer Press.

[332] Wengraf, T. (2001) *Qualitative Research Interviewing, Biographic Narrative and Semi-Structured Methods*. London: Sage.

[333] Whitehead, J. (1989) Creating a Living Educational Theory from Questions of the Kind, "How do I improve my Practice?" *Cambridge Journal of Education*, 19/1, 137-153.

[334] Whitehead, J. (1999) Educative Relations in a New Era. *Pedagogy, Culture & Society*, 7/1, 73-90.

[335] Whitehead, J. (2003) Creating Our Living Educational Theories in Teaching and Learning to Care: Using Multi-media to Communication the Meanings and Influence of Our Embodied Educational Values. *Teaching Today for Tomorrow*, Issue 19, 17-20.

[336] Wikipedia, (n.d.) Experience, in Wikipedia: the free encyclopedia [On-line resource] URL: http://en.wikipedia.org/wiki/Experience (Last Retrieved: 12/03/2006).

[337] Wikipedia, (n.d.) Narrative, in Wikipedia: the free encyclopedia [On-line resource] URL: http://en.wikipedia.org/wiki/Narrative (Last Retrieved: 12/03/06).

[338] Wikipedia, (n.d.) Taoism, in Wikipedia: the free encyclopedia [On-line resource] URL: http://en.wikipedia.org/wiki/Taoist#References (Last Retrieved: 12/09/2006).

[339] Witherell, C., Tan, H. & Othus, T. & J. (1995) Narrative Landscapes and the Moral Imagination: Taking the Story to Heart. In H. McEwan and K. Egan (eds.). *Narrative in Teaching, Learning, and Research* (pp. 39-49). New York, London: Teacher College Press.

[340] Wolcott, H. F. (1994) Transforming Qualitative Data: Description, Analysis, and Interpretation. London: Sage.

[341] Woods, P. (1987) Life Histories and Teacher Knowledge. In J. Smyth (ed.). *Educating Teachers, Changing the Nature of Pedagogical Knowledge.* London: The Falmer Press.

[342] Woods, P. (1986) *Inside Schools, Ethnography in Educational Research.* London, New York: Routledge.

[343] Wootton, M. (1996) *Coping with Stress in Teaching.* Nightingale Teaching Consultancy.

[344] Wragg. E. C. (1999) *An Introduction to Classroom Observation.* London: Routledge.

[345] Wu. Z. J. (2002) *Teachers' "Knowledge" and Curriculum Change: A Critical Study of Teachers' Exploratory Discourse in a Chinese University.* [PhD Thesis] Lancaster University Library.

[346] Wu, Z. J. (2005) Being, Understanding and Naming: Teachers' Life and Work in Harmony, *International Journal of Educational Research,* 41, 307-323.

[347] Xu, S. & Connelly, M. (2009) Narrative Inquiry for Teacher Education and Development: Focus on English as a Foreign Language in China. *Teaching and Teacher Education,* 25, 219–227

[348] Yang, D. & Wu, J. (1999) Some Issues in the Reform and Development of Teacher Education and Training in China. *Teacher Development,* 3/2, 157-172.

[349] Yang, F. (2003) Education in China. *Educational Philosophy and Theory*, 34/2, 135-145.

[350] Yero, J. (2002) *Teaching in Mind: How Teacher Thinking Shapes Education*. Hamilton, MT: MindFlight Publishing.

[351] Yinger, R. & Hendricks-Lee, M. (1993) Working Knowledge in Teaching. In C. Day, J. Calderhead & P. Denicolo (eds.). *Research on Teacher Thinking, Understanding Professional Development* (pp. 100-123). London: The Falmer Press.

[352] Young, B. (1995) Career Plans and Work Perceptions of Pre-service Teachers. *Teaching and Teacher Education*, 11/3, 281-292.

[353] Yuan, Q. (2003) *The Transmitting of Culture: A Comparative Study of Eight Teachers in England and China*. [PhD Thesis] Bath University Library.

[354] Zehm, S. & Kottler, J. (1993) *On Being a Teacher: The Human Dimension*. London: Sage.

[355] Zembylas, M. (2003) Caring for Teacher Emotion: Reflections on Teacher Self-development. *Studies in Philosophy and Education*, 22, 103-125.

[356] Zhao, H. Q. (2008a). Why Did People Become Secondary-school English as a Foreign Language Teachers in China? An Examination of the Pathways, Motivations and Policy. *Educational Research for Policy and Practice,* 7(3), 183-195.

[357] Zhao, H. Q. (2008b) *Ways Forward with ICT-assisted EFL Pedagogy in China: Theories and Practice*. Beijing: National Defence Industry Press.

[358] Zhao, H. Q. & Poulson, L. (2006) A Biographical Narrative Inquiry into Teachers' Knowledge: An Intergenerational Approach. *Asia Pacific Education Review*, 7(2), 123-132.

[359] Zhao, H. Q. (2007) *Interpreting Folkways of Teaching: A Life-history Narrative Inquiry into Characteristics of Chinese Secondary EFL Teachers' Knowledge*. [PhD Thesis] Bath University Library.

[360] Zhao, H. Q. (2009) Realization of the Self, a Process of Discovery and Creation through Cross-cultural Learning. In Scherto, G. (ed.). *Exploring Selfhood: Finding Ourselves, Finding Our Stories in Life Narratives*. (pp. 241-258) Brighton: Guerrand-Hermes Foundation for Peace Press.

[361] Zhou, Z. (2002) The Teaching Profession: To Be or To Do? *Journal of Education for Teaching*, 28/3, 211-215.